973.04 Alv
Alvarez, Alex.
Native America and the question
of genocide

Praise for
Native America and the Question of Genocide

"Professor Alvarez has written a comprehensive analysis which directly confronts the controversial question concerning whether the destruction of the indigenous populations of the Americas was genocide. The book is exceedingly well written and one of the most interesting treatments of the topic I have seen. It should be of interest to students and teachers in a variety of fields including genocide studies, political science, history, and criminal justice."
—Herbert Hirsch, Virginia Commonwealth University

"By addressing issues linked to the term *genocide* and to genocide studies in relationship with the complex histories of Native Americans, Alex Alvarez has put together a thought-provoking volume which will be a valuable resource for study and debate in the classroom."
—Joyce Apsel, New York University

"In this important and fascinating study, Alex Alvarez examines whether the catastrophe that engulfed Native Americans following European colonization amounted to genocide. In his work he balances the scholar's commitment to intellectual honesty with the humanist's empathy for the victims."
—Robert Melson, professor emeritus, Purdue University; former president of the International Association of Genocide Scholars

Studies in Genocide:
Religion, History, and Human Rights

Series Editor: Alan L. Berger, Raddock Family Eminent Scholar Chair of Holocaust Studies, Florida Atlantic University

Genocide is a recurring scourge and a crime against humanity, the effects of which are felt globally. Books in this series are original and sophisticated analyses describing, interpreting, and articulating lessons from historical as well as current genocides. Written from a range of scholarly perspectives, the works in this series articulate patterns of genocide and offer suggestions about early warning signs that may help prevent the crime.

Balkan Genocides: Holocaust and Ethnic Cleansing in the Twentieth Century, by Paul Mojzes
Jihad and Genocide, by Richard Rubenstein
Native America and the Question of Genocide, by Alex Alvarez

NATIVE AMERICA AND THE QUESTION OF GENOCIDE

Alex Alvarez

SALINE DISTRICT LIBRARY
555 N. Maple Road
Saline, MI 48176

ROWMAN & LITTLEFIELD
Lanham • Boulder • New York • Toronto • Plymouth, UK

MAY - - 2014

Published by Rowman & Littlefield
4501 Forbes Boulevard, Suite 200, Lanham, Maryland 20706
www.rowman.com

10 Thornbury Road, Plymouth PL6 7PP, United Kingdom

Copyright © 2014 by Rowman & Littlefield

All rights reserved. No part of this book may be reproduced in any form or by any electronic or mechanical means, including information storage and retrieval systems, without written permission from the publisher, except by a reviewer who may quote passages in a review.

British Library Cataloguing in Publication Information Available

Library of Congress Cataloging-in-Publication Data

Alvarez, Alex.
Native America and the question of genocide / Alex Alvarez.
pages cm. — (Studies in genocide: religion, history, and human rights)
Includes bibliographical references and index.
ISBN 978-1-4422-2581-7 (cloth : alk. paper) — ISBN 978-1-4422-2582-4 (electronic)
1. Indians, Treatment of—North America—History. 2. Indians of North America—Violence against. 3. Indians of North America—Social conditions. 4. Genocide—United States—History. 5. United States—Social policy. 6. United States—Race relations. 7. United States—Politics and government. I. Title.
E93.A42 2014
973.04'97—dc23
2013048466

♾ ™ The paper used in this publication meets the minimum requirements of American National Standard for Information Sciences Permanence of Paper for Printed Library Materials, ANSI/NISO Z39.48-1992.

Printed in the United States of America

To my little brother LeRoy,
with love and respect

CONTENTS

ACKNOWLEDGMENTS

This book could not have been written without a great deal of personal and professional support, for which I am profoundly grateful.

I would like to first begin by thanking a number of friends and colleagues who read early drafts and provided important feedback as I worked on this project. Specifically, my deep appreciation to Janine Schipper, Mike Costelloe, Marianne Nielsen, Neil Websdale, Herb Hirsch, Steffie Kunze, Mark Sogge, Paul Bartrop, and Rene LeMarchand for reading various draft chapters and providing valuable feedback. I especially want to say thank you to Lauren Faulkner Rossi for a very thorough reading of the manuscript and for offering such detailed edits and constructive comments.

Thanks also to Sarah Stanton, Alan Berger, Kathryn Knigge, Jehanne Schweitzer, Brittany Dowdle, and the rest of the staff at Rowman & Littlefield for their hard work and support on behalf of this book.

On a personal level, my love and gratitude to my wife, best friend, and partner, Donna Mae Engleson, for putting up with me. My gratitude also to my children—Ingrid, Joseph, and Astrid—who are a never-ending source of hope, inspiration, and pride.

Last I wish to thank the reviewers for their helpful comments and suggestions. Their time and effort has helped make this a better book. Thank you.

INTRODUCTION

The truth is rarely pure and never simple

—Oscar Wilde[1]

Confronting stories of the West's actual complexity, Americans have worked away diligently, kneading the stories until the complexities of the events they represent have been smoothed, flattened, compressed, and generally made manageable.

—Patricia Nelson Limerick[2]

Living in the American Southwest, it's hard not to be constantly reminded of the long and rich history of the Native peoples of this land. The Southwest is one of the few places in the United States where Native history is still very much in evidence. One of my favorite places is Walnut Canyon, a little-known location just a couple of miles outside of Flagstaff, Arizona. On first arriving, one is greeted by a visitor center that is precariously perched on the edge of a small canyon and which offers the usual fare of a few exhibits, including a nice little diorama depicting life in the canyon a thousand years ago, a gift shop, and an impressive panoramic view into the heart of the canyon. The real treasure, however, is found when one descends the island trail, which leads you down to a limestone knoll in the middle of the canyon. It feels like an island of limestone around which the canyon winds in a horseshoe bend that leaves this central formation isolated from the surrounding walls except for a narrow path down on one end. It's easy to see why the ancient peoples selected this place to live. It is easily defended and offers all the necessities of life: water in the bottom of the canyon, flat areas to grow a few crops, piñon and walnut trees whose nuts provide nourishment, and good hunting opportunities. Even to this day, the area is home to mountain lions, black bear, deer, and plenty of smaller animals. It also offers ample shelter.

A visitor down into the canyon finds the remains of numerous shelters built into the rock face and nestled under the overhanging shelves of limestone. Providing a roof and a back wall, the overhangs were divided up into individual rooms with front and side walls of loose rocks held in place by mortar in a style seen throughout the Southwest. A number of them are still almost entirely intact and allow you to crouch through the doorway and enter into the snug interior. One of the most amazing aspects of this place is that the careful observer can see the hand and finger marks of people who have been dead for close to a thousand years. Preserved in the dried mortar of these shelters, these marks provide a mute testimony to the fact that these lands were once home to a people who are now gone. At its height, more than one hundred people lived in this section of the canyon, and the walls of the gorge must have echoed with the sounds of their lives. The visitor today, however, hears only the wind brushing against the tall ponderosa pines on the rim.

For some reason, Walnut Canyon has always felt like a special place to me—in part because I've always found it peaceful to walk along the ruins and sit and look over the canyon, but also because the place has a timeless quality to it, a sense of agelessness. It's very easy to cast your mind back and to think about the past and the people who once inhabited this land. Who were they? What were their lives like? Did they have the same kinds of hopes and fears that I have? And most important, what happened to them?

In many ways, this book is the result of a convergence between what I do and where I live. Where I live has meant that I have become increasingly sensitized to Native American issues simply because they are so much a part of living here in the American Southwest. The political, social, historical, economic, and cultural landscape is infused with Native American issues, concerns, and perspectives. It is simply inescapable. Flagstaff lies on the edge of the Navajo reservation, the largest reservation in the United States, and Flagstaff has a sizable population of Navajo, Hopi, Apache, and other tribes. Northern Arizona University, where I work, also has a sizable number of Native American students, as well as an indigenous studies program and a cultural center. The city also sits at the foot of the San Francisco Peaks, which are considered sacred to various Native tribes. In other words, Native Americans and Native American issues are a prevalent and important part of living here.

I teach about and study violence. For many years, I have spent a considerable amount of time studying and writing about the various forms of violence that human beings engage in. One particular form of violence that I have focused on is the crime of genocide, which concerns the attempt to eradicate entire populations. Over the years, I have intellectually grappled with many different examples of this most extreme and horrific form of collective violence. These include the Armenian genocide, the Holocaust, the Rwandan genocide of 1994, and the Bosnian experience with ethnic cleansing in the 1990s. But one issue that I have never really addressed up until now concerns historical events in my own backyard, so to speak. As I've indicated, living and working in Flagstaff, Arizona, it's hard not to be aware of the visible and substantial Native American population that comprises such an important part of the history of the Southwest, and in studying genocide, one often comes across claims that Native Americans were the victims of genocide. I have seen this assertion made by students in classes, university faculty, and various community members. In this claim, they are hardly alone. A whole host of writers and activists have made similar assertions. I have also seen this declaration in various scholarly and popular publications. But is this true? Did Native Americans experience genocide? One of the things my experience in studying genocide has taught me is that "genocide" is a word and concept that is often used and misused. The term has a tremendous amount of power, and because of that it has sometimes been applied to highway deaths, abortion, AIDS, slavery, urban planning, and family planning, among other rhetorical excesses.[3] Unfortunately, many of these assertions seem to be based more on a general sense of outrage and horror than on any clear and rigorous understanding about what is and is not genocide. It was with these ideas in mind that I set out to write this book.

I have several connected goals in writing this book. The first is to explore the experiences of the Native populations of North America postcontact through the lens of genocide. As I indicated above, it has become somewhat fashionable to assert that American Indians were the victims of genocide, but all too often those comments appear to be more about political activism or attempts to generate a sense of moral outrage than they are about engaging in scholarly discussion. Genocide refers to a specific concept that is itself subject to various definitions and debates. Scholars and others who study this phenomenon, in other words, interpret the term in multiple ways. By examining the experiences of Native America, I hope not only to shed light on the varied experiences of these indigenous populations, but also to illustrate some of the definitional and conceptual ambiguity of the concept of genocide itself.

I also believe that, given the nature of this crime and its significance to the contested terrain of this nation's history, it is important that claims of genocide be examined rigorously and critically. This is not to suggest that Native peoples in the Americas did not suffer from genocide, but rather that care needs to be taken when applying this label to specific historical events. These assertions are all too often made with sweeping generalizations that seem to suggest the Native experience, and by inference Native peoples, were all the same. This is far from the truth. As we will see, the Americas were and are home to a great many different nations and tribes who have often had dissimilar experiences depending upon their location, the period of contact, who they had contact with, and the various strategies of confrontation and/or accommodation each group adopted.

A more careful and rigorous analysis can reveal some of these differences and provide insight into the various ways in which contact between Natives and Europeans played out. An examination of genocide, therefore, in the context of the Native American experience can reveal much of the complexity of contact and conflict in America after the arrival of the Europeans. Although we often tend to see it as such, it is not as simple as it has often been portrayed. It is more than just a simple morality tale about good and evil, right and wrong, whites versus Natives. The problem with this depiction, aside from being plain wrong, is that it treats all Native people as passive objects who were simply acted upon by those they came into contact with. That is far from the truth. Instead, a closer look reveals that it is a very human story of tragedy and error, missed opportunities and cross-purposes, good intentions and bad, and cruel injustice and violence. Natives sometimes sided with Europeans against other Native tribes, while colonists and settlers sometimes advocated for and assisted Natives.

The individual stories reveal humanity at its best and at its worst and with all of the shades in-between. Native responses to contact varied and evolved over time based on previous experience, contingent circumstances, and individual actors. Some were more successful than others. As the historian James Axtell summarizes well, "In the face of new challenges from a people and world they had never before known or even imagined, the various Indian groups worked mightily and often cleverly to maximize their political sovereignty, cultural autonomy, territorial imperative, power of self-identification, and physical mobility."[4] It is my hope that this book will help illustrate some of these kinds of issues and paint a truer and more human narrative of the past and in the process assist the reader in achieving a better understanding of the contested nature of genocide.

This book is not a definitive account of the entire experience of Native Americans postcontact. I believe that such a volume is largely impossible. There is simply too much material to review with any level of detail and accuracy. Much has also been lost so that what remains is incomplete and sometimes speculative. Instead, this is a more selective and episodic discussion with an emphasis on particular examples and cases that help illustrate some of the complexities of the postcontact experiences. In some ways, this approach is similar to that of the historian Roger Moorhouse who, in his work *Berlin at War*, writes, "my approach has been necessarily *pointillist*, seeking to give a flavor of events, rather than make any grand claims to comprehensiveness."[5] A number of the specific examples I use in this book represent well-known events that have sometimes been used to illustrate the genocidal nature of contact. The Sand Creek Massacre, for example, has often been cited as providing an example of genocide, as has the Navajo Long Walk, and in this book I pay attention to a number of these relatively well-known cases. This approach is necessarily subjective, but I hope that the examples I have chosen are representative and strong enough to support my analysis and discussion. Readers may disagree with some of my choices and explanations, but as one historian reminds us, "All histories are interpretive unless they are dull and shapeless,"[6] and I certainly recognize that any student of Native America and/or genocide can easily find many more examples of specific events and situations that could be used to argue a particular point of view in regard to the subject matter of this book. This book simply represents my choices.

As I stated above, it has not been my intention to provide the definitive work on this topic; instead I have attempted to illustrate the complexities of applying the concept of genocide to the historical treatment of Native America and in so doing, to reveal something of the nature of this thing we call genocide. I also focus my discussion geographically. While I sometimes refer to and use examples from Central and South America, the major focus of this book is North America, specifically that portion which comprises the United States.

At this point, a note about the terminology relied upon in this book is in order. Keep in mind that all terminology is inevitably the result of an imperfect compromise, especially given the fact that there are no universally agreed upon words to describe the groups that are the subject of this book. When speaking generically and broadly, I have tended to rely upon the term "Native American" since that appears to be one of the more innocuous and least offensive descriptors in usage today. "American Indians," "Indians of the Americas," and "indigenous peoples" are also sometimes relied upon to avoid redundant sentences, for narrative flow, and because they are also commonly used. All of these terms have their detractors and adherents, but in recent years, these have all become rather widely accepted. In terms of the groups, I have used tribes, peoples, and nations to describe collective units. Whenever possible, however, I have tried to use the specific names for the tribes being discussed in any particular section. This too has its problems, as the most commonly known names for many of the tribes are often not the names used by the members of the group themselves, but are instead often derogatory names given to them by their enemies and/or neighbors. The Sioux, for example, are one of the more commonly recognized tribal groups, and yet the name "Sioux" comes from the Chippewa word for a kind of snake. Similarly, the name "Apache" comes from the Zuni word for "enemy," while the word "Iroquois" comes from the Algonquian word for "real adders."[7] Others were referred to as "raw meat eaters" or "bark eaters" by their neighbors and enemies.[8] For Native Americans, tribal identities were usually much stronger than racial ones. Natives defined themselves, not as an Indian first and foremost, but as a Lakota, Navajo, Pequot, or Menominee. Whenever possible, therefore, I have tried to use the name that various peoples use to refer to themselves, although sometimes I have also included more common terms that allow for easier identification and ease of discussion.

Writing this book has been an especially difficult process. I have struggled to present this material in as evenhanded a manner as possible and have tried to do justice to the complexities of the issues and ideas under study. In writing this, I have also tried to approach this topic with sensitivity to the suffering and very real human harm experienced by Native peoples, but also with some measure of analytic rigor and honesty in order to assess somewhat accurately what happened. Balancing these two goals has not always been easy or satisfying, but I believe it is necessary.

In closing, I think it is important to point out that this discussion is not intended, nor should it be taken, as a dismissal or a minimization of the harm experienced by the Native peoples of the Americas. In trying to assess the merits of using the term "genocide" to describe the nature of contact between Native Americans and the European explorers, settlers, and colonists, I am in no way trying to trivialize the dimensions of the suffering experienced by various Native peoples. Nor am I trying to justify or excuse the violent excesses inflicted upon Natives by non-Natives. Instead, this book comprises an attempt to present a more evenhanded account and objective discussion of the nature of contact through the lens of genocide in a way that allows us to understand some of the complexities and nuances of those events.

I

BEGINNINGS

The European holocaust against indigenous peoples in the Americas was arguably the most extensive and destructive genocide of all time.
—Adam Jones[1]

Where today are the Pequot? Where are the Narragansett, the Mohican, the Pokanoket, and many other once powerful tribes of our people? They have vanished before the avarice and the oppression of the White Man, as snow before a summer sun.
—Tecumseh[2]

In all likelihood, the first Europeans to set eyes on North America were Norsemen blown off course as they tried to sail from Iceland to their colonies in Greenland, and it was these same Vikings who were the first to make contact with the Native inhabitants of the Americas. Interestingly, this first contact was a direct consequence of a period of climate change known as the Medieval Warm Period. The Medieval Warm Period was an era of about five hundred years of unusually warm and stable weather that resulted in the Norse surging out of their homeland and discovering Iceland.[3] Warmer temperatures, milder winters, and a longer growing period had resulted in a population explosion in Scandinavia, and the resulting pressures of land shortages and higher population densities provided the impetus for young men to take to the seas every summer in search of plunder, land, and opportunity.

This was the era in which the Vikings gained their fearsome reputation as marauders who would strike suddenly from the sea in their fast longships. Coastal communities and monasteries throughout Northern Europe and the British Isles lived in fear of being raided by the Norse, who would suddenly appear—loot, plunder, and kill—and then just as suddenly disappear back out to sea. But it wasn't just an era of pillage. It was also a time of exploration when the Norse forged into previously uncharted waters and explored new territory. Some went east and explored the rivers and lands across the Baltic Sea. This group of Vikings was known as the Rus, and they gave their name to Russia,[4] while others went west into the open ocean. The calmer seas and the retreat of the ice pack northward made it easier and safer to forge out into the vastness of the Atlantic, and in short order, the Orkneys, Shetlands, and Faroes were discovered and settled.

By 874, Iceland had also been found accidently by a seafarer blown off course and was subsequently colonized. In 982, Erik the Red, a belligerent and violent man by all accounts, was outlawed and banished from Iceland for three years after he killed the two sons of one of his enemies. Ironically enough, his father had been banished from Norway for the same reasons and had decided to make a fresh start in Iceland.[5] Now it was Erik's turn. About seventy years earlier, a sailor named Gunbjorn Ulfsson had been forced far west on a voyage from Norway to Iceland and had spotted some islands that are now believed to be just off the east coast of Greenland. A few years after that, a relative of Erik's also had seen these same islands, and now Erik, forced to leave Iceland and deciding to explore westward toward those dimly seen lands, came across Greenland. After exploring Greenland for three years, he returned to Iceland and led an expedition of twenty-five ships back to this land where these voyagers settled in a number of fjords on the southwest coast. He named it Greenland in order to make it more attractive to prospective settlers, but it wasn't a complete fabrication.

At that time Greenland was much more temperate than it is today, with relatively ice-free waters for much of the year and countless inlets and fjords leading deep inland to lush pasturelands. Greenland enjoyed a longer growing season, and was actually more hospitable than Iceland, with better grazing for sheep and cattle and more hay production, crucial for enabling livestock to survive during the long, dark winters.[6] Soon two main colonies were thriving, one in the south and the other further north along the western coast. Recent archaeological evidence suggests that there were about 220 farms in the southern colony and about 80 in the more northerly one, with a total population at their height of 2,000 to 4,000 inhabitants.[7]

Sometime around 986 CE, a Viking by the name of Bjarni Herjolfsson drifted off course because of heavy fog as he was traveling to Greenland in search of his father, who had sailed with Erik's fleet. Unwittingly sailing past Greenland, Herjolfsson and his crew spotted land even farther west, but rather than investigating the "flat and wooded country,"[8] he set course for Greenland, where he was soon reunited with his father. Evidently, curiosity was not Herjolfsson's strong suit. Approximately fifteen years later, Erik the Red's son, Leif Eriksson, decided to explore this land that Bjarni had sighted. Following Bjarni's advice, he first reached modern-day Baffin Island, which he called Helluland, or land of stone. From there he headed south and reached Labrador, which he dubbed land of forest, or Markland. Eventually reaching Newfoundland, he created a small settlement at L'Anse aux Meadows on the very northern tip of the island. Leif was quickly followed by his brother Thorvald, who was eager to settle in this lush new land, and a number of years later by another Viking named Thorfinn Karlsefni.

Using the colony in L'Anse aux Meadows as a base, the Vikings ranged along the American mainland, perhaps as far south as New York state and as far inland as the location of present-day Quebec City. Although they explored, they never really stayed and settled. In fact, the Norse only inhabited L'Anse aux Meadows for a few years. Why didn't they stay? The land and climate were certainly more congenial and resource rich than Greenland was. Part of the problem was the isolation and the difficulties in reaching the new land. Crossing the Davis Strait between Greenland and North America and sailing down the Labrador Sea was a dangerous venture even in the best of times. Storms, floating ice, and fog combined to make it a treacherous crossing. Markland was also a very long way from their bases of operation in Greenland, Iceland, and Norway. In addition to these factors, they also found the new lands to be inhabited by Natives who contested the presence of the Norse at every turn and who were so numerous that it effectively discouraged a permanent settlement.[9]

These were the Beothuk, a hunter-gatherer people living in Newfoundland, whose liberal use of red ochre for adornment led to them being referred to as "Red Indians" by later explorers, and their hostility shouldn't be surprising. During one of Thorvald Eriksson's trips to Newfoundland, for example, the Norse voyagers found three skin boats pulled up on shore with nine Native men sheltering underneath them. For no obvious reason, the Vikings surprised and captured eight of the men and then killed them. Unfortunately for them, one survivor escaped and returned with a large group of warriors who rained arrows down on the Norse. One of the wounded was Leif's brother, Thorvald, who, as he lay dying, recommended that they return to their homes in Greenland. Samuel Morison puts it this way, "Nature in Vinland was kind, compared with Greenland, but colonists would be in constant dread of the natives, none of whom as yet had reached the Greenland settlements."[10] So the first recorded meetings between Europeans and Native Americans were anything but peaceful.

At some point, the Norse in Greenland also made contact with the Natives of the northern regions, the Thule, who were themselves also recent newcomers to the area. These ancestors of the modern Inuit had originated in Alaska and made their way across Canada and into the Northern reaches of Greenland, where they eventually ran into the Norse. What were those first interactions like? Most likely their nature varied from one encounter to the next. A few were doubtless peaceful and involved the exchange of supplies. The Norse probably traded scraps of iron and cloth for ivory and furs, but it doesn't appear as if trade relations ever really developed into anything substantial. Part of the problem may have been the attitudes the Norse held toward the natives, who they called *skraelings* or *skrellings*, a derogatory term meaning "thin, scrawny, weakling, wretch, or screecher," and there's plenty of evidence to suggest that relations were often not amicable.

The Norse presence in Greenland had been made possible by the Medieval Warm Period, which lasted until approximately 1200 CE, and was followed by a global cold snap known as the Little Ice Age, which resulted in much tougher conditions for the Norse in Greenland. It also made life more difficult for the Thule people, who were largely located in the northern reaches of Greenland and who began to move south in response to the colder weather and consequently came increasingly into contact with the Norse settlements. Predictably, relations deteriorated along with the climate. In 1350, a force under the command of Ivar Bardason sailed up the coast toward the Western Settlement in response to rumors that the colony had been attacked and occupied by

Natives.[11] All they found was a settlement deserted by both the Norse and the Thule attackers, or, as a contemporary related, "On their arrival they found no men, either Christian or heathen."[12] A number of years later, in 1379, the Eastern Settlement was also attacked and as noted at the time, "The Skrellings attacked the Greenlanders, killed eighteen of them, and carried off two boys, whom they made slaves."[13] The Norse at that time were barely holding on. Their growing season had decreased, winters were longer and colder, and the fjords along which they lived and traveled were clogged with ice for much longer periods. The sea-lanes back to Iceland and Norway were also increasingly perilous, with fewer ships making the dangerous passage.

The increasing conflict with the Native peoples added to their difficulties and hastened the eventual demise of the Norse toehold in Greenland, an end that was probably inevitable given the change in climatic conditions and the depletion of the few resources that Greenland had offered. The well-known scientist and geographer Jared Diamond suggests that it didn't help that the Norse also seemed unwilling to change their traditional ways and adapt to the land and climate.[14] And so, the first contact between European and Amerindian, between "old" world and "new," ended in conflict, hostility, and bloodshed, although this was arguably one of the few cases in which the Natives came out ahead. As the writer Tony Horwitz succinctly puts it, "In the first recorded contest between Europeans and natives of America, the home team had won."[15] In many ways, this relatively brief prelude set the stage for the many violent clashes that were to come in the decades and centuries to follow.

Tragically, as the Viking experience portended, the history of Native America since contact with the European world is a story all too often filled with misunderstanding, prejudice, hatred, violence, and death. It is a complicated narrative in which American Indians and the European explorers, conquerors, settlers, and colonists were engaged in an often-brutal struggle for physical and cultural survival as each variously fought, resisted, negotiated, accommodated, and adapted themselves to the changing world they found themselves in. Native Americans, in particular, have sometimes been the victims of an entire series of direct and indirect assaults that resulted in widespread physical destruction and forced the survivors to cope with the loss of land, culture, lifestyle, language, and belief. The scale of the destruction is truly hard to grasp.

Millions of Natives died from violence, pestilence, forced assimilation, slavery, relocation, and starvation. Entire cultures were destroyed completely and never seen again, while those that survived were forever scarred and altered by the unrelenting assault on their way of life.

The Native population today is a fraction of what it once was. Estimates of the size of the population of the Americas prior to 1492 vary widely, with some suggesting a low of 2 million to others suggesting a high of 145 million people.[16] The most likely figures suggest a range of between 2 to 7 million inhabitants for the Americas as a whole (North, Central, and South), and a population range for North America alone of between 1 to 5.5 million.[17] The issue of the population size is a difficult one to resolve because, as James Wilson points out, "the evidence is maddeningly sparse, incomplete, and open to wildly differing interpretations."[18] Estimating the Native population of the Americas prior to contact has also been a very contentious subject because of the apparent notion that a smaller Native population makes the European arrival and invasion of the Americas seem more benign because it minimizes the number of lives lost to Europeans.[19]

Regardless of the true number, a figure, incidentally, which will never be known with any certainty, it is clear that the Americas were inhabited by many millions of peoples from a great many different tribes, cultures, and societies. This forces us, in the words of one observer, to "set aside the notion that America was an empty land, sprinkled lightly with aimless nomads."[20] That, at least, is no longer in dispute. Over the course of the next few hundred years, after the arrival of the Europeans, the population of the indigenous peoples of the Americas dropped dramatically, if not catastrophically. At its lowest ebb in the nineteenth century, the population of Native Americans is estimated to only have been around 250,000, with an all-time low of 237,000 in 1900.[21] Many tribes and cultures simply ceased to exist and remain forever unnamed and unremembered. Others are remembered only as place names on maps and atlases.

This great mortality was sometimes intentionally and sometimes unintentionally brought about through a great variety of means, some of which are the focus of this book. The destruction of countless societies and the terrible suffering of millions of human beings whose lives were ended or blighted by the destructive forces unleashed by the conquest of the Americas was and remains a tragedy of immense proportions.

Today, there are 564 federally recognized tribes and just under five million American Indians and Alaska Natives, including those of mixed race,[22] and while this is a significant increase from its nadir in 1900, it truly represents only a tiny fraction of the multitudes who once inhabited this continent.

NATIVE ORIGINS

How did the Indians first arrive? It is generally believed that the first Americans arrived sometime around 14,000 to 35,000 years ago from what is now Siberia.[23] In fact, apart from Antarctica, the Americas represent the last continents to be inhabited by humans. While many Native religious beliefs and traditions teach that the peoples of the Americas originated in place, recent research on mitochondrial DNA places the origins of Native Americans in Siberia, which is consistent with other archaeological and linguistic evidence.[24] This explanation is not meant to dismiss the importance of Native origin beliefs, since these play an important cultural role in helping to define group identity and history, but rather to reveal what science suggests about the nature of the peopling of the Americas. While it is admittedly challenged by other theories,[25] most scholars suggest that over the course of many years family bands of hunter-gatherers moved across the Bering land bridge and down through the North American continent.

The Bering Strait, which separates Alaska and Siberia, is a very shallow body of water, and during periods of heavy glaciation, the ocean was around 300 feet lower than in the present day, exposing a body of land called Beringia that was only 55 miles wide in some places but 1,000 miles long from north to south. It connected the Asian and North American continents.[26] It wasn't a migration in the strict sense of the word, but rather an ebb and flow of people gradually trending eastward with successive generations moving farther and farther afield as the windswept land ahead was explored and as periods of warming opened up ice-free avenues into the heartland of the North American continent. Human movement was in all likelihood tentative and sporadic and stretched over generations.

These Paleo-Siberians lived a nomadic life in search of game, usually consisting of small animals such as rabbits, but larger prey was also sometimes to be had. They also spent a great deal of time foraging for plants, roots, nuts, and berries to supplement their diets. Pollen analysis reveals that the landscape, not much different from the land behind them, was marked by grasses, small bushes, and some deciduous trees. The lifestyle was a precarious one and required the people to be opportunistic and to not rely on any one specific source of food. Because the land was unable to support large numbers of large animals per square mile, the nomadic bands of hunter-gatherers often had to roam far afield to bag enough game and forage.[27]

Imagine the scene when the first family groups from what is now Siberia found grassy steppes stretching away eastward across what had once been the bottom of the Bering Sea and which now harbored a variety of animal life, waterways, and marshes. Across the northern horizon stretched a wall of ice that at different times was nearly two miles thick in places, while the southern edge of Beringia sometimes held deciduous stands of oak, hickory, and beech.[28] Why did they come? Curiosity probably played a role, the same drive to see new sights and explore new lands that has always played such a large role in human history. They were probably also following game, such as the herds of caribou that roamed over Beringia, as well as deer, wooly mammoths, mastodons, and other megafauna.[29] Some of these animals still exist, while others such as the short-faced bears, the giant sloth, and the mammoths and mastodons are now long extinct.

Beringia was a cold and windswept place that was nevertheless suitable for migratory herbivores and the predators that inevitably followed in their wake. Even though vast sheets of ice covered most of what is now Canada, during this Pleistocene era, as it is known, the earth periodically cooled and warmed, forcing the glaciers to alternately advance and recede. During the warmer periods, ice-free avenues to the south sometimes opened up and offered a pathway to the more temperate southern climes. Ultimately, as the earth warmed somewhere around 15,000 years ago, the melting ice sheets released the waters that had been locked in the ice and the shallower western plains of Beringia began flooding, which drove many of the inhabitants of Beringia permanently eastward into what would later be called North America.[30] This didn't necessarily end all migration. The Bering Strait is only three miles wide at its narrowest and some have suggested that, once across this short stretch, the coastal sea-lanes offered a highway south, albeit a fairly hazardous one given the state of seafaring technology at the time.[31] Eventually, over the course of thousands of years, these early Paleo-Indians spread across the Americas and all the way down to Tierra del Fuego, the land of fire, at the southernmost tip of South America.

Over many generations, as these first Indians spread across the continent, they adapted to the specific geographic and ecological conditions they found along the way and developed a great assortment of cultures and lifestyles. Culture, after all, is something that evolves to help a group of people survive and cope with the world around them in all of its varieties and extremes. It consists of the language, values, beliefs, rules, behaviors, and physical artifacts of a society, which is why it has often been called a "design for living."[32] Simply put, culture provides the tools that allow a group of people to cooperate, communicate, live together, work together, and survive as a community. Given the wide variety of climates, geographic features, and weather conditions, we shouldn't be surprised at the diversity of the cultures that were created by the groups that explored the continent. The peoples who settled across North, Central, and South America developed an incredibly rich array of cultural adaptations that reflect an amazing human ability to adapt to geographic differences and extremes.

Those that remained in the north, in what is now Canada and Alaska, created societies that managed to exist in an incredibly demanding climate. Relative newcomers who had crossed over Beringia in subsequent waves of trekkers, the Aleuts, Yup'ik, Inuit, and Athapascan peoples endured in a landscape that is renowned for its extreme and unforgiving nature. The Aleut survived along the Aleutian island chain and relied upon the rich marine environment to provide food, shelter, and clothing while living in small seaside villages of no more than 100 to 200 people.[33]

The Yup'ik, Inuit, and Athapascan, on the other hand, learned to deal with the cold and long, dark winters of the northern coast and interior of North America. Given the scarcity of food and shelter and the difficulties of survival in such a harsh land, these peoples developed cultures that were remarkably communal and supportive in orientation. Living and traveling in small family bands, they became adept at surviving in an environment that could quickly kill the unwary. In the summer they fished and hunted for game such as moose, caribou, beaver, and waterfowl. They also foraged for berries, parsnip, and the inner bark of the poplar tree during the all-too-brief growing season.[34] During the long darkness of the winter, they sometimes roamed far over the sea ice in search of seals, which they stalked at the breathing holes favored by this marine mammal. They weren't the only group to take advantage of the riches of the ocean.

In the Pacific Northwest, Native groups such as the Tlingit, Kwakiutl, and Haida learned to take advantage of the incredibly rich marine environment of the northern Pacific. Every year the rivers of the region were clogged with different varieties of salmon heading upriver to spawn, while the coastal waters teemed with marine mammals and shellfish. In this environment, the people who settled here developed societies characterized by large villages with communal longhouses that allowed for a pooling of resources to better harvest the abundant resources of the region. Intrepid hunters sometimes took to the rolling swells of the open ocean in large wooden canoes to hunt whales during their seasonal migrations offshore. They also created the "potlatch," a ceremonial ritual marking a transition such as a birth, death, or wedding and which involved feasting, dancing, singing, and giving gifts in order to commemorate the occasion and to establish and maintain status, rank, and wealth.[35]

Further south and in a much different climate, the Hohokam peoples of the Sonoran desert coped with the arid climate by creating a series of technologically sophisticated canals that allowed them to irrigate fields and grow crops in a landscape with little rain and high temperatures. Yet the Hohokam and their neighbors not only survived, but also thrived. The Hohokam territory spanned over 25,000 square miles and encompassed many communities, some of which were quite large.[36]

Farther east along the Mississippi River in the Midwest, the Cahokian culture created some of the densest population centers in North America. Their largest city probably had a population at its peak of around 15,000, which made it the largest community north of the Rio Grande River.[37] Surrounded by fields of corn, the network of chiefdoms that constituted their society built small cities identified by large, flat-topped earthen pyramids upon which temple palaces were built for the nobility, whose job it was to see to the prosperity of the people and to ensure successful harvests.[38]

In Central America, the Olmecs, Maya, and Aztecs built empires that were technologically and politically sophisticated societies. As Charles Mann writes of them:

> They invented a dozen different systems of writing, established wide-spread trade networks, tracked the orbits of the planets, created a 365-day calendar (more accurate than its contemporaries in Europe), and recorded their histories in accordion-folded "books" of fig tree bark paper.[39]

They also invented the concept of zero, which has always been a significant milestone in any civilization as it is a necessary prerequisite for science, technology, and mathematics. Even farther south, the Inca built a vast empire along the Andes that encompassed high mountains, coastal plains, and tropical rainforest. In fact, it was the world's largest empire at that time and spanned thirty-two degrees of latitude.[40] In order to run such a large domain, the Inca developed an incredibly sophisticated administrative system that built and maintained large cities, roads, and canals, all of which allowed a vast empire to be efficiently maintained.[41] Europe, at this point, had nothing to compare.

This list could easily be continued to include any of the thousands of other empires, tribes, clans, and peoples scattered throughout the Americas that had created their own unique identities, customs, and traditions. I emphasize this point since all too often popular opinion and even government policy has tended to perceive all Native peoples as being one people. Policies in the United States, for example, have sometimes been uniformly applied without regard for individual tribal differences or experiences. Unfortunately, it has also been a way of "essentializing the other," which makes no allowance for the diversity of experience, culture, and lifestyle among the various indigenous populations and does not acknowledge their individual worth and humanity.

Although usually perceived by the new European arrivals as savages and primitives, the inhabitants of the "new" world were anything but. Ethnocentric to a fault, Europeans judged Natives by the standards of European culture and found them wanting. But we need to remember that Native cultures were not European ones and operated by a different set of principles and standards, or as Frederick Hoxie quite rightly points out: "Indian communities cannot be analyzed as if they were smaller, backward versions of European villages."[42] Socially, economically, politically, and culturally, the Americas were a place of incredible richness, complexity, and sophistication. This is not to suggest, however, that life in the Americas was a Garden of Eden with everyone living in innocence, peace, and harmony.

THE MYTH OF THE NOBLE SAVAGE

It has long been popular in some circles to portray the Native people of the Americas as being noble savages who embody a mythic ideal of humanity in perfect accord with nature. The tendency to romanticize indigenous populations has a long tradition within Western society and reaches back into antiquity, or as John Mohawk points out, "All societies have had their utopian dreams, and in many ancient societies, utopias were envisioned as located in a distant past when human beings and nature existed harmoniously in blissful unity."[43] Often, this kind of perspective arises out of a sense that civilization is somehow corrupting and alienating and that people can only remain uncorrupted when they are left in a "state of nature." In ancient Greece it was the Lotus Eaters who embodied this tradition. According to Greek mythology, the Lotus Eaters were a race of people living on an island who ate only the fruit of the lotus, which is a narcotic, and consequently lived in a state of bliss and peace. In Rome it was the idyllic Arcadia of shepherds, nymphs, and rustic gods that represented an escape from the corruption, violence, and degradation of the "civilized world." Cut off from the rest of the world, Arcadia was envisioned as a land of rural simplicity and harmony. Even the biblical conception of the Garden of Eden fits into this notion, with Adam and Eve living in an earthly paradise free of needs and wants and in a state of absolute innocence.

These kinds of rustic fantasies are easy to understand once we recognize the appeal for those who long to escape into a simpler world. These were the kinds of ideas and images that the new world evoked for many new European arrivals. To jaded eyes, the lands they encountered represented a paradise inhabited by a people who were uncorrupted by greed. The landscape, especially in the Caribbean, was lush and beautiful and appeared to be largely untouched by human hands, while the people were graceful and without the pockmarked and disfigured complexions so common to Europeans. One European commentator remarked that:

> They live in a golden age, and do not surround their properties with ditches, walls or hedges. They live in open gardens, without laws or books, without judges, and they naturally follow goodness and consider odious anyone who corrupts himself by practicing evil.[44]

In a similar vein, the discoverer of the new world, Christopher Columbus, wrote to the king and queen of Spain that:

> They all go naked, men and women, just as their mothers bore them . . . They have no iron or steel or weapons, nor are they fitted to use them; not because they are not well built and of handsome stature, but because they are extraordinarily timorous . . . It is true that, after they become reassured and lose this fear, they are so guileless and so generous with all that they possess, that no one would believe it who has not seen it. Of anything they have, if they are asked for it, they never say no, on the contrary they invite the person to share it and display as much love as if they would give their hearts.[45]

If these positive kinds of perceptions had been maintained, the story of the Americas after contact might have been very different, but unfortunately, these positive images were soon reshaped by the pressures of greed, bigotry, intolerance, and religion into much more negative stereotypes that justified and enabled wholesale slavery, exploitation, violence, and sometimes even extermination. Even the positive image of the Noble Savage was connected to a paternalistic attitude in which the Natives were somewhat like innocent children who needed the guiding and educating hand of the parental Europeans.[46] In the European mind, primitive equated to childlike.

The positive stereotypes, however, never disappeared entirely. Throughout the colonial era, for example, these conflicting images served to reinforce the tensions between those who sought to coexist with and protect the Natives and those who worked to exploit or eliminate them. We've also seen them resurrected in more recent times with Native Americans being portrayed as primitive ecologists, conservationists, and environmentalists living in perfect harmony with nature. In its own way, this stereotype is as dehumanizing and misleading as the many images of Native Americans that depict them as ignorant savages.

Both ignore the individual and cultural diversity exhibited by the different tribes and take away the humanity of those so labeled. The essential point is neither to denigrate the Native people of the Americas nor to justify the violence wreaked upon them, but rather to point out that romanticizing the peoples and cultures of the Western Hemisphere is not very helpful in any attempt to understand and make sense of the Native experiences postcontact.

Ignoring the humanity of those being studied and elevating them to the status of a mythic being, the myth of the noble primitive is ultimately as harmful as the most racist negative stereotypes about savages and barbarians that contributed so much to the conflict and destruction. We must resist the urge to objectify and romanticize the victims. The world of the Natives prior to the arrival of the Europeans was as complex, as wonderful, and as flawed as that found anyplace else in the world and subject to the same kinds of problems, shortcomings, and human weaknesses, as well as achievements and aspirations. The Native peoples exploited and sometimes overexploited their resources and environment to the full extent that they were able.[47]

In some places Native American life was characterized by incessant warfare and raiding. While some have suggested that Native ways of war were less sustained, systematic, and destructive, this argument misses the point and is largely incorrect.[48] Importantly, this perspective contributes to the stereotyping discussed above. Among some tribes warfare did tend to be more ritualistic and were usually shorter-term affairs, but this was probably not a very comforting distinction if you were on the receiving end of the violence. Native warfare was also not always so benign. A great deal of recent research indicates that for many, if not most Native peoples, fighting and war were a constant reality and much of this fighting was quite destructive and deadly.[49] The Inuit routinely practiced a form of ambush raids that involved killing all members of rival bands and settlements except for one person who would be left alive to tell the tale.[50]

During the 1600s, the Iroquois practiced what some have termed genocidal or ethnocidal warfare against neighboring tribes such as the Huron, Algonquians, Montagnais, Erie, and Shawnee, among others.[51] This style of warfare began appearing in the 1600s in response to the economic incentives offered by the burgeoning fur trade and by the increasing availability of firearms, and while this certainly was influenced by the European presence in the region, it nonetheless reflects a very pragmatic approach to warfare and a willingness to embrace destructive tactics. On the plains, the groups that made up the Lakota people, often known as the Sioux, constantly fought against the Cheyenne, Kiowa, Arapahoe, and the Crow, and succeeded in decimating the Omaha and Poncas.[52] They themselves were only on the plains because they had been driven out of their homeland in what is now Minnesota by the more numerous Ojibwa peoples. Similarly, the Nermernuh, better known as the Comanche, nearly exterminated the Tonkawa and decimated the Apache.[53] They were consummate raiders and had no problem attacking other Native Americans.

One expert on early warfare in the Americas suggests that between 20 and 30 percent of all Native males and 3 to 5 percent of females were killed during wars.[54] To compare these rates to European conflict we find that Native American warfare resulted in somewhat higher casualty rates than those found during the Napoleonic Wars and are comparable to those experienced by the losers during the Thirty Years' War, a time of widespread conflict, famine, and destruction.[55] We can also look at the Incan civil war fought in South America just prior to Pizarro's appearance. Two brothers, Atahualpa and Huascar, were contesting the throne of the vast Incan Empire. The war they fought was a brutal one, equal in destructiveness to any European civil war. When the Canari people (a tribe in the northern part of the empire) sided with his brother, Atahualpa engaged in a war of terror against them, which involved numerous massacres of Canari men, women, and children when individual villages and towns didn't surrender unconditionally.[56]

Furthermore, both the Aztec and Incan Empires were just that: empires. Their power and wealth was based upon the subjugation of other tribal peoples who were oppressed and exploited at the whims and needs of the ruling classes. In fact, one important factor in the successful overthrow of a number of Native empires was that the Europeans were often able to find willing allies among various subjugated tribes.

In recent years, scientists exploring the history of Vikings in North America have uncovered a number of Norse settlements on Baffin Island, across the Davis Strait from Greenland, and northern Labrador. These sites have yielded various artifacts that suggest a larger Norse presence in North America than previously believed. Speculating that they were in search of valuables for use in Greenland and in Europe, some scientists now believe that the Vikings actively sought trading partners and found them among the nomadic Dorset people, who had a long history of trading with their neighbors for needed goods.[57] These archaeological sites seem to suggest that the Norse and the Natives developed a friendly relationship based on mutually beneficial trading arrangements and even sometimes lived together within the same settlements. This image of a peaceful transatlantic trading network paints a different story than is often believed. While the Vikings found hostility and conflict further south, in the far north among the Dorset, they found a friendlier reception. As the archaeologist Patricia Sutherland asserts after working on these sites, "I think things were a lot more complex in this part of the world than most people assumed,"[58] and that is precisely the point of this chapter and of this book.

2

GENOCIDE

Some Native American scholarship focusing on genocide oscillates between two opposing camps: those that devote energy simply to proving that genocide did occur in Native American history and those that more liberally apply the concept of genocide without sufficient analytical support.

—Brenden Rensink[1]

Genocide did occur sporadically in American Indian history. While the term enthnocide may be a more appropriate word to describe Indian policies over time, genocide, nevertheless, is a correct term to apply to specific times, places, and events in American Indian History.

—Laurence M. Hauptman[2]

It has become apparent that there are undesirable consequences to enlarging or diluting the definition of genocide. This weakens the terrible stigma associated with the crime and demeans the suffering of its victims. It is also likely to enfeeble whatever commitment States may believe they have to prevent the crime.

—William A. Schabas[3]

What is genocide? At this point it may be useful to spend a bit of time defining the term since it is a primary focal point of this book: to apply the concept of genocide to the experience of the indigenous peoples of the Americas. Genocide, as was previously noted, is an oft-used word that is all too often poorly understood and widely misused. At various times the term has been used to describe integration, birth control, drug distribution, sterilization, abortion, bisexuality, cocaine addiction, dieting, and suburbanization.[4] Clearly, the word is often used for inflammatory or political purposes that have little to do with the intended meaning of the word. Unfortunately, this tends to obscure the generally accepted nature of genocide. It may also serve to lessen the impact of the word when it is truly needed to call attention to this form of violence. If it is used to explain everything, then it explains nothing.

The word itself was first coined in 1944 with the publication of *Axis Rule in Occupied Europe*. Its author was a Polish lawyer named Raphael Lemkin who had fled from the Nazis in 1939 and eventually made his way to the United States where he became a persistent advocate for the plight of those suffering under Nazi rule.[5] Long concerned with international law and human rights, Lemkin believed that existing terms such as "massacre," "war crimes," and the like didn't really capture the scale and systematic nature of the Nazi-perpetrated atrocities. He therefore crafted the word "genocide" from the Greek word for a "race" or "tribe" (*genos*) and the Latin word for "killing" (*cide*). Genocide, then, literally means the killing of a race or tribe. Essentially, it involves the attempt to destroy a population group. As Lemkin envisioned it, genocide referred to a wide range of activities that both directly and indirectly were intended to systematically eliminate a group that had been targeted for annihilation.

Importantly, Lemkin saw genocide as a comprehensive process of destruction rather than a one-time or piecemeal type of event. Individual acts of violence that are not connected to a broader pattern of violence, as horrific as they may be, are not necessarily genocide according to Lemkin's formulation. Genocide, in other words, is a strategy, not an event. Lemkin was a tireless advocate, and after the war ended he helped persuade the newly created United Nations (U.N.) to begin the process of transforming genocide from an abstraction into international law. In this pursuit, he was aided by the well-known Nuremberg trials, which revealed the extent and nature of the horrific Nazi crimes to the world. It is important to note, however, that genocide was not one of the charges leveled against the Nazi leadership since the concept had not yet been defined and codified into law. In 1946 the U.N. passed a resolution condemning genocide, an important symbolic step, but one without much force for preventing the crime.

This was followed by several years of contentious debates and committee work culminating in the General Assembly of the United Nations
adopting genocide as a crime under international law in December of
1948.[6] According to Article II of the U.N. Genocide Convention definition, genocide is defined as:

> any of the following acts committed with intent to destroy, in whole
> or in part, a national, ethnical, racial or religious group, as such:
>
> a. killing members of the group;
> b. causing serious bodily or mental harm to members of the group;
> c. deliberately inflicting on the group conditions of life calculated to
>   bring about its physical destruction in whole or in part;
> d. imposing measures intended to prevent births within the group;
> e. forcibly transferring children of the group to another group.[7]

It might be helpful to break this definition down into its three main
component parts: the acts, the victimized groups, and the concept of
intention.[8] The first element of the definition, the acts, reveals that
genocide encompasses many different behaviors, not all of which are
directly or overtly violent. The first three listed techniques of genocide
(a, b, and c), refer to physical genocide, while the last two (d and e)
refer to biological forms of genocide.[9] When people think of genocide,
they tend to picture cases of mass murder such as the gas chambers of
the Holocaust or the massacres with machetes that were such a prominent feature of the Rwandan genocide. But that isn't the entire picture.
As this definition makes clear, genocide can include many other forms
of destruction, only some of which are overtly violent. What this means
is that genocide can be a relatively short-lived affair, such as directly
killing members of a group, or it can be a longer-term project, such as
preventing births within a group, the effects of which are only destructive over a long period of time.

The second element concerns the victimized groups, and this definition reveals that only the targeting of a national, ethnic, racial, or religious group counts as genocide. For something to be considered genocidal, it must be focused against one of these four categories of populations. These groups, however, are somewhat difficult to define specifically because the terms themselves are vague and arbitrary. Should
someone be considered a member of a religious group even if they do

not practice that faith? What if they convert? Is nationality defined by citizenship or birth? These kinds of questions have never been fully resolved. We also now recognize race as a social construct, not a scientific one, and racial identity is therefore much more fluid than once believed. The practical result of all of this imprecision has meant that the notion of groups has a fair amount of subjectivity built into it, and the group is defined, at least in part, largely by the perceptions of the perpetrator.

What sets genocide apart from other similar kinds of crimes is that people are targeted solely because of their membership in the targeted group. It doesn't matter what kind of person they are or what they do or say; they are slated for elimination simply because they belong to some population that is being persecuted. It doesn't even matter if a particular individual identifies himself or herself as belonging to the victim group or if they deny their membership. As long as they fit into some category as defined by the perpetrators, their intended victimization will be assured. While the indigenous populations of the Americas clearly fit into the category of identified groups, other communities do not. Political groups, for example, were purposively excluded from this definition because it was believed that they were too unstable and impermanent and because inclusion might have endangered support for the U.N. Genocide Convention in countries where action against political groups had occurred or might occur. [10]

The third and perhaps the most important element of this definition concerns the component of intent. This means that the crime of genocide must evidence purposive behavior. It has to be planned and deliberate. This is a basic principle of Western criminal law. For something to constitute a crime, behavior must be intended; it cannot be accidental or unwilling. Legally speaking, proving intent can be a tricky proposition, and this is especially true for the crime of genocide. In regard to genocide specifically, the genocide convention requires a degree of intent that is often referred to as "specific intent," "special intent" (*dolus specialis*), or even "genocidal intent." [11] In order to qualify as genocide, the destructive acts must have been specifically intended to destroy a group. Conversely, destroying a group without that specific intention does not qualify as genocide.

Essentially, then, for something to be considered genocide, it must not only be intentionally committed, but it must also have the express goal of eliminating a population. This is an important point, since not all atrocities and violence can be considered as constituting genocide. War crimes and atrocities, widespread deaths due to disasters and dislocation, and communal and ethnic violence are not necessarily genocide. As horrific, tragic, and terrible as these forms of violence may be, unless they contain the intention to annihilate a group of people, they are not examples of genocide, at least not according to this definition. This has important ramifications for our discussion of genocide and Native peoples, as we shall see.

The U.N. convention has a number of other significant shortcomings, one of which is directly related to the experiences of the Natives of the Americas. In particular, the notion of cultural genocide is not included in this particular definition, although many social scientists continue to include it in their discussions of this phenomenon. Lemkin himself saw this as an important type of genocide. Sometimes referred to as ethnocide, cultural genocide refers to the attempted annihilation of the ties that connect a community and that make them distinct and unique. Culture is all about how groups of people are connected,[12] and cultural genocide targets those cultural qualities instead of human bodies. It leaves the people alive, but destroys the bonds that unite them and kills the collective identity of its victims. Even though it was not included in the United Nations Genocide Convention definition, in 1981 the United Nations Educational, Scientific, and Cultural Organization (UNESCO) declared:

> Ethnocide means that an ethnic group is denied the right to enjoy, develop and transmit its own culture and its own language, whether individually or collectively. . . . We declare that ethnocide, that is, cultural genocide, is a violation of international law equivalent to genocide, which was condemned by the United Nations Convention on the Prevention and Punishment of the Crime of Genocide.[13]

Cultural genocide also has a fairly wide acceptance among scholars who see it as an important conceptual category of genocide.

SOCIAL SCIENCE AND DEFINITIONS OF GENOCIDE

In many ways, the U.N. Genocide Convention definition is the result of a highly politicized process that resulted in a document with a number of shortcomings and problems. Because of this, many social scientists have created alternative definitions of genocide that try to address some of the weaknesses of the U.N. Convention definition and that do not impose such a high threshold of intent. For example, Robert Melson created an alternative definition, which suggested that genocide is:

> a public policy mainly carried out by the state whose intent is the destruction in whole or in part of a social collectivity or category, usually a communal group, a class, or a political faction.[14]

We shouldn't be surprised that Melson, a political scientist, focuses on the state as the principal agent of genocide. This is a theme echoed by other genocide scholars who study this issue and leads to the conclusion that genocide is, for all intents and purposes, a policy designed to achieve some specific end or goal. While not all genocides are state perpetrated, it is also true that most recent examples tend to be the result of either formal or informal state policy.[15] Alternatively, the sociologists Frank Chalk and Kurt Jonassohn contend that genocide is:

> a form of one-sided killing in which a state or other authority intends to destroy a group, as that group and membership in it are defined by the perpetrator.[16]

For Chalk and Jonassohn, what separates genocide from other forms of collective violence is the asymmetry of violence. In other words, the victims are not engaged in mutual combat, and this is what separates genocide from warfare, terrorism, and similar forms of collective violence with combatants on both sides. These ideas are mirrored in the work of the British political scientist Martin Shaw, who argues that genocide, while closely related, is distinct and separate from warfare insomuch as it targets civilian groups and populations rather than combatant soldiers.[17] Another sociologically based definition comes from one of the leading scholars of genocide, Helen Fein, who wrote that genocide consists of:

sustained purposeful action by a perpetrator to physically destroy a collective directly or indirectly, through interdiction of the biological and social reproduction of group members, sustained regardless of the surrender or lack of threat offered by the victim.[18]

Fein offers a definition that emphasizes the notion that genocide is an intentional and systematic process of destruction, which is fairly close in structure to that of the U.N. Genocide Convention definition. These few examples give a sense of the range of definitions offered as conceptual, if not legal, alternatives and help provide an understanding of what a variety of experts believe constitutes genocide.

Another strategy that some have used to address the perceived deficiencies in the official definition is to create other kinds of *"cides."* In an effort to highlight the gendered nature of much of this kind of violence, a number of scholars have developed and used the concept of gendercide.[19] Others have offered politicide, classicide, urbicide, and autogenocide, among others.[20] Keep in mind that these definitions are meant to serve different purposes. While the U.N. Genocide Convention definition is meant to serve as a legal tool to deter and punish, scholarly definitions and variations are designed to clarify and help explain the nature of this crime. In other words, they are conceptual tools rather than legal ones. But there is no single definition that is universally accepted and relied upon.

Perhaps the strongest and most widely applied definition is the U.N.'s, which has the power of international law behind it. It has been successfully incorporated into the tribunals that were established for Yugoslavia and Rwanda, the International Law Commission's Code of Crimes against the Peace and Security of Mankind, as well as the International Criminal Court.[21] We shouldn't forget, however, that it is not the only definition that is used to identify, describe, and encompass this phenomenon. So how do the U.N.'s definition and these alternative definitions fit with the experiences of the Native peoples of the Americas?

NATIVE AMERICANS AND GENOCIDE

Applying the concept of genocide to the history of Native America poses some unique challenges and complications. Typically, when examining cases of genocide, the situation is relatively straightforward as there is usually an obvious outbreak of violence that clearly fits or doesn't fit within the established criteria for genocide. While there are sometimes disagreements about these qualities with reference to exceptional and unusual cases, the classic characteristics of genocide are generally agreed upon by most scholars. Genocide is usually perpetrated by a government that for a variety of reasons intends and plans to systematically eliminate a specific population group using a variety of methods, and victims are chosen because they belong to a racial, ethnic, national, or religious group that is identified as an enemy and which often has a history of victimization.[22] Yet when we look at the case of Native Americans, we find that it doesn't necessarily fit the usual pattern. Since genocide refers to a particular legal and conceptual idea that encompasses specific and intentional acts aimed at the destruction of a population, can this concept rightly be applied to what the Natives of the Americas experienced? Certainly some have suggested that it is absolutely appropriate. The historian David Stannard writes that "The destruction of the Indians of the Americas was, far and away, the most massive act of genocide in the history of the world."[23] Similarly, the controversial activist Ward Churchill argues that "the genocide inflicted upon American Indians over the past five centuries is unparalleled in human history, both in terms of its sheer magnitude and in its duration."[24] Rebecca Frey also makes this point when she writes:

> most of the massacres of Native Americans in what is now the United States during the 18th and 19th centuries involved fewer victims than recent aviation accidents involving jumbo jets, yet few historians would deny that the deaths of the 20 Conestoga Indians in Pennsylvania in 1764 or those of the 180 Cheyenne killed at Sand Creek in Colorado a century later were genocidal killings.[25]

The genocide scholar Ben Kiernan echoes this theme when he asserts that the only way to characterize the Native experience is as genocide. But are these assertions accurate? Is it really that simple? While at first blush it seems easy to accept these claims, when you look a little more closely, the issue becomes a bit more problematic. This is not to suggest that genocides did not occur, but rather that it is more complex a question than we might initially think. There are a number of specific reasons for this assessment.

First, according to the U.N. Genocide Convention, and many of the other definitions as well, genocidal behavior must be intentional. For a crime to rise to the level of genocide, it must have been knowingly committed. Not only that, it must have been intentionally perpetrated with the express goal of eliminating a population. Simply put, according to an interpretation that adheres to this standard, if these definitional criteria are not met, then it's not genocide, or, as one representative involved in the creation of the genocide convention definition suggested, "Genocide is characterized by the factor of particular intent to destroy a group. In the absence of that factor, whatever the degree of atrocity of an act and however similar it might be to the acts described in the convention, that act could still not be called genocide."[26]

Not everyone, however, shares this focus on intention. Some, for example, have tended to focus more on the outcome of the violence, and not so much on intent. Even though this perspective has no legal standing, it makes it much easier, intellectually at least, to apply the label of genocide to the experiences of the Native peoples of the Americas. By focusing on the consequences of contact, rather than on the intentions, it is easier to suggest that the entire postcontact Native experience was wholly genocidal in its impact. But is this a valid approach? Why should we stick with the legal definition when we are only retroactively applying the concept of genocide to the conflicts between Natives and Europeans? We are simply trying to better understand the past, not pursue legal action. Do we need to adhere to the underlying meaning of the term as it has been established and as it continues to be defined and redefined by the various legal bodies with jurisdiction over genocidal offenses? If not, why then limit ourselves to a legalistic definition? Similarly, we can ask if we need to stick to the ideas and parameters as outlined by the originator of the term, Raphael Lemkin. Is it possible that the idea of genocide has moved beyond its original conceptualization? In fact, Lemkin's ideas about genocide were sometimes inconsistent and even contradictory, so how closely do we need to stick to his vision of this crime? There are no easy answers to these questions because they get to the very meaning of the concept of genocide, or, more accurately, how the meanings of genocide are understood and applied. In other words, genocide itself is a contested concept subject to varying perceptions and interpretations.

We can consider the issue of intent, which is so crucial to the U.N. definition of genocide. An advocate of this position might suggest that to ignore it and focus only on outcome is to dismiss one of the most basic principles of law and justice. A person or group's intentions are critical in understanding the nature of the act. In all aspects of life, we make distinctions and judgments based on what was intended. Accidental or unintentional behavior is always perceived somewhat differently than purposeful behavior. From this standpoint, intention is crucial to any understanding of the nature of genocide, and its centrality can be illustrated with reference to another type of crime. Let's examine first-degree murder, for example.

Murder in the first degree is generally considered to be the worst form of criminal homicide and is ranked above second-degree murder and the different forms of manslaughter.[27] Because it is considered to be more heinous, a conviction on first-degree murder charges typically elicits a harsher sentence than the other forms of murder and manslaughter. For a killing to be considered as first-degree murder, it has to be perpetrated with the mental elements of premeditation and deliberation. Premeditation concerns the intention to kill, while deliberation means that the killing was considered and planned.[28] Simply put, first-degree murder requires that the perpetrator had to have thought about their actions, decided to kill, and then carried it out. This thinking, planning, and carrying out does not need to be a long process, but can occur in the minutes and seconds before the actual killing takes place.

Second-degree murder, on the other hand, tends to be a more impulsive and emotional form of murder because it does not include the elements of premeditation and deliberation. This type of killing involves someone exhibiting extreme indifference to life and a desire to seriously harm somebody rather than a clear intention to kill. When we look at manslaughter, considered to be a less serious form of criminal homicide than first- or second-degree murder, we find even less intentionality revealed in the crime. In some ways, manslaughter is about accidental killings caused by reckless or indifferent behavior. The legal responsibility is correspondingly less than it is for murder.

The point of this discussion is to illustrate the centrality of intent for defining different kinds of criminal homicide. As the mental elements change, the definition of the crime also changes. Without premeditation and deliberation, a killing is not first-degree murder. In the same way, advocates of a legalistic definition of genocide argue that without intent, "specific intent" to be exact, a crime is not genocide. International legal rulings have held that genocidal intent is the key or central element in any legal application of the term to acts of genocide. [29] As the genocide scholar Ben Kiernan succinctly states in support of this position, "Comparable acts committed even deliberately but in a reckless manner do not constitute genocide. The crime requires the perpetrator's conscious desire." [30] In his analysis of genocide and ethnic deportations in the Soviet Union, Alexander Statiev examines this issue of intent versus outcome and argues that the ethnic deportations were not genocide precisely because the requisite need of intention was absent. [31] Even though the deportations were callously implemented without regard to casualties and even though large numbers of individuals were killed, the Soviet government never intended the outright extermination of the ethnic groups they deported, or as he puts it, "Had the Soviet government wanted to exterminate these minorities, it would have done so: its punitive capacity was as unlimited as that of the Nazi regime." [32]

One interesting attempt to deal with the problematic nature of intent was developed by the well-known genocide scholar Israel Charny, who suggests that genocide be categorized into first, second, and third degrees, just as with ordinary criminal homicide. [33] This differentiation would be determined by the amount of premeditation and the totality of the destructive effort, among other qualities. Rather than having a single high standard of genocidal intent (*dolus specialis*) that must be met for a crime to rise to the level of genocide, Charny's proposal allows for a more graduated definition of genocide that acknowledges different "levels" of genocide and which would allow for a broader range of events. Furthermore, Charny also proposes the concept of attempted genocide that is analogous to the category of attempted murder. For Charny, the issue of intent is clearly central to his understanding of genocide.

Another interesting take on the issue of intent comes from Kai Ambos, a law professor who suggests that the issue of intent should be applied differently based on whether the actors were top-level, mid-level, or low-level perpetrators and whether or not they were state agents or private citizens. [34] According to Ambos, it is the top-level perpetrators who should be held accountable to the special intent requirement of genocide since they are the ones who formulate the goals and set into motion the plan to destroy a population. But for low-level private citizens who participate:

> this awareness cannot be simply inferred from the genocidal state policy (as in the case of low-level state agents) nor from their essential involvement in the state plans (as in the case of mid-level private actors) but requires a *specific knowledge* in terms of a link of their concrete acts to the overall genocidal policy. Only then can a banalization of the genocide crime be avoided and their qualification as "genocidaires" justified.[35]

This is a much more nuanced understanding of how intent may relate to the different types of perpetrators that are involved in committing genocide.

To further complicate this issue, relatively recent court cases have served to modify our understanding of how the terms of the genocide convention definition can be interpreted and applied in regard to intent. Unfortunately, they haven't necessary clarified the issue. While the framers of the convention definition theorized the nature of genocide, it has been in the courtroom that the meanings of the language and terms used in the convention definition have been interpreted. In regard to intent, for example, a number of courts have provided rulings that illustrate the practical application of the term. The International Criminal Tribunal for Rwanda (ICTR) has upheld the notion that genocide requires the signal aim of explicitly trying to eradicate a protected group. They also, however, decided that proof of this intent need not come from a confession or discovery of a genocidal plan or policy, but rather can be inferred from patterns of destructive action that include such things as the general context of the commission of other systematic violence against a particular protected group, the scale of the attacks, and the deliberate and systematic targeting of people because they belong to a group identified in the genocide convention definition.[36]

On the other hand, in February of 2007, the International Court of Justice (ICJ) ruled on the case of Bosnia v. Serbia and was unable to infer genocidal intent on the part of Serbia. While many have criticized this ruling, it does illustrate the variety of opinions on the matter, even among international legal jurists.[37] When the International Criminal Tribunal for the Former Yugoslavia convicted Goran Jelisic in 1999, he was found guilty on many violations of the laws and customs of war, of murder, inhumane acts, and cruel treatment. He was not, however, found guilty of genocide even though Jelisic had named himself the "Serbian Adolf" and had made various statements about "cleansing" the Muslims and wanting to kill them and then carrying out those stated intentions.[38] The prosecutor appealed this ruling and the subsequent appeals chamber decision supported the trial chamber decision because they couldn't find the necessary level of intent on the part of Jelisic.[39] Even though Jelisic committed many murders against Bosnian Muslims, much of his violence was largely random and, according to the trial and appeals court, not necessarily genocidal in intent. Similarly, both the trial and appeals chamber of the tribunal for Yugoslavia failed to convict Milomir Stakić of genocide even though he had participated in widespread and systematic atrocities against Bosnian Muslims, because the prosecution was unable to establish the *dolus specialis*, or genocidal intent.[40]

More recently, in March of 2009, when the Pre-Trial Chamber of the International Criminal Court indicted the leader of the Sudan, Omar al-Bashir, for crimes against humanity and war crimes, they failed to include the crime of genocide even though the International Commission of Inquiry on Darfur to the United Nations had identified genocidal conditions in Darfur, and even though a number of states, including the United States, had labeled the violence occurring there as genocide.[41] The judges at the ICC later reversed themselves and indicted Omar al-Bashir on genocide charges, but this apparent confusion is revealing. The bottom line is that even in the international legal community there is no complete agreement on how exactly genocide is to be defined, especially in regard to such issues as intent. In short, what this means is that there is no one single definition of genocide, nor even one single interpretation of the U.N. Genocide Convention definition. Evidently, defining genocide is a tricky and sometimes confusing business.

This is what makes the case of Native America so problematic, since intent is not always present when examining different episodes within the postcontact experience of various Native peoples. As we will see, vast numbers of Natives were killed by disease. For the activist Ward Churchill, disease was a weapon that was consciously and intentionally used to facilitate the destruction of Native peoples.[42] In his own words, "the waves of epidemic disease that afflicted indigenous populations during these centuries were deliberately induced or at least facilitated, by the European invaders."[43] Similarly, the historian David Stannard labels the deaths from disease a "deliberate racist purge,"[44] and writes that "Although at times operating independently, for most of the long centuries of devastation that followed 1492, disease and genocide were interdependent forces acting dynamically—whipsawing their victims between plague and violence, each one feeding upon the other, and together driving countless numbers of entire ancient societies to the brink—and often over the brink—of total extermination."[45] Yet, except for a few specific examples that we will examine a bit more closely in a later chapter, this contention is largely refuted by the recognition that many of the deaths produced by disease were unintentionally caused and no evidence supports the notion of widespread facilitated infections.

In fact, the U.S. government created programs to vaccinate Native Americans from smallpox, one of the most virulent killers of the Native population. Beginning with Thomas Jefferson in 1801, the U.S. government attempted to ameliorate the impact of smallpox among Native tribes and passed legislation in 1832 that specified:

> That it shall be the duty of several Indian agents and sub-agents under the direction of the Secretary of War to take such measures as he shall deem most efficient to convene the Indian tribes in their respective towns, or in such other places and numbers and at such seasons as shall be most convenient to the Indian populations, for the purpose of arresting the progress of smallpox among the several tribes by vaccination.[46]

This legislation was not just window dressing since it was supported by a budget intended to help carry out this policy. Thomas Jefferson also wanted members of the Lewis and Clark expedition to carry doses of the smallpox vaccine, or as Jefferson called it, "kinepox," in order to vaccinate the Natives with whom they came in contact.[47] Carrying out these policies proved very difficult, for obvious reasons, but it nevertheless reveals a willingness and desire to protect Native Americans from this particular disease. A close examination of disease and the Native peoples of the Americas reveals a mixed bag of motives, policies, and intentions. This doesn't lessen the tragedy of these deaths or reduce the suffering that was created, but the deaths from disease aren't automatically genocide if one adheres to a definition of genocide that relies upon the notion of intent.

Similarly, applying the same standard of intent to the deaths inflicted through violence leads one to conclude that not all the killing constitutes genocide. Massacres such as the infamous one at Sand Creek and the slaughter at Wounded Knee were certainly atrocities, and perhaps genocide, but not necessarily. It depends on how the term is defined and utilized. These examples reveal the complexity of applying this modern term to historical events. For some, it's all about deciding whether individual massacres or acts of violence were part of a larger pattern of intentional violence aimed at the extermination of the tribes involved. If that is the case, then a strong argument can be made for them being acts of genocide. For others, however, it's more about the end result, regardless of whether it was consciously planned and intended. While the U.S. government sometimes pursued goals that were intentionally and callously destructive of Native peoples, at other times, policies of accommodation and coexistence were also introduced. These initiatives were certainly not benign or even appropriate, but do reveal that the government at different times and places and with different tribes had divergent intentions and goals, not all of which were destructive in orientation or outcome. How do we factor this into our understanding of genocide?

Furthermore, we can point out that not all of the violence was state orchestrated. Remember that most views of genocide suggest that governments largely perpetrate it as part of official or unofficial policy. Militia and vigilante groups, lynch mobs, and other organizations often engaged in violence against Native peoples. Uncoordinated and local in both perpetration and intention, these groups nevertheless engaged in murderous activities that have many or all of the hallmarks of being genocidal. How do these fit in with state policies? What does it mean if the state sometimes tried to protect Native peoples from the genocidal actions of local groups as was sometimes the case? How do these instances fit in with definitions of genocide? There is no simple answer to these questions. In short, the process of applying the language of genocide to Native America is complicated, not always self-evident, and is influenced by the definition or definitions used by those studying the issue, as well as the motives for using the term.

This discussion does provoke one important question. Can the sum total of all the Native experiences be seen as genocide in terms of its ultimate impact? In other words, even though the experiences of individual tribes varied tremendously, the overall effect of the experience of contact was invariably destructive, culturally as well as physically. Is it reasonable to perceive and define it as genocidal? At first glance, it also seems to tie in with the ICTR judgment that proof of intent can be inferred from patterns of destructive action that include such things as the general context of the commission of other systematic violence against a particular protected group, the scale of the attacks, and the deliberate and systematic targeting of people because they belong to a group identified in the genocide convention definition.[48] Clearly, this kind of argument focuses on the end result of contact and doesn't speak to the issue of intent, but it also raises practical questions as well. How is it possible to speak of one genocide when the period spans hundreds of years and involves a number of different governments, organizations, and groups?

The time frame of genocide is an important question when dealing with genocide and the Native American experience. How long can genocide last? We know that genocides sometimes range in time from a few months to a few years. The genocide in Rwanda in 1994 was perpetrated over the span of a hundred days, while in contrast, the Holocaust took place over a period of several years. Can genocide potentially endure over the course of decades and even centuries? Since genocide entails a systematic and coordinated attempt to destroy a population, the longevity of the process shouldn't automatically discount something from being considered genocide. On the other hand, the systematic and coordinated nature of genocide certainly implies a need for sustained intentional effort over time, and if that ends or is lacking, then it is not genocide anymore.

It's also important to note that when we look at the long time frame for the experience of Native Americans postcontact, we find that over the hundreds of years of contact, the formal and informal policies of the Spanish government were never coordinated with that of the French, British, Dutch, or American governments. The French, for example, were never interested in sending over large numbers of immigrants to establish colonies. Land and settlement were less important for them than the lucrative fur trade, and they invested a tremendous amount of

energy in cultivating profitable relationships with Native tribes that
were often far less confrontational and hostile than those experienced
by the British, who were much more interested in acquiring land and
settling it with British subjects. The demands of the fur trade dictated a
more cooperative and diplomatic approach, and the relatively small
number of French trappers, traders, and settlers never posed the same
threat that the British or the Spanish did in the respective territory they
claimed.

Policies also varied over time and place, and individual governments
sometimes pursued contradictory policies at the same time. The Spanish, for example, often struggled between the contradictory impulses of
brutal conquest through wholesale killing versus peaceful conversion to
Christianity through religion. It was conquest versus conversion, or gold
versus god. The Jesuits and Dominicans were largely concerned with
converting the Natives to Christianity, the business leaders were interested in exploiting the labor of Natives in order to get rich, and the
political and military leaders were interested in gaining, consolidating,
and protecting territory. Each of these goals often resulted in tensions
and contradictions within Spanish policies and practices in regard to the
various Native populations unfortunate enough to come under the sway
of the Spaniards. There was never one unified and consistent policy of
extermination. This isn't to suggest that policies of conversion were
benign, but rather that they represent a competing goal to that of physical annihilation. We can see these contradictory impulses in other
places as well.

In 1675, for example, war broke out in Virginia between the Susquehannock people and the white settlers. Using hit-and-run tactics, the
Susquehannock attacked isolated farms and homesteads, killing the isolated families living on what was then the margin of the frontier.[49] The
settlers reacted by appealing to the governor of the colony for permission to exterminate all the Natives, including those not at war with the
settlers. The governor, however, refused permission because he wanted
to maintain profitable trading relationships with the nonhostile tribes
and instead implemented a defensive strategy of building new forts and
defending established territory. Many settlers, unsatisfied with this decision, rallied around the leadership of a prominent young planter
named Nathaniel Bacon, who openly defied Governor Berkeley and
organized attacks against any and all Natives. Berkeley responded by

declaring Bacon guilty of treason, causing the upstart to march his troops against the governor and force him from Jamestown. Reinforced by support from England, Berkeley ultimately defeated the rebellion and hanged a number of Bacon's supporters, although Nathaniel Bacon escaped the noose by dying from dysentery shortly after capturing Jamestown. This little known example illustrates the cross purposes that so often characterized the policies and practices of the Europeans when it came to dealing with indigenous peoples.

Policies and practices also changed over time. The young Thomas Jefferson romanticized the noble and heroic savage, while the older Jefferson saw the Natives as an impediment to westward expansion and plotted to remove them from their lands. Given these facts, how is it possible to talk of *a* genocide? Again, the point is that when talking about genocide and Native populations, the reality appears to be much more complicated and nuanced than some might initially suggest. The purpose of this discussion is not to be unnecessarily pedantic and to split hairs, but rather to point out that if we want to discuss the Indians of the Americas and suggest that they were the victims of genocide, we need to be careful as to how the term is applied and to recognize that the term itself is used in different ways. This doesn't necessarily invalidate any particular claim of genocide in regard to the Native populations, but it certainly forces us to evaluate those assertions more carefully. The late sociologist and genocide scholar Irving Louis Horowitz summarized this position beautifully when he wrote, "It may seem terribly harsh to make surgical distinctions between varieties of death and the varieties of cruelty. But that is precisely the challenge that social science research must confront in the study of genocide. Such careful distinctions are made not for the purpose of choosing between forms of evil but in order to evaluate what consequences these evils bring about."[50] As I have stated earlier, the purpose of this book is not to state definitively whether or not genocide occurred in any particular instance, but rather to examine some of the complexities and discuss what they reveal about the concept of genocide and the varied experiences of the indigenous peoples of the Americas.

The history of the Americas after contact is not the simple story we often assume it to be. We create narratives of good and evil, right and wrong, and believe that this accurately represents reality. We sift through the historical record searching for insight and answers and piece together stories from what little has been left behind, and often don't acknowledge that the information we have is incomplete and represents only a fraction of what occurred. History is a collection of facts, culled from the historical record, that we shape to reflect a coherent story. Yet what about those whose voices were lost, whose stories were never told? While we can never completely overcome the paucity of the historical record, nor the selectivity of historical analysis, we can at least acknowledge that the truth is not as clear-cut as we all too often suggest. It is infinitely richer, more varied, and more complex. That is certainly the case for the topic of this particular book. The historian Karl Jacoby captures this reality when he writes:

> Despite popular perceptions of Europeans inserting themselves into native societies in the Americas through military conquest alone, the actual process of colonization often revolved around a much more ambiguous set of encounters. Seldom absent altogether, violence lurked in the background in these interactions as the participants struggled in quotidian ways over how to deal with the others in their midst.[51]

In other words, the story of Natives and newcomers is not solely one of genocidal violence, but of different civilizations coming together, sometimes peaceably, often violently. It was truly, to borrow Samuel Huntington's notable phrase, a "clash of civilizations."[52] All sides in this long and all-too-often tragic tale exhibited a variety of motives, goals, and alliances. Strategies of compromise and accommodation were tried and sometimes succeeded. Other times, because of misunderstandings, blindness, and folly, the tactics of conciliation and cooperation ended in abject failure. All sides at different times exhibited bravery and heroism, cowardice and betrayal, atrocity and cruelty. In short, the story of the Americas in the years, decades, and centuries after the arrival of the Europeans is a very human story, and it is hoped that this book, in discussing the Native experiences through the lens of genocide, will not only help clarify the issue of genocide in the Americas, but will also assist in revealing some of the complexities and dimensions to the interactions between Natives and Europeans that are all too often ignored or glossed over.

3

DESTRUCTIVE BELIEFS

s in the grasp of a superior.

—orge E. Ellis, Clergyman, 1882[1]

insatiable greed and ambition, is the cause of their villainies. felicitous, the native peoples so t, that our Spaniards have no sts.

—Bartolomé de Las Casas[2]

use our sorrow that so peculiar disappeared from the earth like the world.

—W. E. Cormack[3]

Friday, October 12, 1492, when in what is now the Bahamas. rs after midnight, and the ships 'or day to arrive. On that Friday, and that had been spotted the on the beach. Flags flying, Columbus and some of his captains and sailors rowed ashore to claim the land for King Ferdinand and Queen Isabella and to meet these people.[4] This first contact was peaceful and consisted mostly of trade.[5] As Columbus himself wrote, "In order to win their friendship, since I knew they were a people to be converted and won to our holy faith by love and friendship rather than by force, I gave them some red caps and glass beads which they hung round their necks, also many other trifles."[6] But even though this first encounter seemed relatively benign, we can already make out some disturbing warning signs for the future in his comments. Clearly, the initial friendliness was, at least in part, an expediency designed to make conversion to Christianity easier. Columbus's comments reveal a mind-set that doesn't allow for a live-and-let-live kind of approach. In fact, later in the same passage he goes on to write:

> they should be good servants and very intelligent, for I have observed that they soon repeat anything that is said to them, and I believe that they would easily be made Christians, for they appeared to me to have no religion. God willing, when I make my departure I will bring half a dozen of them back to their Majesties, so that they can learn to speak.[7]

His words speak to a Eurocentric sensibility that devalued the people about whom he was writing. In his words there is no real consideration given to the Natives themselves in terms of their well-being or of treating them as anything other than an inferior kind of person. In his eyes, they were like children. He wasn't thinking about asking for volunteers to come back to Spain with him. Almost certainly, he was simply planning to kidnap some just before departure.

But the image of the Natives that we derive from Columbus isn't completely negative. In some instances, we find that Columbus displayed a fair amount of respect and understanding of the Natives he encountered. In many ways, Columbus's writing reveals a complicated and deeply ambivalent attitude. On the one hand, he was impressed with their friendliness, openness, and generosity, yet on the other, he looked down on them as being uncivilized savages who were almost childlike in their openness and naiveté. In one letter, for example, Columbus wrote:

> I gave them a thousand pretty things that I had brought, in order to gain their love and incline them to become Christians. I hoped to win them to the love and service of their highnesses and of the whole Spanish nation and to persuade them to collect and give us of the things which they possessed in abundance and which we need. They

have no religion, and are not idolators; but all believe that power and goodness dwell in the sky and they are firmly convinced that I have come from the sky with these ships and people. . . . In this belief they gave me a good reception everywhere, once they had overcome their fear; and this is not because they are stupid—far from it, they are men of great intelligence, for they navigate all those seas and give a marvelously good account of everything—but because they have never before seen men clothed or ships like these.[8]

Yet, these positive sentiments were often contradicted by other more negative perceptions. The graciousness and humility he saw displayed by many of the Natives was typically interpreted as subservience. In his eyes, they were acting as servants and slaves, and what could be more natural than to treat them as such? People often hold inconsistent and contradictory feelings, impulses, and beliefs, and Columbus was no different. Keep in mind that he was coming from a society in which non-Christians from around the Mediterranean region served as slaves in many households.[9] We shouldn't be surprised, therefore, when over the course of four voyages, Columbus's interactions with the people he met devolved increasingly into violence and exploitation. In fact, in some ways he welcomed it.

The first time that violence broke out after a disagreement about a trade deal, Columbus wrote that it was a good thing because the Natives needed to learn to fear the Christians.[10] In the face of mounting evidence that he had not found the fabled lands of Asia, Columbus increasingly turned his attention to that other prize he had promised his imperial sponsors: gold. A deeply ambitious man, Columbus showed little tolerance for the increasing unwillingness of the Natives to submit to Spanish demands for gold or for their resistance to being enslaved, and so the situation deteriorated into violence and reprisals. In one extreme case, on the island of Hispaniola, the situation was so bad after Columbus had imposed a tribute system, enforced by murdering and torturing those who resisted, that rather than submit, 50,000 Natives destroyed their food stores and committed mass suicide.[11] One contemporary chronicler suggested that at least two-thirds of the Natives of Hispaniola died between 1494 and 1496, while in 1548 a census found only about 500 Natives on the entire island out of an initial population of many hundreds of thousands.[12]

This initial Spanish experience in the Caribbean was not unique in the sense that many subsequent interactions between Europeans and Natives followed the same basic pattern. So often we find that initial interactions were relatively friendly and peaceful, perhaps tinged with wariness, but open nonetheless. Typically, the Europeans found the first Natives they encountered to be helpful, friendly, and willing to engage in trade. The newcomers often needed basic supplies such as food, while the Natives quickly realized the value of the metal supplies and firearms that the Europeans could provide for them. Soon, however, and often, these initial encounters devolved into mistrust, hostility, and outright conflict and violence. For the Natives, trading often had symbolic and ceremonial overtones, with exchanges of gifts serving to connect people in a reciprocal web of mutual obligation and duty.

When they traded with the Europeans, however, these traditional practices proved to be insidious and destructive because the new arrivals felt no such sense of reciprocity and often treated the Natives with extreme arrogance and condescension. These qualities, combined with the Europeans' unpredictable willingness to use violence, threats, and intimidation, quickly ensured that the initial friendliness frequently eroded into fear, anger, and conflict. Sometimes the trigger was some theft or minor infraction that the Europeans reacted to with extreme brutality. Because of this common pattern, it's easy to ask if the relationships between these vastly different societies were always predestined to be so bloody and brutal. Was cohabitation and peace truly even possible? In many ways, the answers to these perplexing questions lie within the beliefs held by many, if not most, Europeans of the time. While the extent and virulence of the attitudes varied somewhat between various European nations and populations, and while there were always exceptions within every group, it is safe to say that the explorers and colonists commonly held certain kinds of mind-sets that helped increase the risk of misunderstanding and conflict and, ultimately, of genocide. These attitudes were in large part a legacy of the European cultures from which they came.

This is a very important issue when addressing the issue of Native America and genocide since genocides don't just happen or spontaneously erupt. A great deal of research has shown that they are planned and that certain attitudes, perceptions, and ideologies are often necessary for genocide to take place.[13] Perpetrator groups, for example, invariably dehumanize their intended victims in order to make it easier to harm them. It is a way of distancing oneself psychologically from the victims in order to see them as "the other," a being that is separate and distinct from one's own group. They are also often defined as deserving of their fate because of what they have done in the past or plan to do in the future. Frequently, this involves invoking notions of self-defense because of some imagined threat that the victims pose.

It is also now well established that people who plan and perpetrate genocide are generally not monsters, even though they perpetrate monstrous crimes. The individuals and groups who carry out policies and plans of destruction are typically ordinary human beings who have become convinced, persuaded, and/or coerced into participating in the attempted elimination of entire population groups. Human nature being what it is, these same people need to engage in certain kinds of social-psychological processes that make victimizing others possible and easier.[14] It is safe to say that many Europeans held the kinds of attitudes and beliefs that served these destructive ends. These kinds of perceptions are common to all populations because of a built-in predisposition to see one's own group as superior and better than all others.[15] This is called ethnocentrism, and in many ways it's only natural for human communities to have developed this tendency. If a group is to survive, then individuals must value their membership in that collective and feel loyalty to it, and this can only happen if people feel that their beliefs, traditions, values, and behaviors are not only different from other cultures, but are also better. From there, it's only a short step to believing that not only is one's own culture superior, but that those from other cultures are inferior. In other words, it's a way of emphasizing that "we" are distinct from "them."[16] This is just basic human nature. The biologist E. O. Wilson believes that natural selection played a powerful role in developing this human tendency. The ability to quickly identify and ward off potentially dangerous strangers helped provide a modicum of safety for one's own group.[17] This tendency is present even at a very early age as scientists have shown that three-month-old infants will react fearfully to strangers, but will smile and coo for parents and other familiar caretakers.[18]

When encountering the indigenous peoples of the Americas, or anywhere else for that matter, the Europeans tended to act ethnocentrically. In truth, however, Native American peoples were no different and also exhibited ethnocentric tendencies. The Navajo name for themselves is "the Dineh," which simply means "the people." The same is true for the O'odham, Apalachee, Inuna-ina, Issa, Ani-Yun'wiya, Tsetchestahase, and Anishinabe among many, many others.[19] Each name describes that group as some variation of "the people."[20] Similarly, Zulu in Africa referred to other tribes as "animals," while to the ancient Greeks, foreigners were known as "barbarians."[21] There is certainly a level of ethnocentrism inherent in referring to your own group as "the people" or "the human beings" because it automatically suggests that nonmembers of your group or tribe are not people or are a different kind of people.

EUROPEAN CULTURE AND VIOLENCE

It's no exaggeration to suggest that the Europeans who arrived in the Americas came from a continent steeped in intolerance and violence. Centuries of warfare, persecution, and religious pogroms had left an indelible mark on European culture. If we take the Spanish as a case study, we find that they were profoundly influenced by the Spanish wars of reconquest in the centuries leading up to the voyages of Columbus, as Christian kingdoms fought to recapture the Iberian Peninsula from the Muslims. It began in 711 CE, when a Muslim army crossed over from North Africa and invaded the Iberian Peninsula.[22] The Visigoths who ruled Spain at that time were politically fractured and vulnerable to invasion, and it didn't take long before Islamic forces had taken over all of Iberia except for several small Christian kingdoms in the north, specifically Asturias, León, Castile, Navarre, Aragón, and Catalonia. Calling the land *al-Andalus*, or "land of the Vandals," the North African invaders created an Islamic kingdom, based in the southern city of Cordoba, that was remarkably tolerant and progressive for the time and renowned for being a center of education and medicine.[23] Students and scholars from all over Europe and the Near East flocked to the libraries and universities that were established in Islamic Spain.[24]

Despite this, the small Christian kingdoms in the north began a centuries-long struggle that ultimately ended with the defeat of the Islamic kingdom of Granada in 1492.[25] They saw it as their mission to recapture the land of Spain from the Muslims, and this period became known as the Reconquest or *Reconquista*. The Reconquest was a complicated affair, with the various Christian and Muslim principalities often feuding and fighting amongst themselves and changing alliances, sometimes even across religious lines.[26] The fighting was characterized by raids into Islamic territory with the intent of destroying crops, orchards, and villages, and of killing and enslaving any Muslims they came across. This kind of conflict, with its shifting coalitions, fast-moving raids into enemy territory, and never-ending fighting, created a society that was heavily militarized and viewed outsiders with hostility and suspicion, since one didn't always know who was an enemy.

The result of this struggle was that hatred of the "other" and intolerance of differences was a quality that became deeply embedded in Spanish culture throughout the centuries of endemic warfare. In many ways, it was also a society that had become desensitized to violence and brutalized by the never-ending fighting and the ensuing death and destruction. In short, the Reconquest created a land in which soldiers were glorified for having liberated their homelands from foreign invaders. Importantly, they were seen not only as foreign invaders, but also as infidels. Keep in mind that much of the era of the *Reconquista* occurred during the period of the Crusades, when Europe was inflamed with the desire to free the Holy Land from the clutches of Islam. Many Europeans saw the conflict in Spain as part of a wider struggle against nonbelievers. In fact, Christian crusaders sometimes fought in Iberia as part of their Christian duty.[27] The Reconquest was consequently defined as a holy war and violence in its cause was, therefore, a virtue.

As the Reconquest ended, Spain was a heavily militarized society without an enemy, and it was easy to transfer this crusading zeal toward the exploration and conquest of the New World. The exploration of the Americas provided a safe outlet (at least for the Spanish crown) for the militaristic aggression of the young men who had come of age during the endless wars and whose only real skill was that of fighting. As the historian David Weber puts it, "The Spanish struggle to control the New World and its peoples became, in effect, an extension of the Reconquista—a moral crusade to spread Spanish culture and Catholicism to pagans in all parts of the Americas."[28] Notice, if you will, that the end of the *Reconquista* coincided with the first voyages to the New World in 1492.

At the same time, the savagery of the Spanish Inquisition was in full swing as Catholic Spain sought to root out heretics and Jews, especially those who had converted to Christianity but secretly practiced Judaism. These *conversos*, as they were known, were subject to the full fury of the Inquisition. As the historian Lauren Faulkner Rossi suggests, "The physical violence of the Reconquest went hand-in-hand at this point with the spiritual violence of the Inquisition."[29] In a very real sense, the Spanish saw their incursions in the Americas as a new crusade. Thomas Berger captures this beautifully when he writes:

> War with another race, on behalf of Christ, had become a way of life for Spanish men-at-arms. Once the Reconquest of Spain was complete, the Spanish soldiery were suddenly without adversaries, yet unsuited to commerce or labour. Providentially, it seemed, the discovery of the New World offered a new adventure; they would not have to put up their swords. Instead they could pursue their warlike ways against a new enemy.[30]

Hardened and brutalized by war, imbued with a sense of righteousness and Christian piety, the Spanish arrived in the Americas with attitudes, beliefs, and perceptions that helped enable the conquest and justified their violence against the Native peoples they encountered. They believed that God favored them and that Native peoples were inferior and deserving of whatever fate the Spanish inflicted on them, and because of these beliefs, they were capable of a level of cruelty and gratuitous violence that is shocking in its extreme brutality.[31] A Spanish priest named Bartolomé de Las Casas, who spent many years in the Caribbean and Central America, described in nauseating details some of the atrocities perpetrated by the Spaniards. He wrote, "And Spaniards have behaved in no other way during the past forty years, down to the present time, for they are still acting like ravening beasts, killing, terrorizing, afflicting, torturing, and destroying the native peoples, doing all this with the strangest and most varied new methods of cruelty, never seen or heard of before."[32] An eyewitness to many of the events described, Las Casas details specific barbarities that make quite gruesome reading. According to Las Casas, for example, during the conquest of Hispaniola, the Spanish attacked the towns and spared neither the children nor the aged nor pregnant women nor women in childbed, not only stabbing them and dismembering them but cutting them to pieces as if dealing with sheep in the slaughter house. They laid bets as to who, with one stroke of the sword, could split a man in two or could cut off his head or spill out his entrails with a single stroke of the pike. They took infants from their mothers' breasts, snatching them by the legs and pitching them headfirst against the crag or snatched them by the arms and threw them into the rivers, roaring with laughter and saying as the babies fell into the water, "boil there, you offspring of the devil!" Other infants they put to the sword along with their mothers and anyone else who happened to be nearby. They made some low wide gallows on which the hanged victim's feet almost touched the ground, stringing up their victims in lots of thirteen in memory of Our Redeemer and His twelve Apostles, then set burning wood at their feet and thus burned them alive. To others they attached straw or wrapped their whole bodies in straw and set them afire.[33]

This kind of cruelty was not unique to this island, but instead was all too characteristic of Spanish rule. It is terribly ironic that the Spanish, who recoiled in horror from the Aztec practice of human sacrifice and condemned it as barbarism, had almost no qualms about their own wanton acts of cruelty. Clearly, as the above quote illustrates, there was a religious dimension to the violence that allowed them to see their violence in Manichean terms as a struggle of good versus evil, Christian versus Pagan, and Godly versus Satanic. In many ways, the violence in the New World mirrored the violence of the Inquisition back in Spain. Brutalized by their history and training, provided with beliefs justifying the violence, and bolstered by dehumanizing stereotypes, the conquistadors often resorted to levels of violence that are shocking in its savagery.

The Spanish were not the only ones with this kind of cultural and historical legacy. Similarly, the British experience in North America was also influenced by their earlier experiences with conquest and colonization, most notably in Ireland. Throughout much of the 1500s, England was engaged in consolidating their control of Ireland and brutally suppressing Irish resistance and recalcitrance to British rule. So widespread were the massacres and so extensive the destruction that some scholars have labeled it genocide.[34] While other scholars strongly disagree with this characterization, no one disputes the brutality and violence of the conquest of Ireland. When England set her eyes on the Americas, it was to many veterans of the conquest of Ireland that she turned. Men like Humphrey Gilbert, Sir Walter Raleigh, Richard Grenville, and others brought their hard-won and brutal skills to the New World. Is it any wonder that at the first sign of difficulty or trouble in the New World, these men would resort so quickly and easily to extreme measures? After all, these same tactics had brought them success in Ireland, so why not in the Americas? The past always shapes the present and future, and the history of Europe played an important role in helping to mold the attitudes and mind-sets of the European arrivals in the Americas.

What is ironic is that the conquistadors tended to be highly legalistic, although perhaps this shouldn't be a surprise since laws and legal formalities have always served to provide a sense of legitimacy to some forms of violence. The law is a powerful force for validating and legitimizing behavior since it is often perceived as reflecting standards of right and wrong. Law not only guides behavior through deterrence and punishment, but also by helping shape and influence morality and ethics. Therefore, when law protects and sanctions something, it typically enjoys a fair amount of automatic acceptance, especially given our predisposition to defer to authority. When the Spanish arrived in a new area or region, one of their first acts would be to recite a royal decree known as the *requerimiento*. This document was required to be read to the Natives and informed them that God, through the pope, had given the Spanish authority over all the lands of the Americas and that the Natives had to accept the authority of the Spanish and their Christian missionaries. As the *requerimiento* itself asserted in part:

> Wherefore, as best we can, we ask and require you that you consider what we have said to you, and that you take the time that shall be necessary to understand and deliberate upon it, and that you acknowledge the Church as the Ruler and Superior of the whole world, and the high priest called Pope, and in his name the King and Queen Doña Juana our lords, in his place, as superiors and lords and kings of these islands and this Tierra-firme by virtue of the said donation, and that you consent and give place that these religious fathers should declare and preach to you the aforesaid. [35]

Ironically, it wasn't even required to have the document translated into the language of those it was being read to or even to have any Natives present. As long as it was read aloud, regardless of the lack of comprehension or attendance of those to whom it was purportedly for, the legal requirements as laid out by Spanish law were met. Essentially, it provided a pretext for war and conquest. Once the terms were satisfied, the Spanish could move forward with absolute brutality, yet with clear consciences knowing that they acted in the interests of the Spanish monarchy and of God. Religious-based violence can often be and has often been quite extreme because at some level, the responsibility for the acts is removed from the perpetrator and placed upon God. This means that any sense of guilt or shame is removed because the violence has been divinely sanctioned. In a very real sense, the violence is ordered, authorized, justified, and even demanded by a higher authority and is thus transformed from an evil into a virtue.[36] European explorers and colonists often saw their violence against the Natives as an act of faith and a defense of their deepest religious beliefs and traditions. In short, especially in the early years of conquest, the Europeans were arriving from a world in which religious-based violence had been a very powerful and omnipresent part of their experience.

Violence against Native Americans was, in many ways, simply an extension of the killing and torture that Europeans had long inflicted on each other because of various religious differences, schisms, and heresies. Of this, the historian Olive Dickason writes, "Their superior technology, coupled with their belief that man was made to dominate nature, and Christians to dominate the world, did nothing to mitigate their conviction that Europeans were indeed the 'true men,' and that New World men were of an inferior order."[37] But the conflicts and violence that arose with such regularity were not solely the product of history, religion, and culture, but also of economics and colonialism.

COLONIALISM AND GENOCIDE

Economics lay at the root of much of the conflict between Europeans and Natives. The driving imperative for exploration of the Americas was wealth, pure and simple. Columbus's voyages were all about finding a quick and easy way to reach the riches of the Orient, but after realizing the potential of this new land, European nations were not slow to awaken to the possibilities the Americas offered. For the Spanish, it was all about gold; for the French, it was the abundant fur, especially beaver pelts that were in such demand back in Europe; and for the British, it was land. Over time, these goals evolved, but this was the essence of it. The Natives were perceived in a number of ways that related to these ever-changing goals, especially as mediated by the process of colonialism. Colonialism refers to the practice by which states and other political entities assume political, economic, and military control of other territories. Essentially, it is about one country or empire expanding and taking over another country or region.[38]

While we generally think of colonialism as a European practice, we should recognize that it is a rather old and widespread process of acquisition that has occurred in many places and times. Throughout history, empires have expanded their sway over adjacent or distant lands in order to acquire more territory for their people, spread their influence and ideas, and harvest more resources. From a colonial mind-set, Native populations were usually seen in one of two ways: at best, they were a resource to be exploited, and at worst, they were an impediment to be removed. If their labor couldn't be used to mine gold or silver or to work on plantations, for example, then they needed to be relocated or eliminated. It's easy to see how, with this kind of mind-set, violence seemed to go hand-in-hand with colonialism and colonial policies.

Some have suggested that settler colonialism is intrinsically genocidal. One of the most prominent proponents of this argument, the historian Patrick Wolfe, asserts that "Settler Colonialism destroys to replace."[39] In other words, settler colonialism is predicated on the notion of destroying indigenous populations to make room for the incoming waves of settlers who want to create a replica of their home society. Removing the Natives ensures that the settlers are able to build, cultivate, and rework an area into the mirror image, or at least a close approximation, of the land from whence they came. In many ways, settler colonialism is about erasing the past in order to create a new vision of the future, one based not on indigenous peoples and traditions, but upon the colonists' home country. Think of all the places in the Americas that were named, or to be more accurate, renamed, after European cities or regions—New England, New Brunswick, New Orleans, New York, and New Jersey, to name just a few. The historian

Tony Barta echoes this theme in his analysis of the Australian colonial experience and its effect on the Aborigines.[40] Similarly, Ben Kiernan, Ann Curthoys, and A. Dirk Moses, in their respective works, reiterate this notion with respect to indigenous genocide in Australia and Tasmania.[41] For Barta and others, whether or not the attitudes of the colonialists were intentionally destructive, the process of colonial occupation was itself inherently exterminatory. The colonists, by taking land and imposing their own values and ways of life on the geographic and social landscape, created a conflictual relationship with Native populations and a way of life that ultimately destroyed that which had existed there previously.[42] One recent powerful and provocative argument explicitly compares the American West and Nazi East in making the case for the genocidal characteristic of both examples of colonial expansionism.[43]

These arguments are in many ways based on Lemkin's original thesis on genocide, in which Lemkin argues that the process of colonialism is innately genocidal and suggests a two-stage process of colonial destruction. In stage one, the native cultures and traditions are destroyed, and in stage two, they are replaced with those of the home country of the invaders. In many ways, this is a compelling argument that accentuates the destructive nature of settler colonialism and is true to the original vision of the creator of the term "genocide." It goes a long way toward explaining the destructive violence that all too often characterized relations between the different cultures and makes a powerful case for describing the motive and methodology as being ultimately genocidal. These scholars are essentially asserting that genocide should not be understood just as an intentional form of destructive action, but can also be seen as a type of relationship that is fundamentally or inherently genocidal. In other words, the asymmetry of power and political, economic, and social relationships is such that the net result of colonial structures and arrangements is genocidal, or as A. Dirk Moses summarizes nicely, "Genocide is to be explained as the outcome of complex processes rather than ascribable solely to the evil intentions of wicked men."[44]

In some ways, this mirrors the concept of structural violence, which suggests that discriminatory social arrangements can also be construed as violent in the same way that we understand interpersonal aggression, such as rapes, assaults, and homicides, to be violent. First proposed by the sociologists Peter Iadicola and Anson Shupe, this categorization asserts that certain discriminatory social arrangements have a destructive impact on specific populations and are therefore best understood as constituting a form of violence against that group.[45] In the same way, this argument about colonialism and genocide also highlights the negative impact of the social structures created by settler colonialism and asserts that they can best be understood as genocidal.

These arguments, however, as powerful and compelling as they are, do tend to discount or at least minimize some of the complexities of the colonial and genocidal processes. In many ways they also fundamentally alter what is meant by the word "genocide" and transform it from a concept based on specific intentional actions to one based on the outcome of inequitable relationships. This is certainly a different lens through which to view this phenomenon we call genocide. There is also a tendency to simply assume that all colonialism is genocidal. But we have to recognize that there are a variety of forms of colonialism, and these divergent types tend to produce very different types of colonies. The experience of colonialism, in other words, is not uniform.

The historian Jürgen Osterhammel notes that there are a number of different types of colonies, including exploitation colonies, maritime enclaves, and settlement colonies.[46] The British colonies of the Eastern Seaboard are best understood as settlement colonies in which the main goal was to import large numbers of colonists and reshape the new territory into a distant version of the original. This is the kind of colonialism that Patrick Wolfe and others suggest is intrinsically genocidal because it often involves removing or eliminating any indigenous populations that happen to conflict with the idealized imagery of the society being created. In this type, native labor is much more dispensable than it is in exploitation colonies, which are best understood as those in which a small population from the home country works to develop and exploit the resources of a conquered territory for the benefit of the society from which they came. These colonial rulers tend to be few in number and view the native populations as one more resource to be used. Rather than trying to destroy the native inhabitants, in this type of colonialism their labor is harnessed for the benefit of the home country. Osterhammel suggests that Spanish America sometimes followed this model.

While it is certainly possible that exploitation colonies may be genocidal, it isn't necessarily so. The French in North America pursued a different path than either the Spanish or British. They saw the fur trade as their vehicle to riches, and in order to successfully harvest the beaver pelts they needed, they cultivated extensive trade relations with many tribes. Many tribes, in turn, saw opportunity in alliances with different colonial powers and exploited those relationships in order to increase or sustain their own power. Writing about the French experience, one historian succinctly notes, "the French soon realized that it was in their best interests to work out means of cooperation and accommodation rather than to insist that Amerindians become Frenchmen. In trade, they sought to engage Amerindian self-interest."[47] Sometimes, as the French model illustrates, colonialism was not so much imposed as it was negotiated. Natives were not simply passive objects that the impersonal forces of colonialism destroyed, nor were colonists simply the unthinking tools of colonial exploitation.

We should recognize that the goals of colonialism can also change. One of the first British settlements was the Jamestown colony on Chesapeake Bay, and the Virginia Company, which sponsored the expedition, wanted the settlers to exploit the Natives in order to survive and to get rich quick by finding gold and other valuables, just as had been done by the Spanish conquistadors in Mexico and South America. Instead of spending time planting crops, the new settlers spent their time fruitlessly searching for gold, or as one of the colonists wrote in his diary, "There was no talke, no hope, no worke, but dig gold, refine gold, load gold."[48] Unfortunately for the British, however, the Natives in the region of Jamestown were part of the Powhatan confederacy and refused to play along and submit to the colonists' needs. They also didn't have any gold. The Jamestown colony teetered on the edge of survival, and so dire was their predicament that at one point the starving survivors even resorted to cannibalism. It took the directors of the colony several years to acknowledge that this colony was not working and that they needed to modify their plan if it was to succeed. Ultimately, as Daron Acemoglu and James A. Robinson succinctly state,

> It took the Virginia Company twelve years to learn its first lesson that what had worked for the Spanish in Mexico and in Central and South America would not work in the north. The rest of the seventeenth century saw a long series of struggles over the second lesson: that the only option for an economically viable colony was to create institutions that gave the colonists incentives to invest and to work hard.[49]

   The example of Jamestown teaches us that colonialism itself, including its goals and practices, often changed and evolved over time as needs and circumstances changed and evolved. Because of this reality, it is perhaps more accurate to understand that violence and genocide, when they did occur, were not preordained by some intrinsic logic of colonialism, but were instead the outcome of contingent circumstances in particular areas and/or eras, and influenced by the choices and compromises made by those involved.

   To further confound the issue, we can also recognize that there were often profound differences between settlers and governmental officials and other concerned groups and organizations. Oftentimes, those on the cutting edge of colonialism, the settlers on the frontier, were those most overtly antagonistic, hostile, and even genocidal in their attitudes and actions, while governmental officials sometimes found themselves working to ameliorate the worst excesses of their colonists. Caught in a catch-22 situation, governmental officials sometimes found themselves trying to protect Native Americans from the depredations of their own people eager to acquire more land and more resources. Sometimes the colonial governments would cave in to the pressures from the settlers and would try to come to some new arrangement with the tribes that were perceived to be in the way. Often the Natives would resist this new renegotiation, and conflict and war would be the result, with the Natives usually on the losing end of the equation. But not always. Colonialism was not always inescapable nor was it always completely successful, at least not in the short term.

   One example of this comes from what was called the province of Santa Fe de Nuevo Mexico, now known as New Mexico. The Spanish had been in the area since the 1500s and had subjected the Pueblo peoples to ever-harsher rule. The Pueblo people, a diverse population of small and relatively independent tribal groups, lived primarily in small villages throughout the region that were often situated on top of mesas and other plateaus. Descendants of the Anasazi, the Puebloan peoples had developed lifestyles well suited to the semiarid climate of the Southwest and a distinctive adobe architecture that is still recognizable today.[50] The similar design of the towns led the first Spanish in the region to call them all Pueblos, the Spanish word for "town," even though different villages often had different social structures, traditions, and languages.[51] The Spanish also perceived the Puebloan people as being superior to other Native tribes that they encountered because they were farmers and lived in long-established settlements with substantial buildings.

Beginning in 1598, the Spanish under Don Juan de Oñate y Salazar and a small group of colonists established the colony of New Mexico and began an era in which the Pueblo peoples increasingly found themselves in conflict with the newcomers, who styled themselves as the rulers of these diverse indigenous peoples.[52] Much of the friction revolved around two primary issues. The first was the system of *encomiendas* and the related right of *repartimiento. Encomiendas* were land grants issued to soldiers to encourage them to settle in the new colony, while the *repartimiento* basically gave these colonists the ostensible right to make the Natives living on the land work for them.[53] Needless to say, this system of forced labor was not popular among the Pueblos. The other issue was that of religion. The Spanish, with typical missionary zeal, attempted to stamp out the Katsina religion and replace it with Christianity. While many converted, others refused to give up their traditional faith. In the face of such continued resistance, the Spanish resorted to increasingly heavy-handed tactics, such as executing some religious leaders and whipping a number of others. The 1660s and 1670s also saw an era of long-term drought that coincided with increasing raids from a number of plains tribes. The inability of the Spanish to prevent raiding attacks and to control the weather taught the Pueblo that the Spanish and their gods were not all-powerful. They and their gods, in other words, were neither infallible nor omnipotent.

Things came to a head in 1680, when the varied Pueblo tribes under the leadership of a number of religious leaders, most notably a prominent San Juan Indian named Popé, executed a well-planned surprise attack on all the Spanish within the New Mexico colony. Most of the hated Franciscan Friars were killed, as were many other colonists, and the survivors were driven completely out of the territory within a matter of weeks. What is interesting is that the Pueblo people, even though they profoundly rejected Spanish rule and the much-detested Christian religion, nevertheless retained some of what had been imposed on them, such as continuing to grow crops and raise livestock that had been first introduced by the Spanish. As the historian David Weber writes, "Just as they had been selective in adapting aspects of Hispanic culture, so too were they selective in rejecting them."[54] While there had been many smaller insurrections previously that had met with mixed success, this one was successful because for the first time the various Pueblo tribes in the area united in the face of harsh Spanish rule. For thirteen solid years the Pueblos were able to resist subsequent attempts by the Spanish to regain this lost colony, and the Spanish were only able to reenter the territory when the unity of the Pueblos fell apart. Whether or not one judges the Pueblo revolt a success depends largely on one's perspective and the timescale used to assess the rebellion. The bottom line, however, is that colonialism was not simply a monolithic process, nor were the groups in its path simply passive objects of exploitation or annihilation.

Certainly, colonial policies and practices could and oftentimes did lead to genocide, but not always and not everywhere. Typically, violence tended to erupt after land and resources grew scarcer, which served to intensify competition and exacerbate tensions.[55] These conflicts played out in various ways that reflected local dynamics, personalities, and decision-making processes. Individuals could and sometimes did profoundly influence how things played out. By all accounts, it was Popé's leadership and implacable hatred of the Spanish that was crucial to the Pueblo revolt of 1680. Something of a mysterious figure, Popé was evidently one of over forty traditional religious leaders of the Pueblo who had been arrested in 1675 for practicing sorcery. Three were hung and one committed suicide, while the remainder, Popé among them, were publicly whipped.[56] Instilled with a desire for vengeance, Popé became an implacable foe of the Spanish overlords and was instrumental in planning and carrying out the revolt. Without him, the revolt might never have happened. His leadership was absolutely crucial. After the revolt, he faded into history, and no one knows definitively what happened to him, although it is conceivable that his fate was passed down in the oral traditions of his Pueblo peoples and simply never shared with non-Natives. Many others in the long and turbulent history of Native and European relations played similarly influential roles.

The famous Spanish priest, Bartolomé de Las Casas, for example, was a powerful and forceful advocate for Native Americans after having overcome his initial prejudice against them and worked tirelessly to protect and defend them from his fellow countrymen. Although some of his accomplishments were honored more in the breach than in actual practice, he nevertheless became the conscience of the Spanish in the New World and was successful in influencing imperial decrees and legislation.[57] Others arrived at a place of compassion and understanding rather late in their lives. Perhaps the best example of this concerns the experience of a Spanish conquistador named Álvar Núñez Cabeza de Vaca, whose family name literally means "head of a cow."

Cabeza de Vaca came from a fairly well-known military family when he was appointed treasurer of an expedition to search for gold and glory in Florida under the direction of Pánfilo de Narváez.[58] Narváez was an experienced conquistador who landed on April 14, 1528, with around four hundred men, on the west coast of Florida near present day Tampa Bay in search of gold and fame. He hoped to repeat the success Cortés had had in finding and plundering a wealthy and great empire. With visions of gold and everlasting fame prodding him on, Narváez had successfully petitioned the king of Spain to raise an expedition to Florida, which had been discovered by the Spanish but not successfully explored. After landing, Narváez split up his force, and his men spent a futile and frustrating summer trekking northward through the Florida landscape and coming to the realization that there was no wealthy Native civilization awash in gold for them to conquer. Instead, they found hunger, illness, and often-hostile Natives who ambushed and killed expedition members with their long bows. Cut off from his ships, Narváez eventually made the coast, where he and his starving men built five barely seaworthy boats to take the survivors across the gulf to Mexico, the passage south to Cuba being deemed too treacherous. They believed they could skirt the coast westward toward Spanish communities more safely and thus find rescue. Unfortunately for them, things did not go as planned, and a few months later, Álvar Núñez Cabeza de Vaca and a handful of near-naked survivors were all that remained of the once-proud Spanish expedition. Shipwrecked on the coastal islands of Texas, losing almost all their possessions and clothing to the surf, this handful of men was slowly whittled down by exposure, starvation, disease, and violence. The violence came not only from various Native groups but also from each other, as some of the beleaguered explorers resorted to cannibalism. Ultimately, Cabeza de Vaca and three others were all that were left alive.

For the next few years, these conquistadors slowly made their way across what is now Texas, New Mexico, and Northern Mexico before finally coming across a Spanish slaving expedition and finding rescue in April of 1536, a full eight years since they had first landed in Florida. But Cabeza de Vaca was not the same man who had set out all those years ago. That man had been arrogant, proud, and shared the common attitudes of the other conquistadors toward the Indians. This new person was a much humbler man who had come to recognize that the Natives were fellow human beings and worthy of respect and tolerance. When the rafts had foundered and the survivors washed up on what is now Galveston Island, the Spanish were starving and freezing. They had no supplies or possessions, and they were also quite literally naked to the world, as most of their clothes had been lost when the rafts were lost. As Cabeza de Vaca himself described the scene, "The rest of us who escaped were naked as the day we were born and had lost all that we had with us at that time. And since by then it was November and the cold was very great and we were in such a plight that one could have counted our bones without difficulty, we looked like the very image of death."[59] At this point, when they were close to death, a group of Natives from the area came to their rescue.[60] Upon finding the distressed Spanish in such dire straits, they broke into tears and then made plans to help the hypothermic survivors. They built bonfires at regular intervals from the site of the shipwreck to their village and then carried the survivors from fire to fire, allowing them to warm themselves on the cold journey to the village. Upon arrival, the Spanish were provided with a large house for shelter and with food supplies.

It's hard not to be moved by such a showing of compassion and humanity, and for Cabeza de Vaca, it was the start of his transformation from an arrogant conquistador into a more humane person who saw past the ideology he had grown up with and began to understand the common humanity he shared with these Native Americans. In his years among the Natives, Cabeza de Vaca and his comrades became slaves and beggars, shamans and healers, and everything else survival or their Native hosts required or needed. Many times they were absolutely helpless, their lives dependent upon the goodwill and kindness of those they had once despised and judged as savages, and over time these situations could not help but impress themselves upon the hapless travelers. Finally, in 1537, Cabeza de Vaca and his surviving companions found themselves in Spanish territory in what is now northern Mexico and their ordeal was finally over. Upon his return to Spain,

Cabeza de Vaca wrote about his travels and experiences for the king and in 1540 returned to the Americas, although this time to South America, where he founded a settlement in what is now Argentina. While never questioning the right of the Spanish to colonize, his tenure was nevertheless considerably more benevolent than many others of the time.[61]

In many ways, the conflicts during the colonial and postcolonial eras were the result of a variety of factors that include not only the structures and ideologies of colonialism and expansionism, but numerous other issues as well. The conflict and violence were ultimately enabled by something deeper and more fundamental to human beings and the communities they create. Whether ultimately deemed genocidal or not, certain kinds of mind-sets and certain kinds of ideas appear to be universal in helping make violence possible. Regardless of the time period, the location, or the specific form of violence, humans need to engage in a variety of psychological processes that allow for the victimization of others, and the history of Native America certainly seems to bear this out. Europe, on the eve of first contact, was a world brutalized by generations of political, social, and religious conflict and war, seething with ignorance, intolerance, and bigotry. Coming from this background, the Europeans who arrived in the Americas often displayed attitudes that helped facilitate the exploitation and harm done to the Native peoples they encountered, but it is important to note that these were not unique to these new arrivals. Rather, they are mind-sets that are unfortunately common to all people.

4

DISEASE

The white invaders never would have conquered the Americas so readily had they not had a far more lethal weapon than their primitive guns and Old World tactics. European disease vanquished the New World's natives, not powder and ball.

—R. G. Robertson[1]

If the Black Death was an ecological disaster, then the invasion of the New World was a biological Armageddon.

—Andrew Nikiforuk[2]

One cannot talk about the history of Native America without looking at the significant role that disease played in the destruction of the indigenous peoples subsequent to first contact, although as we will discuss, only rarely is it possible to characterize it as genocide. However, whether genocidal or not, disease played a pivotal role in shaping and influencing the course of events in the Americas, and an understanding of its impact is therefore crucial for helping us make sense of what happened. In point of fact, disease has been one of the most pivotal factors in all of human history. It has overthrown empires, humbled dictators, and destroyed countless lives, communities, traditions, and customs.

In Athens, typhoid fever forever ended the intellectual, military, and political dominance of this once-powerful city-state. In Europe, the Black Death reinvigorated the Church and helped bring about an end to serfdom that ultimately helped bring down feudalism. Napoleon's invasion of Russia was thwarted not only by the onset of winter, but also because of a massive outbreak of typhus that severely depleted his Grand Army.[3] Out of the 450,000 men he began the invasion with, only 6,000 made it back to France. Typhus and dysentery killed by far the largest number of his men. Smallpox helped pave the way for Islam to spread into much of the Mediterranean and parts of Europe during the seventh and eighth centuries.[4] In India, cholera wracked the subcontinent during the 1800s and reportedly killed over fifteen million people. And in North, Central, and South America disease also played its deadly role as a shaper of human affairs. As we've seen, prior to 1491 and the subsequent waves of European colonists, adventurers, explorers, and nation builders, the Americas were home to a remarkably diverse set of cultures, tribes, and nations populated by millions of people. In contrast, the first Europeans to wash up on the shores of the Americas were relatively few in number and sometimes remarkably ill-equipped to survive and prosper in what was a very alien environment. How, then, did they succeed in displacing the indigenous populations they encountered? In the face of overwhelming numbers and well-established stable societies, how were the new arrivals able to carve out a place in the New World?

The traditional narrative explaining the success of the Europeans argues that it was largely technology that allowed the new arrivals to gain the upper hand and survive in the face of native hostility. This argument suggests that the combination of steel weapons, firearms, armor, and horses is what allowed the new arrivals to frighten, awe, and subdue the native populations into surrender and defeat. According to this line of reasoning, large native armies were rather easily defeated by very small numbers of invaders because they were frightened of armored humans on horseback, and because their weapons were ineffective against armored soldiers clad in steel helmets and breastplates and handling loud and smoky firearms. In many ways, this kind of argument reflects a certain kind of racist attitude that assumes the superiority of the Europeans over the superstitious and primitive savages of the Americas.[5] Certainly, military technology played a role, but the problem with this argument is that, upon closer examination, it doesn't completely explain the success of the invaders. Firearms at that time, while loud and obnoxious, could only fire a single round and were very slow and cumbersome to reload. For all intents and purposes, after the first shot they were nothing more than cumbersome clubs, and while steel swords and armor offered a significant tactical advantage, they were not necessarily sufficient to overcome the often extreme numerical disadvantage experienced by the new arrivals.

Keep in mind that not all Natives were overawed by European technology and weapons. Native weapons, while perhaps neither as technologically advanced nor as effective, were nonetheless still lethal weapons when wielded by experienced warriors. A steel helmet, breastplate, and sword provided only so much protection. In the Southeast, for example, Spanish armor proved ineffective against the long bows of the Aute Indians, whose arrows could transfix a person completely even if he was wearing breast and back plates.[6] One Spanish expedition lost ten foragers to arrows, and in the words of one of the expedition members, "We found their bodies pierced all the way through, although some of them wore good armor."[7] So what then was the cause for the European success if superior weapons were not the reason? As with most explanations about human behavior, there is no one single answer. Human beings are complicated and act and react for a multitude of reasons and causes. Certainly religious beliefs sometimes played a role, as did differing traditions of warfare. There are other factors as well, but the single most important reason was disease. This reality can be best illustrated with reference to two specific case studies: the Aztec and the Inca. Although these are not the only examples, they certainly provide very clear object lessons for illustrating the impact of disease in shaping the course of events.

CORTÉS AND THE AZTECS

In 1519, the Spanish conquistador Hernán Cortés and about 500 men landed on the Yucatan peninsula determined to bring the territory of what is now Mexico under Spanish rule and, hopefully, to profit from the endeavor.[8] Armed with a few cannons, firearms, crossbows, and a blind faith in the rightness of their cause, the Spanish set out to subdue a new world. At Veracruz, Cortés famously burned his ships, thus committing himself and his troops to either victory or utter defeat and death. Retreat was no longer an option. It was also here that Cortés tried to set up a meeting with the ruler of the Aztecs, Moctezuma, and after being refused, decided to proceed anyway and marched toward the heartland of the empire.

The Aztec Empire at that time was the preeminent political and military entity in the entire region. Centered at their capital of Tenochtitlan, the Aztecs were relative newcomers to the broad valley of Lake Texcoco, situated in the mountainous central region of what is now Mexico. In fact, the present-day capital of Mexico City is built on the site of the former lake. The capital city of Tenochtitlan was a floating city that housed 200,000 to 250,000 inhabitants and was a marvel of architecture characterized by broad canals, great squares, two-story stone houses, and magnificent temples. It was far larger than any European city of the time and could hold more people than London and Paris combined.[9] Three great stone causeways, the longest of which was six miles long and on which eight horsemen could ride abreast, led into the city. Particularly noteworthy were the floating gardens, known as chinampas, that were irrigated and provided year-round crops for the city. Also notable was a system of ceramic pipes that fed public fountains, public baths, steam rooms, and toilets. Even the brash Spanish invaders were awed when they finally saw this city. One eyewitness wrote:

> When we saw so many cities and villages built in the water and other great towns on dry land we were amazed and said that it was like the enchantments (. . .) on account of the great towers and cues and buildings rising from the water, and all built of masonry. And some of our soldiers even asked whether the things that we saw were not a dream? (. . .) I do not know how to describe it, seeing things as we did that had never been heard of or seen before, not even dreamed about.[10]

This city the Spanish were so awed by represented the beating heart of a relatively new empire. Even though they were recent arrivals to the region, the warlike Aztecs succeeded in quickly conquering and pacifying a large area that stretched from the Gulf of Mexico in the east to the shores of the Pacific and to the rain forests in the far south. The Aztecs controlled an empire that covered about 125,000 square miles in all.[11] Warfare was very important to Aztec culture, and they were very good at it. Bravery and skill in battle were expected from young males, and at its height the Aztec Empire could field an army of 200,000 men. The

Aztecs created a highly ritualized form of warfare whose aim was not only to kill the enemy and take territory, but also to provide captives who would later be sacrificed to the Aztec pantheon of gods. In short, the Aztecs were a powerful, technologically advanced, and highly militaristic society. Against such a powerful and warlike empire, how could Cortés and his small force ever have succeeded?

On their way to Tenochtitlan, the Spanish expedition fought a number of battles against various tribes, which helped provide them with Nahuatl speakers who could translate for Cortés and his men, and ultimately proved useful in helping secure alliances, especially with disgruntled vassals of the Aztec Empire. Like any empire, the success of the Aztec had been built upon the subjugation and oppression of various other tribes, many of whom resented their overlords. By the time they crossed the mountain passes that led into the central valley of the Aztecs, the ranks of the expedition were swollen with many thousands of recent native allies who saw in Cortés's expedition a chance to overthrow their Aztec oppressors.

In their advance, the Spaniards were also aided by an Aztec religious belief suggesting that a white-skinned god named Quetzalcoatl, who had sailed away in ancient times, would return in a year named One Reed. It just so happened that, according to the Aztec calendar, Cortés appeared on the horizon shortly after that year had arrived.[12] Moctezuma's ambivalence and attempts to deflect and parlay with the Spanish owes much to the confusion over the identity of Cortés. Essentially, they wondered if he was Quetzalcoatl come back to claim his rightful place as ruler of the Aztecs.[13] Greeted initially as guests and made welcome, it wasn't long before the Spanish responded by throwing Moctezuma in chains and ransacking his palace. Fearing the increasingly restive and angry citizens of Tenochtitlan, Cortés and 250 of his men left for the coast after hearing that some Spanish ships had made landfall. According to a contemporary chronicler, one of the new arrivals was "a black African stricken with Smallpox, a disease which had never been seen here before."[14]

The Spanish had recently begun importing African slaves to replace the Taino Indians of the Caribbean, who were dying in large numbers from disease and the depredations of the conquistadors, and this African was undoubtedly one of those unfortunates. That smallpox-infected slave must have passed on smallpox to soldiers in Cortés's band. When he had left Tenochtitlan, Cortés had put a conquistador named Pedro de Alvarado in charge of his remaining troops, who promptly massacred a celebration of young Aztec nobles. Not surprisingly, the Aztecs rose in rebellion, even though Cortés still had their king as hostage, and forced the Spanish to retreat out of the capital. Cortés rushed back with reinforcements, among them at least one smallpox-infected soldier, but was unsuccessful in staving off defeat and had to beat a hasty exit from the Aztec capital. Their retreat from Tenochtitlan became known as *La Noche Triste*, or the Night of Sorrow. Approximately three-fourths of the Spaniards died in the retreat, along with several thousand of their allies.[15] For all intents and purposes, the European conquest of the Aztecs had failed. Unfortunately for the Aztec, however, the Spanish left something behind that was to prove crucial to their return and eventual success. That something was the smallpox virus.

Smallpox had already made an appearance on the islands of the Caribbean, most notably on Hispaniola, Cuba, and Puerto Rico in the early 1500s, with disastrous results.[16] Probably introduced from Spain or Portugal, the disease exterminated entire tribes and decimated many others. Cortés had left Cuba for his rendezvous with the Aztecs on the mainland several months after smallpox had arrived on the island, and it wasn't long before it had reached the shores of the Yucatan and spread to the margins of the Aztec Empire. Shortly after Cortés and his adventurers had been forced from Tenochtitlan with heavy casualties, smallpox broke out in the densely populated capital city. Remember that this was a city of approximately 200,000 to 250,000 within the city proper, and estimates suggest that the large valley within which the city was located was home to approximately 1,000,000 inhabitants.[17] Not surprisingly, in the packed confines of the city and the surrounding countryside, the disease spread like wildfire, killing many thousands of the Aztec. In the words of one Spanish witness, "When the Christians were exhausted from war, God saw fit to send the Indians smallpox and there was a great pestilence in the city."[18] According to a contemporary translator, the Aztecs themselves saw it this way:

> And before the Spaniards had risen against us, a pestilence first came to be prevalent: the smallpox. It was the month of Tepeilhuitl when it began, and it spread over the people as great destruction. Some it quite covered with pustules on all parts—their faces, their heads,

their breasts, etc. There was great havoc. Very many died of it. They could not walk; they only lay in their resting places and beds. They could not move; they could not stir; they could not change position, nor lie on one side, nor face down, nor on their backs. And if they stirred, much did they cry out. Great was its destruction.[19]

This single outbreak crippled the ability of the Aztecs to organize and resist the Spanish, who were largely immune to the epidemic they had unwittingly imported. Importantly, it also killed Moctezuma's successor, Cuitláhuac, who was by all accounts an able political and military leader and who was the focus of Aztec resistance to the Spanish invaders. Many other Native leaders were also struck down by smallpox, thus removing possible sources of leadership against the invaders. Cortés returned to Tenochtitlan and destroyed the city after a siege, eventually defeating the Aztecs. While it took a number of months and numerous battles, the single most decisive factor in the eventual success of the Spanish invaders was the smallpox virus, or as one historian put it, "Had there been no epidemic, the Aztecs, their war-making potential unimpaired and their warriors fired with victory, could have pursued the Spaniards, and Cortés might have ended his life spread-eagled beneath the obsidian blade of a priest of Huitzilopochtli."[20] It was said at the time that when the Spanish took Tenochtitlan, the dead covered the ground so thickly in places that one couldn't avoid stepping on the dead bodies.[21] In subsequent years, smallpox made numerous repeated visits and helped bring about a population reduction from a height of 25.2 million to 1.1 million.[22]

PIZARRO AND THE INCA

In many ways the mirror image of what occurred in Mexico to the Aztecs, the Incan defeat at the hands of the Spanish conquistador Francisco Pizarro also provides an object lesson in the role that disease played in the conquest of the New World. As with the Aztecs, the Incan Empire encompassed a tremendous amount of territory and a great many peoples and, in fact, was the largest single empire in the world at that point in time. How, then, did such a powerful empire fall to such a small number of military adventurers? Pizarro had even fewer troops with him than Cortés and yet was able to win the vast riches of the Inca even in the face of apparently insurmountable odds. The answer to this puzzle is disease, which again played a critical role in facilitating the overthrow of the mighty Inca.

Smallpox actually reached the Inca Empire before the Spanish did. In fact, it's quite possible that it was part of the same epidemic that struck down the Aztecs about four years earlier. From the initial outbreak in Mexico in 1520, the smallpox virus traveled south along various trade routes, appearing in various locations, such as Guatemala in 1521, and continued southward to arrive finally at the Incan homeland in the Andes, where it spread rapidly throughout the empire. The Inca had created a vast and efficient road system that unintentionally aided in the rapid transmission of the disease.

In 1527, the emperor of the Inca, Huayna Capac, was traveling when he received word that many of his relatives, including his brother, sister, and uncle, had died from a disease that had broken out in the capital city of Cuzco.[23] As he hurried back, he also fell ill with what was presumably smallpox and died before reaching the city. Thousands died in the subsequent epidemic, including many of the empire's political and military leadership. Importantly, among the dead was the chosen successor to the throne. One consequence of these deaths was to convulse the empire in civil war as the two surviving sons of the now-dead emperor, Huáscar and Atahualpa, vied for power. In 1532, after a long and bloody conflict, Atahualpa won the contest just in time to greet the Spanish invaders.

The leader of this expedition was Francisco Pizarro, who was accompanied by less than 200 men, a minuscule number to take on an empire that could routinely field armies of 100,000 men or more.[24] In fact, one of Pizarro's men wrote to the king of Spain that, "All of us were full of fear, because we were so few in number and we had penetrated so far into a land where we could not hope to receive reinforcements."[25] But fortunately for Pizarro and his men, the empire was in extreme disarray. While the exact mortality rate of the smallpox epidemic is unknown, some scholars of this period suggest that the Incan Empire could have lost about half of all its inhabitants.[26] Add to that the dislocation, death, and destruction during the Incan civil war that followed on the heels of the epidemic, and it's easy to see how a daring adventurer could have exploited the situation to his advantage. At their first meeting, Pizarro actually captured Atahualpa and eventually had him put to death. During this time period, the Inca were hit by another smallpox epidemic that further decimated the ranks of the Inca. The death toll was such that a witness to the effects of the disease commented that:

> The Incas died by the scores and hundreds. Villages were depopulated. Corpses were scattered over the fields or piled up in the houses or huts. . . . The fields were uncultivated; the herds were untended; and the workshops and mines were without laborers. . . . The price of food rose to such an extent that many persons found it beyond their reach. They escaped the foul disease, only to be wasted by famine.[27]

These catastrophes were simply too much for the mighty Incan Empire to endure, and so it fell rather easily to the Spanish invaders. By the end of the century, the Incan people were reduced to less than a quarter of their former numbers. Some have even suggested that by 1630, because of the combined effects of disease, slavery, and various other problems, the Andean population was only about 7 percent of what it had been at its height.[28]

As these two examples illustrate, disease played a significant role in allowing the Europeans to survive and conquer the peoples of the Americas. The Aztec and Incan experiences were not unique, but were rather the norm. Time and again, in location after location, the same basic scenario played itself out with devastating effects for the Natives, but, importantly, not for the Europeans. These epidemics also affected the Europeans and sometimes killed them, but to nowhere near the same extent. They were generally much less lethal for the Europeans. Why was this so?

NATIVES, EUROPEANS, AND THE IMPACT OF DISEASE

By all accounts, Native populations had almost no resistance to the diseases introduced by the Europeans. In 1491, Native America was a remarkably healthy place, at least in terms of disease and especially in comparison with Europe. This is not to say that disease didn't exist in the Americas, but it was nowhere near as much of a problem as it was in Europe. There are a number of reasons for this relatively disease-free existence. It may well be that the slow migrations over Beringia had served to weed out those who were sick. Essentially, the cold and inclement environment filtered out many diseases that couldn't cope with the frigid temperatures and those who were sick or infected didn't typically survive the long passage. Northern climates still tend to be much less disease-ridden than tropical locations, where diseases are much more numerous and endemic. In large part, this is simply a function of temperature and humidity since many viruses and bacteria have a more difficult time surviving in cold and arid climates.

Second, the population density of the Americas tended to be much less than that of Europe. There were some exceptions to this rule, such as in the Aztec heartland, but generally speaking Native populations were not packed together as densely as was common in Europe. This meant that diseases often tended to burn themselves out and were not as easily transmitted between different communities and tribes, but it also meant that the more urbanized populations of Europe had greater resistance to the common diseases of the time. They had earned this relative immunity the hard way as generations of city dwellers had suffered from various deadly diseases that had only spared those who were naturally resistant. Those who survived tended to pass on their resistance to their children so that over time the population as a whole became much more able to withstand outbreaks of disease.

Third, the Natives of the Americas had not domesticated nearly the same amount of animals as the Europeans had. For many hundreds of years, Europeans had lived in extremely close proximity to many domesticated species of animals including chickens, ducks, pigs, cows, horses, and dogs, to name some of the more common types. Often, the rural European poor lived in the same one-room huts as their animals. These animals provided a reservoir for what are known as zoonotic diseases, or diseases which can be transmitted from animals to humans. Consequently, many diseases repeatedly coursed their way through Europe and could be considered endemic. Cattle, sheep, goats, chickens, pigs, and dogs have all contributed their share. Influenza, for example, originated from birds, but was passed along to people from pigs, chickens, and ducks.[29] Over generations, this endless cycle of disease resulted in populations developing resistance to diseases that were initially more deadly.

In contrast, the Natives of the Americas only domesticated a few animals and consequently didn't have the same zoonotic diseases to contend with. In addition to these sources of transmission, not only did the indigenous populations of the Americas not have the same acquired immunity that Europeans had developed over time, but some have suggested that they also had a much lower natural immunity.[30] Genetically, the indigenous populations of the Americas tend to be very homogenous. This lack of genetic variability has meant that the Native populations were remarkably vulnerable to the diseases introduced by the Europeans. With greater genetic variation there are more individuals who may be able to better resist a specific disease.

In short, because of a lack of acquired and natural immunity, the Native populations of the Americas were remarkably vulnerable to disease. This same situation has been found elsewhere as well. The historian Sheldon Watts, for example, points to the case of an isolated Scottish island whose people had been largely cut off from the main populations of Scotland and England and had avoided the all-too-common diseases that were prevalent everywhere else. When smallpox finally arrived in the 1700s, 90 percent of the Foula islanders died from the outbreak. They simply had no acquired immunity to the disease and were thus lethally vulnerable when it did strike. As with other diseases, over time and place there were various strains of smallpox, some more virulent than others. Anyone, however, who survived even a very mild strain was immune to other versions of the disease. The isolation of the Foula islanders, however, ensured that their immune systems were unable to resist the onslaught when smallpox eventually made its first appearance on these remote isles. In many ways, the Natives of the Americas were like the Foula islanders, whose lack of exposure to smallpox did not allow them to develop resistance to the disease so that when smallpox finally did arrive, the consequences were lethal.

The diseases introduced into the New World included smallpox, measles, the bubonic plague, cholera, typhoid, pleurisy, scarlet fever, diphtheria, mumps, whooping cough, colds, gonorrhea, chancroid, pneumonia, typhus, and tuberculosis.[31] Of all of these, it was smallpox that was the most deadly, and it is to this particular disease that we now turn.

SMALLPOX

Smallpox is a very old disease that has probably killed more humans throughout history than any other single source of human mortality. In truth, it is an absolutely horrid disease that has always been rightly loathed and feared. Known as the variola virus (from the Latin *varius*, which means spotted), smallpox is caused by a tiny brick-shaped virus that is essentially a very simple form of life. It is an organism composed of DNA (deoxyribonucleic acid) that is encased in a layer of protein. It can reproduce only within the living cells of a host, such as a plant, animal, or bacteria, and does so by burrowing into the cells of an organism and inserting its own genetic code into that cell. That hijacked cell then stops doing what it normally does and begins to produce more viruses, becoming a virus factory until it dies. Once a cell has been taken over, it can only be stopped from producing the virus by killing the cell, a fact that greatly complicates treatment. In these cells, the new viruses build up and begin to leak out and infect surrounding cells or are dramatically expelled when a cell gets full to the bursting point and ruptures. When enough cells in a body are hijacked or killed by the variola virus, the host begins to manifest sickness and can eventually die.

In human beings, the infection usually begins in the more vulnerable cells lining the mucous membrane within the lungs and then diffuses to other cells within the body and its organs. Smallpox is highly communicable and is therefore very contagious. It is often transmitted by being inhaled after an infected person sneezes or coughs, but it can also be contracted through touching and handling the clothing of someone with smallpox or even the corpse of a smallpox victim. Unfortunately, the smallpox virus is also incredibly hardy and can survive outside of a human body for up to two years.[32] This durability combined with contagiousness means that a smallpox outbreak can easily turn into an epidemic very quickly with little chance of containment. Villages in the Americas that had been ravaged by the disease remained hot spots of contagion long after the victims had died, and anyone passing through an abandoned community could easily contract the disease from the unburied corpses, their clothing, or anything else that had been exposed to the virus.

An infected person usually doesn't exhibit any symptoms for the first eight to fourteen days while the virus is building up in that person's system, during which time that infected individual can infect others. In the Americas this characteristic meant that, once introduced, the disease was guaranteed to spread. When someone came down with the symptoms, others within that community would often flee the onset of the illness and unwittingly carry the disease with them to infect those they sought shelter with. In this way, smallpox often raced ahead of the new European arrivals, with tribes becoming infected that had never even experienced contact with the invaders. Animals also helped spread the disease in advance of the European newcomers.

Once symptoms appear, the effects are catastrophic for the victim. It starts with a sudden and rapid rise of temperature accompanied by fatigue, extreme backache, headache, chills, convulsions, and nausea. In some cases, the infected person may also experience delirium and even coma. Often the patient develops a red color in the face that may spread over the entire body. After about four days, the victim may experience a significant lessening of symptoms and may think that he or she is on the mend. This lull, however, is just temporary and is quickly followed by the most severe and often lethal stage of the infection. It's at this point that the most identifiable indicator of smallpox makes its presence known: a rash appears, first on the face, then everywhere on the body. Over the course of the next couple of days, this rash develops into raised pimples, then blisters, and then pustules. In severe cases, the pustules may grow together with massive sections of the skin actually sloughing off and opening up the unfortunate sufferer to bacterial infection. The smell from the pustules is very nauseating and compounds the suffering. It literally smells as if the person is rotting. If the victim lives long enough, these pustules eventually dry up and turn into scabs. During this period, the victim often dies. Importantly, the dried-up scabs of the pustules, as well as any clothing or bedding that had come into contact with the pustules or subsequent scabs, remain contagious for a very long period. Underneath the surface of the skin, the virus has worked its deadly way through the body, attacking and destroying various organs such as the heart, lungs, liver, and intestines.

If the victim developed the hemorrhagic strain of smallpox, the fatality rate was nearly 100 percent, but thankfully only a small number of those infected developed this type of smallpox. For most others, the fatality rate averaged about 30 percent, although some populations suffered a mortality rate of 50 percent or more. Among many Natives in the New World, the fatality rate was much higher. Ironically, smallpox was not as destructive to the Europeans who introduced it into the Americas because over the years a natural process of acquired resistance had developed. As R. G. Robertson eloquently points out:

> After the fall of Rome, smallpox visited the villages of medieval Europe every five or ten years, exacting its toll from those who had been born since the last outbreak. Most adults of childbearing age had survived the virus and gained lifelong immunity from future attacks. In a process that evolved over many generations, immune parents passed to their offspring an increased resistance—but not immunity—to the illness. [33]

Those who survived smallpox were almost always indelibly marked by their experience. Since the virus destroys sebaceous glands, which are most numerous in the face, survivors often have pockmarked faces. In some cases, the virus targets the eyes and leads to permanent blindness. Survivors are also often sterile after their encounter with the smallpox virus. A smallpox epidemic for smaller Native tribes could therefore be absolutely devastating for the long-term survival of that people, since the few who lived were often incapable of reproducing. Smallpox doomed many tribes to extinction.

The eruption of smallpox in a region was guaranteed to spread panic and cause massive dislocation as those unaffected (or at least believing they were unaffected) fled from the sources of infection. Tragically, many of them only succeeded in spreading the disease further afield. When George Vancouver led the first British expedition to explore Puget Sound in the Pacific Northwest in the late 1700s, he found its shores littered with skulls and bones and the few survivors he encountered often had the telltale pitting of the skin. Many were also blind. [34] Smallpox had already coursed its way across the continent and preceded the arrival of the Europeans.

While many Natives fled the onset of disease, others, perhaps bound by the powerful ties of kinship, concern, and love, stayed to help their afflicted family and relations and in the process usually succeeded only in condemning themselves. Natives in New England, for example, had a tradition in which friends and family of the stricken would gather around the victim to give support and try to wait out the sickness, which increased the risk of transmission dramatically.[35] On the Great Plains, the standard practice was to bring in a medicine man who tried to treat the illness with prayers and rituals that, as often as not, simply spread the virus. Medicine men, for example, sometimes tried to suck out the illness with their mouths and then would spit out the poison into the air for the benefit of the onlookers. Needless to say, this was a very effective way of spreading the disease.[36]

It also didn't help that Natives often didn't understand the nature of disease and modes of infection and contamination, or in the words of one Blackfoot, "We had no belief that one man could give a disease to another any more than a wounded man could give his wound to another."[37] Especially with smallpox, it didn't take much to infect even those who came into brief contact with those infected. Charles Mann recounts the story of a Blackfoot raiding party that came across a Shoshone camp in 1781 in Alberta.[38] Sneaking up on what they thought was a sleeping campsite, the Blackfoot burst into the tents by slitting them open with their knives and were horrified to find the Shoshone were either dead or dying from smallpox. Reportedly, they left immediately and did not touch any of the infected, but they nonetheless managed to bring the disease back with them to infect their village, with predictably deadly results.

We must keep in mind that these diseases did not just erupt one time, never again to reappear, but instead came and went in deadly waves. Native Americans suffered from a whole series of epidemics, and in fact, some have suggested that there were at least ninety-three epidemics from the 1600s through the 1800s.[39] Smallpox was probably first introduced in the Caribbean in the first years of the sixteenth century, spreading like wildfire throughout the islands and ultimately reaching the Central American mainland in 1519, with devastating consequences for the Aztecs, as we've previously seen. From there, it moved south to reach the Incan Empire shortly thereafter and probably spread north as well. In all likelihood, that wasn't the only source of smallpox infection in North America. During the same time period, European fishermen and whalers were plying the bountiful waters off Canada and New England. Basque fishermen had been fishing the waters of Newfoundland since the Middle Ages, but since they had no territorial ambitions and wanted to keep their fishing grounds secret, history has generally ignored their presence.[40] They were followed by fur traders in search of the highly lucrative beaver pelts used in the making of fur hats that were so fashionable in Europe.

Not surprisingly, the contact these early arrivals had with the Native Americans soon introduced a variety of diseases, the most significant of which was smallpox. Between 1612 and 1613, for example, the Paw-tucketts, who lived in what is now Massachusetts, were completely wiped out by a disease that was most likely smallpox.[41] When the Puritans arrived at Plymouth Rock in 1620, they found a land emptied of its people. They also found empty villages littered with the bones of its former inhabitants. As one new arrival wrote, the Indians

> died on heapes, as they lay in their houses; and the living, that were able to shift for themselves, would runne away and let them dye, and let their Carkases ly above the ground without burial. . . . And the bones and skulls upon the severall places of their habitations made such a spectacle after my coming into these partes, that as I travailed in the Forrest, nere the Massachusetts [Bay], it seemed to mee a new found Golgotha.[42]

At Cape Cod and later at Plymouth, the starving and ill-prepared Puritans ransacked recently deserted villages for food and supplies. They dug up graves and searched through the village homes in search of whatever they could find. Luckily for them, they did find corn,[43] and as Edward Winslow, a future governor of the Plymouth colony wrote, "And sure it was that God's good providence that we found this corn, for else we know not how we should have done."[44] These ten bushels of corn were crucial to the survival of these Pilgrims who, not having the backing of the government, had set out without many crucial resources or the skills necessary to create a successful colony.

The famous Tisquantum, more commonly known as Squanto, who helped the Puritans survive in their early years in New England, was himself the last surviving member of the Patuxet tribe, an affiliate of the Wampanoag people that had largely succumbed to disease. From the 1600s onward, the Indians of New England were ravaged by numerous diseases, including smallpox, bubonic plague, and pneumonic plague, with the result that approximately nine out of every ten coastal Natives died from one or more of the diseases that engulfed them. In the early 1600s, Samuel de Champlain wanted to set up a French base on Cape

Cod, but quickly gave up because there were simply too many people already living there. Similarly, Sir Ferdinando Gorges tried to establish a settlement a year later in southern Maine, but abandoned the project in the face of Native resistance. There were simply too many well-armed Indians who didn't want the new arrivals to settle on their land. By the time the Puritans arrived around fifteen years later, the entire region had been almost entirely depopulated by disease and the entire course of history changed. When Tisquantum returned to his home after being kidnapped and taken to Europe, he first made it to Maine and from there caught a ship sailing for Massachusetts captained by a Thomas Dermer. In the words of Charles C. Mann:

> What Tisquantum saw on his return stunned him. From southern Maine to Narragansett Bay, the coast was empty—"utterly void," Dermer reported. What had once been a line of busy communities was now a mass of tumbledown homes and untended fields overrun by blackberries. Scattered among the houses and fields were skeletons bleached by the sun. Gradually Dermer's crew realized that they were sailing along the border of a cemetery 200 miles long and 40 miles deep. [45]

It seems doubtful that the Puritans could have survived if disease hadn't run its course prior to their arrival. Other regions of the country fared similarly with massive population die-offs more the norm than the exception. There is much truth to Francis Jennings's statement that "The so-called settlement of America was a *re*settlement, a reoccupation of a land made waste by the diseases and demoralization introduced by the newcomers." [46]

In 1539, the Spaniard Hernando de Soto landed in Florida and spent the next few years looking for gold in Florida, Georgia, the Carolinas, Tennessee, Alabama, Mississippi, Arkansas, and Texas. [47] He traveled through the heart of some of the most densely inhabited regions of North America and encountered numerous towns and villages and many, many thousands of Natives. He and his men plundered, destroyed, stole, and killed prodigiously as they wandered the land. Eventually, de Soto fell ill and died on the banks of the Mississippi, and the survivors of his expedition built a few boats and descended the river and then the Gulf Coast until they reached Spanish territory in Mexico. No European would revisit the area for more than a century. In 1682, a small French expedition, led by Rene Robert Cavalier, Sieur de la Salle, descended the Mississippi with the goal of reaching the Gulf of Mexico. Instead of a land full of towns and people, they found a deserted landscape emptied of its inhabitants. Where de Soto had found at least fifty large settlements along one stretch of the Mississippi, La Salle found fewer than ten. Disease, introduced by the de Soto expedition, had done its deadly work and depopulated the lower Mississippi River region and the entire Southeast. Ironically enough, it appears that de Soto's men were not actually responsible for the outbreak, but rather it was the pigs which they had brought along with the expedition as a mobile food source.[48] Pigs are a potent reservoir of disease, and by sharing the pigs with Natives or because a few may have escaped into the forest where they continued to breed, a potent new disease vector was introduced to the region, causing the collapse of the population in the southeastern part of North America.

DISEASE AND GENOCIDE

This same kind of process occurred time after time, in region after region. While the individual names and places were different, the story was always the same. Native peoples became exposed to different diseases introduced by the Europeans, with death, devastation, and dislocation as the result. How terrible it must have been to see everyone around you die and to know that you would soon follow them; to know that your people and all their accomplishments, aspirations, knowledge, traditions, and culture would soon vanish from the earth. This did not just happen a few times, but rather occurred over and over again in location after location throughout the Americas. Entire civilizations and tribes that had slowly matured and developed and struggled and survived over long periods of time were snuffed out in the span of a few short years. The suffering engendered by this is incalculable. An important question to raise at this point is whether or not the die-off of American Natives due to disease constitutes genocide. The question of genocide doesn't diminish the scale of the tragedy, but it is nonetheless an important question that helps us better understand the nature of this calamity and how it came to pass.

One approach to looking at the question of genocide, as we have seen, is to examine the issue of intent. From this perspective, the important question is whether or not the disease-related deaths were knowingly caused with the express purpose of eradicating the Native peoples of the Americas. If yes, then these deaths can clearly be construed as constituting genocide. If not, then the issue becomes much less clear. On the one hand, it can be argued that, given their long experience with disease and epidemics, Europeans had a good working knowledge of how disease worked, even if they didn't quite know the exact mechanisms by which it was transmitted and how it operated. Europeans knew, for example, the general principles of quarantine, having learned through long and hard experience that when an infection erupted, those infected needed to be isolated. Public health measures were also adopted in many places with varying degrees of success. Susan Scott and Christopher Duncan write of some of these measures:

> With the benefit of hindsight, we can see that not all of these measures would have been equally effective, but it is clear that even in the fifteenth century, people understood the rudiments of infectious diseases, distinguishing them from the prevailing blind superstitions.[49]

In addition, Europeans had sometimes practiced basic forms of biological warfare, usually consisting of throwing the corpses of plague victims over the walls of cities under siege. In 1346, for example, the Tartar army was besieging the Crimean city of Caffa and used catapults to toss the corpses and carcasses of people and animals killed by plague over the city walls.[50] There are many more cases similar to this, which seems to suggest that there existed an awareness of exploiting disease in the New World as a tool of warfare. Certainly, the attitudes of many of the new arrivals were such that genocide would not have been unwelcome. Many of the Europeans despised, hated, and feared the Natives they encountered and wanted nothing more than for these Indians to disappear, which all too often they did because of disease and violence.

On the other hand, there are a number of significant obstacles to making a definitive case for disease as genocide. First, especially in the initial years of contact, many Europeans could have had no inkling about the deadliness of the diseases they were introducing into the New World. Over generations, Europeans had built up resistance to many of the more common diseases found in Europe and couldn't credibly have known that the illnesses they introduced would be so absolutely lethal to the Natives they encountered. Diseases like measles, scarlet fever, diphtheria, mumps, whooping cough, colds, and tuberculosis had become progressively less lethal as European communities built up their resistance over many years and many generations.

This is not to say that Europeans didn't die from these diseases, but rather that their lethality levels had decreased substantially over time. Disease was still a concern for Europeans in the New World and plenty of the colonists died from the very same causes as the Native Americans, but their mortality rates were generally much, much lower. This challenges the notion of intentionality, at least in the early years of contact. Europeans had no real knowledge that the newly discovered continents were virgin soil for the multitude of diseases of which they were carriers and for which the Natives had no acquired resistance. Over time, however, as epidemic after epidemic decimated the Native tribes, the connection must have become obvious for many. In fact, many Europeans saw God's hand in the death toll of the Natives and believed that God was aiding them in their quest for wealth, land, and a new life in the Americas. Pilgrim governor Bradford suggested that "the good hand of God" was responsible for the diseases that "favored our beginnings" by "sweeping away great multitudes of the natives. . . . that he might make room for us."[51] Many others also saw divine providence in the death of the Natives and even rejoiced in the mass death of the Amerindians. This does not, however, necessarily equate to genocide. Hateful, callous, and cruel, not to mention self-serving, these racist attitudes by themselves are not necessarily indicative of genocide. In other words, even though many colonists and settlers interpreted the epidemics as a sign from God and certainly took advantage of the subsequent depopulations, these actions and attitudes are not automatically proof of genocide.

If we assume, however, that at some point the invaders recognized the lethality of their diseases for Natives, did they intentionally act on this to foster the spread of disease? Unfortunately for the sake of clarity, it appears that the best answer is maybe. There appears to be only a handful of cases for which evidence exists that illustrate the intentional infection of Natives, but even here there are some questions. We also have to ask if it is reasonable to assume that all of the various Spanish, British, Dutch, and French officials, settlers, soldiers and officers, and administrators had similarly genocidal intentions and the willingness to use disease as a weapon. Evidence to the contrary suggests that attitudes and policies were much more mixed in regard to Native Americans. The second major handicap to pronouncing genocide is that contact was sometimes accidental. The resulting diseases, therefore, were also consequently inadvertent. When the pilgrims, for example, were scavenging through the deserted villages in search of hidden stores of corn, they were reportedly surprised to find a blond-haired corpse in one of the graves. Evidently, he had been a French fisherman who had been shipwrecked along with some of his shipmates. Held captive by the Patuxet who had found them, these shipwrecked sailors bequeathed the deadly gift of disease, most likely viral hepatitis, which swept through New England, killing almost all of the Amerindians there.[52] This can hardly have been part of any plan.

Other accidental infections resulted from animals being introduced into Native America and unintentionally setting off outbreaks, such as the pigs of the ill-fated de Soto expedition discussed above. While a case can be made that Europeans had a working grasp of disease, the same cannot be said about zoonotic diseases. It's one thing to understand that when disease breaks out one has to flee and those infected must be quarantined, but it's another to understand that seemingly healthy animals can be reservoirs of infections. The accidental nature of some infections, therefore, also weighs against the disease-as-genocide argument in some cases. In short, the question appears to be much more complicated than is sometimes acknowledged by writers and scholars who adopt a particular position on one side or the other of this issue. Unfortunately, it doesn't appear to be a question that is very easily resolved. Even the well-known cases of intentional infection appear to be a little less definitive when examined more closely. This is certainly true when we take a closer look at an example that is often cited as clear evidence of genocide through disease.

Throughout the first half of the 1700s, Britain and France had increasingly come into conflict as each side competed for territory and resources in the lucrative new world. Things came to a head in 1753, when the French sent troops into the Ohio River Valley of western Pennsylvania with orders to take permanent possession of the region for France by building forts in strategic locations.[53] The British responded by building some of their own military forts, things escalated, and before long both sides were at war, although it wasn't officially declared until 1756. Because of the difficulties in bringing troops into the American backcountry, the irregular nature of the combat, and the small populations of colonists, both sides in this war relied heavily on their Native allies.

In 1759, Major General Jeffery Amherst took control as commander in chief of the British forces and won a number of military victories, which helped ensure England's eventual dominance in North America and ultimately provided victory over France.[54] A peace treaty in 1763 ended hostilities with France, but all was not peaceful on the frontier. That same year a group of tribes from the Great Lakes region, dissatisfied with the influx of the British and their heavy-handed policies, launched a series of attacks against English forts and settlements with some initial success. The victorious British had invested themselves in the former French forts and settlements of the Great Lakes region, but whereas the French had cultivated alliances and cemented their relationships with important symbolic gifts and trade goods, the British simply treated the Natives as a conquered people.[55] Not surprisingly, resentments built up and exploded in a series of attacks that resulted in eight British forts captured and many British soldiers and settlers killed. At one council in which he was drumming up support for the conflict, an Ottawa chieftain named Pontiac reportedly said:

> It is important for us, my brothers, that we exterminate from our lands this nation which seeks only to destroy us. You see as well as I do that we can no longer supply our needs, as we have done from our brothers, the French. The English sell us goods twice as dear as the French do, and their goods do not last. Scarcely have we bought a blanket or something else to cover ourselves with before we must think of getting another; and when we wish to set out for our winter camp they do not want to give us any credit as our brothers the French do. . . . When I go to see the English commander and say to him that some of our comrades are dead, instead of bewailing their death, as our French brothers do, he laughs at me and at you. If I ask for anything for our sick, he refuses with the reply that he has no use for us. From all this you can well see that they are seeking our ruin. Therefore, my brothers, we must all swear their destruction and wait no longer. Nothing prevents us: They are few in numbers, and we can accomplish it.[56]

These words, as reported by a French chronicler of the occasion, reveal many of the ostensible reasons behind the outbreak of hostilities, and because of this kind of vocal leadership, this conflict has often been called "Pontiac's War," or "Pontiac's Rebellion." In terms of the fighting, those forts that were not taken initially through subterfuge were put under siege and before long British forces were trapped in Fort Detroit, Fort Pitt, and Fort Niagara.[57] The question of genocide specifically arises in regard to the defense of Fort Pitt and attempts to relieve the garrison there (later to become Pittsburgh, Pennsylvania).

In attempting to break the siege, Jeffery Amherst dispatched Colonel Henry Bouquet with a force of just under 500 men.[58] In a series of letters exchanged between Amherst and Bouquet, the topic of biological warfare was first raised.[59] On July 7, 1763, in a letter to the commander of his relief force, Amherst wrote, "Could it not be contrived to send the Small Pox among those disaffected tribes of Indians? We must on this occasion use every strategem in our power to reduce them."[60] Next, in a postscript on a letter from Bouquet to Amherst dated July 13, 1763, Bouquet, who was approaching Fort Pitt at the time, suggested:

P.S. I will try to inoculate the Indians by means of Blankets that may fall in their hands, taking care however, not to get the disease myself. As it is pity to oppose good men against them, I wish we could make use of the Spaniard's method, and hunt them with English dogs, supported by Rangers, and some light Horse, who would I think effectively extirpate or remove the Vermine.

Amherst's reply, dated July 16, 1763 contains the following postscript:

P.S. You will do well to try to Innoculate the Indians by means of Blanketts, as well as to try Every other method that can serve to Extirpate this Execrable Race. I should be very glad your scheme for Hunting them Down by Dogs could take Effect, but England is at too great a Distance to think of that at present.[61]

These written comments are clear and convincing evidence of what can only be construed as genocidal attitudes and intentions toward the Natives on the part of these colonial officers. The callous indifference to human life, or more specifically Native American life, is appalling. If carried out, this would arguably constitute genocide, at least in this instance. But even if Amherst's genocidal wishes were carried out, it still does not establish genocide as a more widespread practice or policy. It's also important to point out that there is no credible evidence that the policies were actually put into practice. No letters have ever been found detailing that this practice had actually been put into effect. Given the openness with which they discussed exterminating the Natives, one would not expect them to have been reticent in writing about the success or failure of this tactic afterward if they had carried it out, and yet there is no evidence that they did. Are we to assume that the infection plan was carried out or was Amherst's suggestion not followed through by Bouquet? It's doubtful that the truth will ever be known. The situation gets even more confusing when we look at the events at Fort Pitt itself.

At the same time that the above-cited letters were being drafted and sent back and forth, the commander of Fort Pitt, Captain Simeon Ecuyer, decided on a similar course of action as that suggested by Amherst, although it's unclear whether or not he thought it up on his own. After Fort Pitt became crowded with refugees, smallpox had broken out within the fort. It is possible that hearing about the outbreak of smallpox had given Amherst the idea to spread contagion further among the Indians. Regardless of how the idea was first conceived, Captain Ecuyer evidently decided to take two blankets and a handkerchief from the fort's hospital, where smallpox patients were being treated, and give them to two visiting Delaware Natives, Turtle's Heart and Mamaltee.[62] According to the diary of William Trent, a militia commander who was present in the fort when the exchange occurred, "Out of regard to them, we gave them two blankets and a handkerchief out of the smallpox hospital, I hope it will have the desired effect."[63] This passage is often cited as further proof of genocide on the part of the British, but the entire passage of the journal reads as follows:

> [May] 24th [1763] The Turtles Heart a principal Warrior of the Delawares and Mamaltee a Chief came within a small distance of the Fort Mr. McKee went out to them and they made a Speech letting us know that all our [POSTS] as Ligonier was destroyed, that great numbers of Indians [were coming and] that out of regard to us, they had prevailed on 6 Nations [not to] attack us but give us time to go down the Country and they desired we would set of immediately. The Commanding Officer thanked them, let them know that we had

everything we wanted, that we could defend it against all the Indians in the Woods, that we had three large Armys marching to Chastise those Indians that had struck us, told them to take care of their Women and Children, but not to tell any other Natives, they said they would go and speak to their Chiefs and come and tell us what they said, they returned and said they would hold fast of the Chain of friendship. Out of our regard to them we gave them two Blankets and an Handkerchief out of the Small Pox Hospital. I hope it will have the desired effect. They then told us that Ligonier had been attacked, but that the Enemy were beat of.[64]

This more complete quote appears to suggest a more benign motive in giving the blankets to the two Delawares. Is it possible that the blankets from the hospital were from a storeroom or otherwise unused? On the other hand, did they really think that giving gifts that might transmit smallpox was a friendly gesture? That seems hardly likely given the context of the journal.

To further complicate the matter, later that same month, Levy, Trent, and Company sent an invoice that contained "Sundries got to Replace in kind those which were taken from people in the Hospital to Convey the Smallpox to the Indians,"[65] which appears to confirm the genocidal intentions of the gift. The outbreak of smallpox in the region cannot be used to verify that these tactics were successfully employed, or even employed at all in the case of Amherst's suggestions to Bouquet, because smallpox had already broken out among the tribes of the region earlier in the year. This eruption occurred well before Amherst, Bouquet, and Ecuyer had a chance to wreak their mischief. So where are we left at the end of this sad episode? Essentially, we can argue that many of the British officers had genocidal intentions in mind, but it is less clear if they actually were able or willing to carry it out. As the historian Fred Anderson writes, "Appalling as they were, Amherst's orders did not occasion genocide so much as reflect his and his colleagues' genocidal fantasies."[66] In other words, while it is certainly possible that they carried out their genocidal ideas, it is not definitive that they did. This uncertainty is also evident with the other well-known case of intentional infection, this time with the Mandan in 1837.

While some have suggested that the U.S. army intentionally infected the Mandans,[67] a plains tribe that lived along the upper Missouri River in what is today North Dakota, by providing them with smallpox-infected blankets, the evidence indicates otherwise. Based on testimony derived from eyewitnesses to the outbreak that ravaged the Mandan people at Fort Clark in 1837, the source of the epidemic was a trading boat named the *St. Peter* that was plying its trade along the Missouri River.[68] It appears that several of the passengers were infected with smallpox upon boarding in St. Louis and only began showing symptoms several weeks after having departed. These passengers, a Mr. and Mrs. Halsey, were kept under quarantine on the steamboat. Some accounts suggest that when docking at Fort Clark, a Mandan snuck aboard and stole a blanket in use by the infected passengers, while other versions place the blame on a Native American hitchhiker who boarded the *St. Peter* in order to gain passage to his people and managed to come down with the disease after disembarking at Fort Clark. Still another account suggests a drunken party one night as members of the crew caroused with the Mandan and Arikara. Regardless of which story is accurate, after the two-week incubation period, the disease exploded among the tribes of the high plains and absolutely devastated them. None of these versions, however, suggest that the Mandan Indians were intentionally infected, let alone as part of a plan to eliminate them.

To summarize, then, disease played a tremendous role in facilitating the conquest of the Americas by various European groups, including settlers, conquerors, and colonists. By depopulating vast stretches of land and throwing into disarray the surviving Native tribes and cultures, it paved the way for the new arrivals. It does not appear, however, that a strong case can be made that most of the deaths from disease can be considered as constituting an example of genocide. As horrific and as tragic as this great mortality was, it is hard to paint a convincing story that it was largely intentional. Except for a few specific cases, which are by no means certain, the deaths from disease were largely unintentional, and this calls into question the connection between genocide and most Native deaths from disease.

L'Anse aux Meadows Viking Longhouse. Vikings were among the first Europeans to settle in the Americas. They didn't stay long, however, due in large part to conflict with local Native people. ThinkStock.

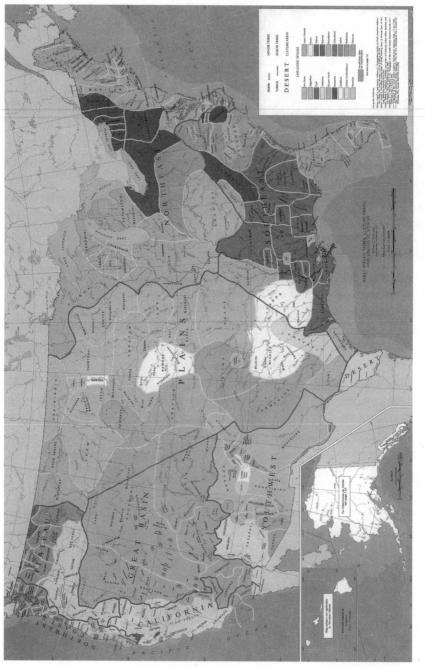

Early Native American languages in the United States. Looking at the great variety of linguistic stocks, it's easy to the diversity of Native cultures. USGS map, 1970.

**Hopis on their housetop. Notice the distinctive Puebloan style of architecture.
Library of Congress Prints and Photographs Division.**

Native slaves building Mexico City on the ruins of Tenochtitlan. After the conquest, the Spanish largely destroyed Tenochtitlan and built a European-style city that became present-day Mexico City. ThinkStock.

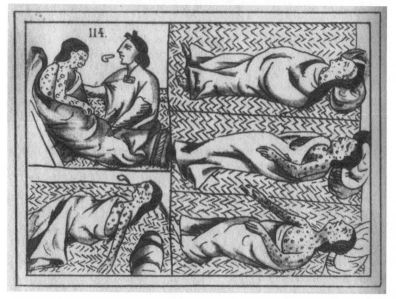

Sixteenth-century Aztec drawing of smallpox victims. Smallpox ravaged the Aztec Empire and contributed to their defeat by the Spanish conquistadors. This image originally comes from fol. 54 of Book XII of the Florentine Codex, the sixteenth-century compendium of materials and information on Aztec and Nahua history collected by Fray Bernardino de Sahagún. This digitized version was taken from Wikimedia Commons.

What's left of Bigfoot's band. Library of Congress Prints and Photographs Division.

Ghost Dance—Cheyennes and Arapahoes. Fears of the Ghost Dance fueled white paranoia and suspicion and led directly to the Wounded Knee Massacre. Library of Congress Prints and Photographs Division.

Big Foot, leader of the Sioux, captured at the battle of Wounded Knee, South Dakota. Here he lies frozen on the snow-covered battlefield where he died, 1890. National Archives and Records Administration.

Big Foot's camp three weeks after the Wounded Knee Massacre (December 29, 1890), with bodies of several Lakota Sioux people wrapped in blankets in the foreground and U.S. soldiers in the background. Library of Congress Prints and Photographs Division.

Site of the Sand Creek Massacre today. Alex Alvarez.

Band of mounted Navajos passing through Cañon. Library of Congress Prints and Photographs Division.

Group of Omaha boys in cadet uniforms, Carlisle Indian School, Pennsylvania. National Archives and Records Administration.

5

WARS AND MASSACRES

Damn any man who sympathizes with Indians! . . . I have come to kill
Indians, and believe it is right and honorable to use any means under
God's heaven to kill Indians.

—Colonel John Chivington[1]

The only good Indians I ever saw were dead.

—General Philip Sheridan[2]

It was a cold dawn on the banks of Sand Creek on the morning of
November 29, 1864, when a troop of Colorado cavalry reined in their
horses on a small rise overlooking the dry creek bed. With their horses
snorting and pawing the ground, the troopers surveyed a Native encampment. Nestled amid the bare cottonwoods and willows on the
riverbed stood a group of about 115 lodges of a Cheyenne band under
the leadership of Black Kettle, as well as a smaller number of Arapahoe
lodges under Chief Left Hand.[3] Weary of the fighting that had been
raging in the southern plains for most of the last year, they had traveled
to Fort Lyon to surrender to the military and arrange a peace. Lacking
the rations to feed the Natives, and needing official permission to accept them as prisoners, the commanders of the fort instructed the surrendering Natives to stay in their camp about forty miles away on the
banks of Sand Creek, where they should continue to hunt and feed
themselves.[4]

Sand Creek is a wide dry riverbed in eastern Colorado that had long
been a wintering ground for the Cheyenne. The camp was sheltered

from the brutal winds of the high prairie by the high bluffs on each side of the wide and well-treed river valley. It was also close to a number of springs that could provide fresh water even in winter. So, having been assured that they would be treated as friendlies and believing themselves to be under the protection of the military, the Cheyenne and Arapahoe had settled in for the winter, unaware of the calamity that was soon to befall them.

The men who reined in their mounts on that long-ago morning were members of the Third Regiment, a volunteer unit of mounted troops who had signed up for a hundred-day stint of military service. The man in charge of the forces that appeared on the skyline above Sand Creek on the morning of November 29 was a former Methodist minister named John. M. Chivington whose nickname was the "Fighting Parson."[5] An ambitious man, Chivington had considered leading his troops north to the Republican River, where large numbers of actively hostile Natives were wintering, but instead decided to head to the Sand Creek encampment of Black Kettle, even though he was fully aware that they had already surrendered. It had the double advantage of being both closer and safer. Evidently, to his way of thinking, all Indians were fair game, regardless of whether they were hostile or not. He is famously reported to have advocated the killing of all Indians, including infants, because "nits make lice."[6] The Colorado newspapers and popular sentiment that often castigated Chivington and his troopers for not being active enough in fighting the Natives doubtless were also an influence on his decision to attack the peaceful encampment.[7] His troopers had been dubbed the "Bloodless Third" by the local press, a fact that undoubtedly rankled Chivington and his men.

Not all his men agreed with his decision. A couple of his officers argued that an attack on Black Kettle's band violated the pledge of safety given to them and amounted to murder. Chivington reportedly flew into a rage and shouted, "Damn any man who sympathizes with Indians! I have come to kill Indians, and believe it is right and honorable to use any means under God's heaven to kill Indians."[8] As dawn broke on that cold November morning, Chivington deployed his 700 men, some to get between the horse herd and the village and the others to advance along Sand Creek to the lodges. Some early risers heard the noise and thought it was buffalo, while others correctly identified the riders as soldiers. But for most of the Cheyenne and Arapahoe, the first warning they had was of the pounding of hooves and the crackle of rifle fire.

The troop, deployed in a wide line, quickly swept toward the encampment, firing indiscriminately at whoever appeared. Many of the Cheyenne and Arapahoe never had a chance. They awoke to bedlam and were shot as they scrambled outside to figure out what was going on. Some managed to flee up the creek, although many were shot as they ran. Subsequent testimony described how some soldiers reportedly made a sport of shooting the children as they ran away.[9]

The victims were primarily women and children, since most of the men were out hunting buffalo as they had been instructed to do by the soldiers at Fort Lyon. Of the approximately 500 people in camp, only about 60 were warriors or old men, the rest were women, children, and infants. As the attack began, one eyewitness described how Chief Black Kettle waved an American flag on a pole and told his people not to be scared because the camp was under the protection of the U.S. government. Reports indicate a white flag was also flown during the attack, but to no avail. After seeing many of his villagers shot down, including children and infants, Black Kettle eventually ran for it and survived the massacre. Another prominent Cheyenne leader, White Antelope, walked toward the troops with his hands in the air and then stood in the middle of the creek with his arms crossed over his chest trying to show that he and his people didn't want to fight. This gesture, as brave as it was, was also futile, and he was simply shot down. As the soldiers rampaged through the village, most of the Cheyenne fled up the creek bed, while the few warriors present fought desperately to hold back the troopers and allow their families to escape.

Not all of the soldiers participated in the shooting. Captain Silas Soule, one of those who had earlier opposed the plan to attack the village at Sand Creek and had been threatened by Chivington for his qualms, did not order his men to open fire. Horrified at the treacherous attack engineered by Chivington, he took the men under his command away from the butchery and simply stood by as a passive observer to the violence. Within a few short hours it was over. While accounts varied, it appears that about 150 Cheyenne and Arapahoe were killed. After the initial attack ended, many soldiers reportedly went on an orgy of destruction, looting the lodges, killing the wounded, raping and killing women, and scalping and mutilating the corpses.[10] Eyewitnesses' testimony at subsequent hearings revealed that many of the bodies had fingers and ears cut off, as were the scrotums of some of the male victims in order to make tobacco pouches. Women had their genitalia excised and displayed on saddle horns and sticks.

Captain Soule, in a letter to his former commanding officer, detailed a horrible list of atrocities and wrote that, "You would think it impossible for white men to butcher and mutilate human beings as they did there, but every word I have told you is the truth, which they do not deny."[11] The "Bloodless Third," as the Denver press had previously dubbed this troop, was no longer bloodless. While still in the field, Chivington began sending dispatches to his commanding officer and to the newspapers trumpeting the massacre as a great battle and victory. Captain Soule, however, and a number of other officers, took a different view and began to advocate for the prosecution of Chivington.[12]

To further examine the Sand Creek Massacre, as it became known, we can assess the reaction to the slaughter. We find that even though the local press and many Coloradans thought the attack was justified and appropriate, at the national level many others did not. One of the most vocal critics was Kit Carson, no pacifist when it came to Native America, who said that:

> Jis to think of that dog Chivington and his dirty hounds, up thar at Sand Creek. His men shot down squaws, and blew the brains out of little innocent children. You call sich soldiers Christians, do ye? An Indians savages? What der yer 'spose our Heavenly Father, who made both them and us, thinks of these things? I tell you what, I don't like a hostile red skin any more than you do. And when they are hostile, I've fought 'em, hard as any man. But I never yet drew a bead on a squaw or papoose, and I despise the man who would.[13]

This kind of sentiment was shared by many, and as word got out about the massacre, a number of investigations were formed, two conducted by the army and one by a Congressional Joint Committee on the Conduct of the War. In its report, the congressional committee was especially scathing. Words such as murder, barbarism, and savage cruelty were used to describe the killings, and Black Kettle's band was depicted as "friendly to the whites, and had not been guilty of any acts of hostility or depredations."[14] Furthermore, the committee wrote that "it is difficult to believe that beings in the form of men, and disgracing the uniform of United States soldiers and officers, could commit or countenance the commission of such acts of cruelty and barbarity as are detailed in the testimony."[15] In regards to Chivington himself, the committee concluded that

> As to Colonel Chivington, your committee can hardly find fitting terms to describe his conduct. Wearing the uniform of the United States, which should be the emblem of justice and humanity; holding the important position of commander of a military district, and therefore having the honor of the government to that extent in his keeping, he deliberately planned and executed a foul and dastardly massacre which would have disgraced the veriest savage among those who were the victims of his cruelty. Having full knowledge of their friendly character, having himself been instrumental to some extent in placing them in their position of fancied security, he took advantage of their inapprehension and defenseless condition to gratify the worst passions that ever cursed the heart of man. It is thought by some that desire for political preferment prompted him to this cowardly act; that he supposed that by pandering to the inflamed passions of an excited population he could recommend himself to their regard and consideration. Others think it was to avoid being sent where there was more of danger and hard service to be performed; that he was willing to get up a show of hostility on the part of the Indians by committing himself acts which savages themselves would never premeditate. Whatever may have been his motive, it is to be hoped that the authority of this government will never again be disgraced by acts such as he and those acting with him have been guilty of committing.[16]

The committee report to Congress then concluded by demanding that "for the purpose of vindicating the cause of justice and upholding the honor of the nation, prompt and energetic measures should be at once taken to remove from office those who have thus disgraced the government by whom they are employed, and to punish, as their crimes deserve, those who have been guilty of these brutal and cowardly acts."[17] The creation of these investigations and the strong condemnation of the massacre raise a number of important questions about how best to understand and characterize the massacre. Was the massacre at Sand Creek part of a larger plan of annihilation that can only be defined as genocide? While it is true that no charges were ever filed, it is also true that Chivington was forced to resign and his career ruined. If the massacre fit into a government plan of genocide, one would hardly expect that the army or Congress would have implemented these investigations. Given the sentiments of the time, one would also not expect that these investigations were purely cynical maneuvers designed to disguise the true policies or intentions of the government. Instead, from reading through the various reports, one gets a sense that there was genuine outrage over the mistreatment of Black Kettle's band of Cheyenne, at least at the national level.

This is not to suggest that the government pursued benign or just policies toward Native Americans, nor to argue that the government was hesitant to wage war against them, but rather that the Sand Creek Massacre does not appear to have been part of a larger plan of extermination, at least not as governmental policy. On the other hand, just because some objected to the massacre does not necessarily invalidate any claims of genocide. Mixed opinion and internal opposition to the attempted extermination of a population group characterizes many examples of state-perpetrated genocides. Additionally, it is also fairly evident that Chivington's attitudes and actions can be perceived rightfully as genocidal and, in this, he was supported by large numbers of men and women in the Colorado territory. Keep in mind that Colorado at this time was a frontier region in which many of the newly arrived settlers and fortune seekers felt under threat by the various local Native tribes. The spring and summer of 1864 had also seen a fair number of stories about massacres and attacks against whites by Indians, with a number of well-publicized killings of settlers.[18] In June 1864, for example, the Hungate family was killed in a way that evoked a widespread sense of panic among those living in the Colorado Territory. As one eyewitness recounted:

> The party from the mill and himself, upon reaching the place, had found it in ruins and the house burned to the ground. About 100 yards from the desolated ranch they discovered the body of the murdered woman and her two dead children, one of which was a little girl of four years and the other an infant. The woman had been stabbed in several places and scalped, and the body bore evidences of having been violated. The two children had their throats cut, their heads being nearly severed from their bodies. Up to this time the body of the man had not been found, but upon our return down the

creek, on the opposite side, we found the body. It was horribly muti-
lated and the scalp torn off.[19]

Stories like this abounded in the months preceding the massacre and
they served to engender a sense of hysteria and panic among Coloradans. It is revealing that as the massacre began, Chivington reportedly
told his men to "remember the murdered women and children on the
Platte."[20] Throughout the investigations and to the end of his days,
Chivington defended his actions at Sand Creek through reference to
Indian atrocities. In a speech in 1883, for example, he stated that "What
of that Indian blanket that was captured, fringed with white women's
scalps? What says the sleeping dust of the two hundred and eight men,
women, and children, emigrants, herders, and soldiers who lost their
lives at the hands of these Indians? I say here, as I said in a speech one
night last week—I stand by Sand Creek."[21] It didn't matter that only
one white scalp had reportedly been found at Sand Creek. The rhetoric
trumped reality. It certainly didn't help that racist and dehumanizing
attitudes toward Natives on the part of whites were fairly commonplace
in Colorado and led many to conclude that extermination was the answer to the problem. One prominent editor of a Colorado newspaper
wrote that "If there be one idea that should become an axiom in
American politics, it is *That the Red Man Should be Destroyed*" (emphasis in original).[22] Similarly, a minister visiting Colorado in 1864 reported that "There is but one sentiment in regard to the final disposi-
tion which shall be made of the Indians: 'Let them be exterminated
men, women and children together.' They are regarded as a race ac-
cursed, like the ancient Canaanites, and like them, devoted of the al-
mighty to utter destruction."[23] Very similarly, another missionary wrote
to his wife that "There is no sentimentality here on the frontier respect-
ing Indians. Cooper and Longfellow are regarded with disgust. Indians
are all the same, a treacherous and villainous set. I would rejoice, as
would every man in Colorado to see them exterminated."[24]

If this then was the general opinion of the white population of Colorado, should we be surprised when most of the recruits of the Third
Regiment shared these kinds of genocidal hatreds? One participant in
the Sand Creek Massacre, years after the attack, wrote that

At the time the 3rd Colorado regiment was raised, the idea was very
general that a war of extermination should be waged; that neither sex

nor age should be spared; and women held these views in common
with men . . . and one often heard the expression that 'nits make lice,
make a clean thing of it.'[25]

So what we see is a real schism in attitudes and actions between those in
Colorado and those government officials and the wider public, many of
whom resided in the east. Chivington and his men were products of a
frontier culture that, out of fear and racism, despised and hated the
Indian and sought to exterminate them, while those farther removed
from the immediacy of frontier life tended to hold somewhat more
humane attitudes and ideas about Native Americans. This kind of dy-
namic was often present in the frontier. Rob Harper's analysis of the
less well-known Gnadenhütten massacre in 1782 on the Ohio frontier
suggests a very similar kind of situation in which frontier attitudes,
hardened and brutalized by war, created a climate of vengeance and
savagery that resulted in the massacre of about a hundred Natives who
were murdered and scalped.[26]

The victims of the massacre were Christian converts who had fallen
into the hands of a militia that had been searching for hostile warriors
raiding white settlements. In this case, the commander of the militia
told the members of the band to decide whether "to carry the Indians
as prisoners to Fort Pitt, or to kill them."[27] But while some militia
members did not support killing these Christian converts, "The traumas
of war, together with the chronic insecurity of frontier existence, mag-
nified such suspicion and intolerance, leading to hostility and even violence against dissenters."[28] In other words, those for killing carried the
day over the qualms of those who didn't support it. So here again, we
can see frontier attitudes, so often shaped by the exigencies of frontier
violence, helped fuel violence and facilitated massacres.

Sadly, the ill-fated Black Kettle met his end almost four years to the
day after the massacre at Sand Creek on the banks of the Washita River
in a similar type of surprise assault when George Armstrong Custer and
elements of the Seventh Cavalry attacked an encampment of Cheyenne
on the banks of the Washita River in November of 1868.[29] General
Philip Sheridan had organized a winter campaign against the Cheyenne
with the intent of destroying their shelters and supplies, thus forcing
them to surrender. According to Custer, he and his men had followed a
war party's trail back to the camp and, after riding through much of the

night, attacked at daybreak.[30] Custer's orders were "to proceed south in the direction of the Antelope Hills, thence toward the Washita River, the supposed winter seat of the hostile tribes; to destroy their villages and ponies, to kill or hang all warriors, and bring back all women and children."[31]

Custer and his 800 men encircled the camp and assaulted what was essentially a peaceful band of Cheyenne. Even though he had lived through the Sand Creek Massacre, Black Kettle had still sought peace and had moved down to the Washita in Indian Territory to avoid the conflicts raging farther north. Sadly, that was not to be. Black Kettle was truly one of those tragic figures of history whose voice of toleration, peace, and moderation was never heeded and who paid the ultimate price for his stand. Black Kettle, the survivor of the Sand Creek Massacre, didn't survive this attack, as he and his wife were shot down early in the attack while trying to cross the river and escape.[32] Even though Custer reported over a hundred Natives killed, more reliable evidence suggests twenty to fifty killed, while the Seventh Cavalry lost twenty-one soldiers, most of them from a small detachment that, while chasing down escaping Cheyenne, ran into a group of warriors from nearby villages who overwhelmed and killed this isolated group of soldiers.[33]

Even though Custer and his men took the women and children prisoner instead of killing them as Chivington had done,[34] and even though the troopers had a significant number of casualties, the Washita is best understood as a massacre rather than as a battle. Many newspapers and letters from private citizens castigated Custer and the army for the massacre and in fact compared it to the massacre at Sand Creek.[35] As opposed to Sand Creek, however, there were no official inquiries or repercussions. In fact, Custer's commanding officer, General Sheridan, offered his congratulations for a job well done. The difference in reaction was due to Custer acting under orders, rather than independently as Chivington had done. The army rallied around Custer and defended him vigorously. General Sheridan dismissed comparisons with Chivington and the Sand Creek Massacre by suggesting that Custer had been following orders and had spared noncombatants, as opposed to Chivington, who had not. Additionally, Sheridan suggested that the Natives at the Washita had been involved in hostilities and that, furthermore, they had never been offered protection as those at Sand Creek had been. While this defense protected Custer from legal consequences, it did nothing to diminish the criticism and controversy. Here again we see a significant distinction in attitudes between those on the frontier and those farther removed from the violence and conflict.

Perhaps the most infamous of massacres during the Plains Wars occurred in the last days of 1890 at a place called Wounded Knee Creek. For a couple of years preceding the attack, the Ghost Dance religion had been sweeping through the plains of the American West. Spread by a Paiute mystic named Wovoka, this new belief system, a mix of Christianity and traditional Native beliefs, asserted that if Natives embraced peace among the various tribes, lived purely, shunned alcohol, and performed various rituals, especially the Ghost Dance, then the earth would soon be reborn. All of the whites, who had brought such violence and misfortune, would disappear and Natives would inherit the earth. Their ancestors would return to this world and the buffalo would fill the prairies again. It would be a time of peace, harmony, and perfect health. One of Wovoka's followers, a Hunkpapa Sioux named Kicking Bear, told his people, "My brothers, I bring to you the promise of a day in which there will be no white man to lay his hand on the bridle of the Indians's horse; when the red men of the prairie will rule the world. . . . I bring you word from your fathers the ghosts, that they are now marching to join you, led by the Messiah who came once to live on earth with the white man, but was cast out and killed by them."[36] To people whose traditional lifestyles and land had been brutally taken away through numerous broken treaties, wars, and disease, and who were often starving, such a vision often proved irresistible.

As this millenarian movement spread like wildfire throughout the Plains tribes, many whites found the rituals and fervor associated with the Ghost Dance scary and disturbing. The Indian agent for the Standing Rock reservation referred to it as, "demoralizing, indecent and disgusting," while local settlers and newspapers worried that this religion was leading up to war. These fears were exacerbated by an extreme strain of the Ghost Dance that was much more aggressive and which included the belief that special Ghost Dance Shirts could be worn that would make the wearer invulnerable to bullets. While most who embraced this faith followed Wovoka's pacifistic doctrine of not fighting, not harming others, and of doing right,[37] among the Sioux, the "plea for peace was transformed into a call to arms."[38] Reservation police tried in vain to halt the spread and practice of the Ghost Dance to no avail, and in response, the U.S. government built up the military presence on the reservations to such an extent that at one point half of the entire U.S. army was deployed on various reservations.[39] It was in this atmosphere of heightened fears and tensions that the army ordered the arrest of Chief Sitting Bull in order to prevent him from furthering the cause of the Ghost Dance. During his arrest, a brawl broke out and Sitting Bull was shot and killed. One other chief who was supposed to be arrested was Chief Big Foot, a Miniconjou Sioux who lived with his band on the banks of the Cheyenne River.

A prominent supporter of the Ghost Dance, Big Foot had been invited to Pine Ridge, not to join supporters of the Ghost Dance, but to participate in a council of leaders who wanted to find a way to defuse the troubles. Perhaps news of the murder of Sitting Bull, as well as the buildup of army troops, influenced the decision, but on December 23, Big Foot and his band set out southward across the frozen prairie toward the Pine Ridge Agency in order to join the council. In fact, evidence suggests that Big Foot wanted to stay put, but acceded to the desire of the majority of his band to go. Fearing the worst, the army decided to pursue the group and finally caught up with them on December 28 after the band had traveled over 200 miles from their starting point. Surrendering to elements of the Seventh Cavalry, the wayward band agreed to be escorted to Pine Ridge and, as evening fell, made camp on the banks of the Wounded Knee creek. Five hundred soldiers and scouts from the Seventh Cavalry were assigned to guard the encampment. The troopers also set up four rapid-fire Hotchkiss cannons on a nearby hill overlooking the campsite. By some accounts, on the night of the 28th of December, a local trader supplied the troops with alcohol so they could celebrate the capture of Big Foot. It was to be a gift with tragic consequences.

On the morning of December 29th, the commander of the Seventh Cavalry, Colonel James Forsyth, ordered that Big Foot's band be disarmed. By some accounts, he was still drunk.[40] If that is true, then it is quite possible that many of his troopers were also intoxicated. What isn't in doubt is that the soldiers handled the search for weapons badly. They roughly handled the women and looked up dresses and skirts for firearms, conducting the search without much respect or deference to the people they were unnecessarily antagonizing. Finally, the inevitable happened. As the soldiers continued to search for weapons, one man named Black Coyote protested that he had paid a lot of money for his rifle and that it was his. As soldiers manhandled him, the rifle discharged; whether intentionally or not is unknown.[41] In the superheated atmosphere of the search, the rifle shot was galvanizing and the soldiers reacted with indiscriminate rifle fire into the crowds while the Sioux rushed around trying to arm themselves.[42] Some accounts also assert that immediately preceding this accidental rifle shot, one member of the band began singing and dancing a portion of the Ghost Dance and at one point grabbed some dirt and threw it at the soldiers, who interpreted it as a signal for an attack.[43] Keep in mind that many rumors had been circulating among both groups, the Natives and the Soldiers. Each side essentially believed that the other was planning an attack. Given this extraordinarily tense encounter, it shouldn't be all that surprising that it ended up so badly.

At first, the fighting was hand-to-hand, but as the melee spread, the Hotchkiss guns opened up and raked the encampment, killing warriors, women, and children wholesale as they attempted to flee. Very few Natives escaped. Estimates suggest that at least 153 Natives were killed out of the total of around 350, and perhaps more.[44] In fact, one estimate suggests that up to 300 lost their lives.[45] Among the victims was Big Foot, who even though frail, elderly, and suffering from pneumonia, was nonetheless shot down by soldiers of the Seventh Cavalry. The troopers had twenty-five of their own killed and another thirty-nine wounded, although many of these victims may have been struck down by friendly fire. The fight, which neither side seems to have specifically wanted, erupted with appalling speed and brutality and would forever become emblematic of the worst excesses of the treatment of the Native Americans.

MASSACRES AND GENOCIDE

In many ways, the massacre at Wounded Knee marked the end of the Indian Wars of the American West. The frontier was gone, and even though there would be a few more small-scale clashes, never again would large numbers of Native Americans and soldiers engage in military warfare. In the aftermath of the debacle at Wounded Knee, Colonel Forsyth's commanding officer tried to reprimand Forsyth for his incompetent handling of the situation, but was in turn overruled by his commanding officer. So here again we have another infamous example of a massacre. In fact, the image of the frozen body of Chief Big Foot in death has become an iconic symbol of the violence so often inflicted against Native America. One survivor of the massacre poignantly captured the meaning of Wounded Knee this way:

> I did not know then how much was ended. When I look back now from this high hill of my old age, I can still see the butchered women and children lying heaped and scattered all along the crooked gulch as plain as when I saw them with eyes still young. And I can see that something else died there in the bloody mud, and was buried in the blizzard. A people's dream died there. It was a beautiful dream.[46]

What are we to make of these massacres? How can they be best understood? Are they examples of genocide as some have suggested, or are they something else?[47] Since genocide refers to a systematic and comprehensive plan of extermination, any massacre by itself is not necessarily genocide, although if it is part of a larger plan of extermination, then it may legitimately be perceived as being genocidal. The sociologist Brenda Uekert, for example, studied government massacres and concluded that there are two primary types: politicidal massacres, which refers to those committed in order to maintain a lock on power, and genocidal massacres intended to wipe out a population.[48] Not all massacres are the same, in other words, and not all are genocidal.

Since genocides are often perpetrated through a series of massacres, can we perceive this massacre as being a small part of a more comprehensive pattern of exterminatory violence? Context is everything, especially when trying to assess genocidal actions.

The historian Paul Bartrop suggests that in trying to differentiate between genocide and massacres, three questions need to be considered:

1. the extent to which a murderous attack by one group against another is an isolated event, or part of a total campaign the intention of which is the destruction of every member of that group regardless of where they may be located;
2. whether the attack is part of a coordinated series of actions that are replicated elsewhere; and

3. whether, given these considerations, the attack was committed by the state (or a state sanctioned proxy) as an act of policy—that is, that the attack was within the law as determined by the governing authorities of the locality in which the action took place. [49]

Given these criteria, Bartrop concludes that the Sand Creek Massacre was an example of a genocidal massacre. Yet given the official reaction to the Sand Creek Massacre, it is not clear that it meets the threshold of genocide, at least in terms of official government culpability. It is more certain, however, to suggest that Chivington's attack was an example of genocide perpetrated at a more localized level. The intention of Chivington and that of many Coloradans, as reflected in the common sentiments of that time, certainly seem to indicate the desire to wipe out the Natives of the Great Plains. From that perspective it appears absolutely appropriate to perceive it as genocidal.

It is also possible to suggest that the Sand Creek Massacre might be an example of what a number of genocide scholars have termed "genocidal massacres."[50] These are a more common phenomenon than genocide itself and consist of more limited cases of mass murder that bear many of the hallmarks of genocide, albeit on a smaller scale. Not intended to eliminate the target population in its entirety, these smaller-scale killings are much more localized in duration and scope. Even though this concept was not explicitly recognized in the U.N. Genocide Convention Definition of 1948, the U.N. definition allows for acts intended to destroy a population *in whole or in part*, a clause that could be seen to encompass massacres. Additionally, the legal expert Bill Schabas points out that genocidal massacres are considered crimes against humanity and also as war crimes.[51] This kind of characterization may well serve to define many of the massacres that were such a feature of the wars of the Great Plains during this era.

Less well-known than the examples briefly discussed above, but perhaps more explicitly genocidal in nature, were the massacres of the Natives of California. In 1769, when the Spanish first arrived in what was to become California, it has been estimated that there were 310,000 to 340,000 Native Americans living there.[52] At the end of Spanish rule in California in 1821, that number had decreased by about a third to 200,000. After the discovery of gold in 1848, however, the population decline became precipitous, and by the end of the 1850s the population was only about 30,000.[53] This dramatic decline was largely the result of unrestrained violence and savagery against California's Indians during the Gold Rush period.

THE CALIFORNIA GOLD RUSH AND GENOCIDE

Prior to contact, the Natives of California belonged to many small tribes and clans and inhabited an extremely varied landscape. These groups included the Pomo, Miwok, Tolowa, Chumash, Cupeno, Yana, Maidu, and Salinan, to name only a few. Tribes along the northern coast fished and hunted sea mammals, while those who lived along the central valley of California foraged for game and relied extensively on the ubiquitous acorn for subsistence. Other tribes inhabited riverine systems and fished and trapped for their food. The foraging nature of many of their lifestyles meant that tribal units often tended to be fairly small and mobile.[54] Because of the richness of the environment and the mild climate, California was, according to some, the most densely populated region of North America.[55] Rich cultures had been created and maintained along with extensive trading networks that linked many of the groups together in an intricate web of affiliation and commerce, culture and conflict. For these tribes, life had gone on relatively unchanged for generations, but that all began to end in 1769 when the Spanish built their first mission in what is now San Diego.

The arrival of the Spanish ushered in an era of exploitation and colonization.[56] In the name of conversion and civilization, the Spanish created a series of missions along the coast and worked assiduously to convert the Natives to Christianity, although it appears the ulterior motive was often more about creating a docile and obedient labor force than it was about anything else. This process typically involved compelling Natives to live on or near the missions in virtual slavery and to subject them to floggings, incarceration, and other punishments in order to enforce Spanish dominance. Soldiers helped coerce the Natives to come to these missions and hunted down those who tried to escape. Children were taken from their families and made to live in barracks. Single women were put into dormitories until they married. This served the dual purpose of allowing for religious indoctrination and deterring the parents and families of those being held hostage. Rape and murder were fairly common.[57] In response, Natives found various active and passive ways to resist the Spanish missionaries that included work stoppages and slowdowns, becoming fugitives, guerrilla warfare, and sometimes even outright revolt. Finally, in 1836, the mission system collapsed, but not before many Native peoples had been killed and their cultures traumatized. It should be noted that many thousands also perished from the waves of diseases that were inadvertently introduced by the Spanish and which periodically swept through Native Californian communities.

Spanish rule was officially ended as a result of the Mexican War of 1846–1848, in which Mexico lost sovereignty over California, and, in fact, many Natives sided with the Americans in order to help throw out their hated oppressors. Unfortunately, they had only exchanged one set of persecutors for another. There was one important difference, however. The Spanish, for all the violence and injustice they perpetrated, sought to establish a society in which Natives belonged, albeit as converts to Christianity and as virtual slaves. The Americans, on the other hand, especially those who immigrated to California during the Gold Rush era, wanted the Native peoples completely gone.[58]

In 1848, workers at Sutter's Mill on the American River discovered gold and set off a stampede that was to have tragic consequences for California's Native population. After word got out, hundreds of thousands of prospective fortune seekers converged on California from all over the world. Some came overland on the trails that had been pioneered by earlier cross-country travelers, while others, especially those from abroad, arrived by sea. After docking in San Francisco, many ships were unable to set sail again since their crews often deserted en masse in order to join the rush. The numbers tell the story of the size of the influx. In 1845, there were only about 7,000 non-Natives living in California. That number jumped to 60,000 within six months of the discovery of gold, and by 1850 it had a population of more than 150,000.[59] This demographic explosion fundamentally altered the relationship between whites and Natives.

Whereas the Spanish had been concentrated almost exclusively in a thin strip along the southern coast, these newcomers roamed throughout the state looking for gold and established mining camps, settlements, and land claims. Inevitably, this led to many violent clashes, which in turn led to more violence. The "49ers," as the prospectors were known, polluted streams in their quest for gold, hunted out the game, felled trees, and appropriated Native lands. Hydraulic mining techniques, for example, involved spraying hillsides with streams of water, destroying plants and shrubs and filling the streams with sediment and erosion runoff. Those who relied on the waterways for fish and drinking water increasingly found the fish dead and the water fouled. The woodlands, especially the oak trees and their acorns, which had been such an important staple, were chopped down for pastureland and for farms, while the acorns of those that remained were fed to hogs. The impact of these new arrivals on the ability of Native Californians to support themselves and live in their traditional ways was significant and universally harmful. Sometimes Natives would attack prospectors, immigrants, and/or settlers, while other times they were accused of stealing something, but regardless of the ostensible provocation, retribution was usually swift and excessive. It was also usually collective and indiscriminate. Any Indian or tribe would serve. Entire villages and tribes were wiped out for incidents both real and alleged that they had nothing to do with.

In looking at this period, we find various groups throughout California committed many massacres, both large and small. One massacre can serve to illustrate the process. This particular one erupted in 1849 after two white ranchers established a ranch near Clear Lake, which is a bit north of San Francisco and the Bay area. They exploited and coerced a number of local Pomo Indians who they had forced to work for them and reportedly also raped a number of women. Enough was finally enough, and the Pomo killed the two men. In response, the army arrived in May 1850, surrounded the village, and proceeded to kill everyone they could. One participant described it as "a perfect slaughter pen."[60] One hundred thirty-five men, women, and children were killed in this one particular massacre. Another participant said that the victims fell "as grass before the sweep of the scythe."[61]

The Clear Lake Massacre was hardly unique and was repeated in many places all over California. Four hundred and fifty Tolowa were killed in 1853 by the Smith River, and the infants that survived the butchery had weights tied to them and were then thrown into the river.[62] In another well-known massacre in February of 1860, whites rowed out to an island in Humboldt Bay and killed 188 Wiyot men, women, and children. Afterward, a visitor wrote in an official report that

> I have just been to Indian Island, the home of a band of friendly Indians, where I beheld a scene of atrocity and horror unparalleled not only in our own country, but even in history—babies with brains oozing out of their skulls, cut and hacked with axes, a two year old child with its ear and scalp torn from the side of its little head, and squaws exhibiting the most frightful wounds, their heads split in twain by axes. [63]

These few horrific examples give a sampling of what was, for all intents and purposes, genocide of the California Indians. This process of killing accelerated through much of the 1850s and 1860s. Towns began offering rewards for proof of a dead Native American. The proof could be offered with different body parts, such as scalps, arms, or hands. [64] The city of Shasta, for example, gave five dollars for every head presented, while the town of Honey Lake paid twenty-five cents per scalp. [65] Local communities sometimes formed militia groups whose sole function was to hunt down and murder any Indians they came across. Many of these groups routinely submitted claims to the state government for expenses that were paid. In 1851 and 1852, $1 million in such expenses were paid out.

The state government clearly was in support of these exterminatory policies, and for all practical purposes, these volunteer militias served as unofficial and informal agents of state policy. Several California governors endorsed extermination against the Natives, most notably John McDougal and Peter Burnett. Governor Burnett told the state legislature in 1851, "A war of extermination will continue to be waged between the races until the Indian race becomes extinct." [66] Burnett's successor as governor was John McDougal, who warned that the state would "make war upon the [Indians] which must of necessity be one of extermination to many of the tribes." [67] This kind of sentiment was often echoed by many California newspapers, which advocated similarly genocidal rhetoric. The *Sacramento Placer Times* wrote, "It is now that the cry of extermination is raised"; the San Francisco *Daily Alta California* wrote, "There will be safety then, only in a war of extermination"; while the *Marysville Herald* wrote, "The northern settlers [will visit] their savage enemies with a thorough and merciless war of extermination." [68]

The Shasta *Herald* wrote, "The initial steps have been taken, and it is sage to assert that the extinction of the tribes who have been to settlers such a cause of dread and loss, will be the result."[69] The *Humboldt Times* ran a headline that went, "Good Haul of Diggers—Band Exterminated" and another that read, "Good Haul of Diggers—Thirty-eight Bucks Killed, Forty Squaws and Children Taken."[70] Other newspapers described the killing as a "White Crusade" and thereby revealed a mind-set that equated the violence against Native Americans with a holy religious struggle.[71]

This indiscriminate mass killing was facilitated by popular images of the California Indians that depicted them as less than human. It is no accident that the language of extermination was so often utilized by the white settlers to describe the destruction being meted out to the Natives. "Extermination" is a term that is used to refer to eliminating insects and rodents, and the reliance on this term reveals that to many settlers the Indians of California were scarcely human. Killing them, therefore, did not elicit the same reaction that killing a fellow human being would. They were defined, to borrow the sociologist and genocide scholar Helen Fein's term, as existing outside of the "circle of human obligation,"[72] or as one contemporary commentator summarized the situation, "In all the frontier settlements of California, there are many men who value the life of an Indian just as they do that of a coyote, or a wolf, and embrace every occasion to shoot them down."[73] Remember too, that many of these recent arrivals had been raised in a society replete with images and stories about the depredations of the "red savages." California newspapers also fanned the flames of bigotry and intolerance by printing horrific stories about the outrages and atrocities supposedly inflicted by Natives against whites, or dehumanized the Natives with descriptions that they "grazed in the fields like beasts and ate roots, snakes, and grasses like cattle, like pigs, like dogs . . . and like hungry wolves" or, "We can never rest in security until the red skins are treated like the other wild beasts of the forests."[74]

Not everyone, however, subscribed to these derogatory attitudes. Some whites were repulsed and dismayed by the unrestrained violence visited upon Native Americans, while others only changed their opinion over time. One former participant in the violence, for example, felt a bit of remorse for his actions and wrote, "To say the truth, I was not entirely satisfied with myself. . . . We invade a land that is not our own, we arrogate a right through pretense of superior intelligence and the wants of civilization, and if the aborigines dispute our title, we destroy them."[75] This sense of remorse, as mild as it was, indicated some sense of awareness as to the injustice of the situation. This kind of sentiment was echoed in an editorial in a Sacramento paper written in 1855:

> The accounts from the North indicate the commencement of a war of extermination against the Indians. The latter commenced the attack on the Klamath; but who can determine their provocation or the amount of destitution suffered before the hostile blow was struck.
>
> The intrusion of the white man upon the Indians' hunting their grounds has driven off the game and destroyed their fisheries. The consequence is, the Indians suffer every winter for sustenance. Hunger and starvation follows them wherever they go. Is it, then, a matter of wonder that they become desperate and resort to stealing and killing? They are driven to steal or starve, and the Indian mode is to kill and then plunder.
>
> The policy of our government towards the Indians in this State is most miserable. Had reasonable care been exercised to see that they were provided with something to eat and war in this State, no necessity would have presented itself for an indiscriminate slaughter of the race.
>
> The fate of the Indian is fixed. He must be annihilated by the advance of the white man; by the diseases, and, to them, the evils of civilization. But the work should not have been commenced at so early a day by the deadly rifle.[76]

As this editorial indicates, even for those who did not approve of the wholesale slaughter of the Native American, there was a widespread sense of the inevitability of their annihilation. Many believed that for their own safety, Natives should be removed from contact with whites. In fact, the creation of the reservation system was originally pioneered in California as an alternative to annihilation. Importantly, this did not happen at the state level, but rather at the federal.

Beginning in the early 1850s, federal negotiators traveled around the state of California signing treaties with various tribes, and their attitude seemed to be one of "extermination or domestication."[77] In exchange for ceding their lands, the Natives were granted federal protection on reservation land that was to be set aside solely for Indian usage.[78] These tribes were forced, coerced, and cajoled into signing, and while the process was often unfair, the ostensible intent was the preservation of the Native Americans, although we can't discount the role that gaining their land played in this process. Not surprisingly, California's citizens and legislators strenuously opposed this initiative. Ultimately, Congress, succumbing to pressure from prominent Californians, buried the treaties, but the forces advocating removal persisted, and in 1853 Congress passed legislation creating five Indian reservations of 25,000 acres each. Those Natives who had survived the carnage were rounded up and hounded or forced onto the reservations, with many being killed along the way. One group, for example, bragged that they had forced 292 Indians onto the reservation and killed 283 others.[79] So even though the reservations were created out of a desire to save Native Americans, they were still subjected to a great deal of violence. The outcome of this period of unrestrained anti-Native violence was that by the turn of the century, there were only around 20,000 Natives left alive in California.[80]

The case of the Natives of California illustrates one of the clearest examples of genocide in North America. The evidence appears quite compelling that many, if not most, within the Anglo community intended to eliminate Natives from within the state of California. The intent, in other words, was genocidal. The massacres, instead of being somewhat isolated instances, appear to have been part of a much larger and systematic pattern of harassment, violence, and outright annihilation. Where this example differs from more recent examples of genocide is that it doesn't appear as if the genocide in California was the result of one unified and coordinated policy instigated and implemented by the government, especially the national government. On the contrary, it seems to reflect a kind of decentralized, grassroots violence that was predicated upon extremely racist and denigrating views of the "diggers," as California Natives were often referred to. The trigger needed to escalate these kinds of attitudes into genocidal action was provided by the Gold Rush. The resulting population explosion pushed further and further into Indian territory in the quest for gold while the Natives, forced increasingly into marginal territories and unable to sustain themselves according to traditional ways, often resorted to raiding for supplies and livestock. They also increasingly attacked prospectors and settlers for self-defense or out of a sense of revenge. The Anglos, already predisposed to despise and hate Indians because of the prejudices and stereotypes that were so prevalent, vented their fear and hatred in extreme and widespread acts of brutality and violence. The violence of the Natives, whether justified in our eyes or not, only served to intensify and reinforce the dehumanizing stereotypes and hostilities. The state government, rather than directing the violence, mostly served to validate and legitimize the genocide, as well as to lend monetary support to the various endeavors. The federal government, on the other hand, found itself in the situation of trying to ameliorate the plight of the Natives and protect them.

There were no wars as such in California during this era. Certainly nothing like the Plains Wars. What occurred in California was largely about extermination, and ultimately this is perhaps what helps differentiate the massacres in California from some of those on the Plains. Sand Creek and the Washita occurred during the course of the Plains Wars and the evidence suggests that the Indian wars of the plains were just that: wars. Unjust and undoubtedly brutal, they were nonetheless still wars, and as such were prone to various atrocities such as the Sand Creek Massacre. The goal of the U.S. government in pursuing these wars was the subjugation of the Native tribes of the plains. These were wars of expansion and empire, but not necessarily wars of extermination, and the atrocities perpetrated during them are perhaps best understood as either war crimes or genocidal massacres. Importantly, however, they appear to be qualitatively different from that which the Natives of California typically experienced, which is why it is much easier to apply the label of genocide to the latter.

THE PEQUOT WAR

One war that is often held up as having been genocidal is the Pequot war of the 1600s between the Pequot and the Puritans, and it represents the first large-scale conflict between the recent arrivals and the Natives in New England.[81] The Pequot were one of many southern New England tribes that included the Patuxet, Wampanoag, Nipmuch, Massachusett, Mohegan, and Pennacook tribes. Relative newcomers to the southern part of Connecticut, Rhode Island, and Massachusetts, the Pequot were a large, aggressive, and warlike tribe according to both Native and non-Native accounts.[82] After the Puritans had established

Plymouth colony in 1620, they enjoyed a fairly long period of peace with the various tribes in the immediate area. Over time, however, the amity became increasingly frayed as the new arrivals increased in numbers and began encroaching more and more into Indian lands.

The Puritans often relied on the principle of *Vacuum Domicilium*, which asserted that vacant lands did not belong to anyone and could therefore be taken over and cultivated.[83] What they failed to recognize was that the local Natives relied on the supposedly unoccupied land for hunting, fishing, and harvesting. In fact, the seemingly empty landscape that the Puritans experienced was, for all intents and purposes, a game reserve that had been managed and altered for generations. Through slash and burn methods of agriculture and selective harvesting, the Indians had created a sustainable way of life that was disrupted by the presence of the Puritans. The high-handed policies and attitudes of the settlers also served to alienate many Natives, who resented the dismissive way they were treated. Moreover, the presence of the European colonists served to disrupt and heighten intertribal tensions and rivalries. During this era, both Dutch and British traders sought to procure trading rights and privileges along the Connecticut River and this situation ultimately helped lead to the Pequot war, along with a massive smallpox epidemic that reduced the population of the Pequot from 13,000 to 3,000.[84]

Weakened by disease, the Pequot tried to reassert some of their previous power in 1634 by attacking members of other tribes coming to trade with the Dutch in the Connecticut River valley. They wanted to monopolize trade in the area and prevent other Natives from doing business with the Dutch. In retaliation, Dutch traders captured a Pequot tribal leader named Tatobem and killed him, even though a ransom had been paid. Subsequently, the Pequot attacked a Dutch trading post, which was followed shortly thereafter by the murder of a trader named John Stone.[85] The new leader of the Pequot, Sassacus, sought then to ally his tribe with the Massachusetts Bay settlers in order to prevent war from breaking out and to help protect them from the pressures of the Dutch, as well as from various other Native tribes that the Pequot were having increased difficulties with.[86]

Part of the negotiations allowed the British to buy land and settle along the Connecticut River valley, which they promptly did. The peace held for two years, but things finally came to a head in 1636 when the body of a trader was discovered after unknown Natives had killed him and the Puritans launched a retaliatory campaign. In this they were aided by the Narragansett and Mohegan, who were pressured to help the Puritans, but also assisted the Puritans because of their longstanding rivalry with the Pequot.[87] In fact, some suggest that the conflict between the Pequot and the Puritans was fostered and manipulated, in part, by Native rivals of the Pequot.[88] The Pequot war raged throughout much of 1637 with Puritan expeditions ranging into Pequot territory and killing and slaughtering as many Pequot as could be found. An early expedition went to nearby Block Island where every male Indian was killed, although ironically these were mostly Narragansett and not Pequot.[89]

One of the worst massacres occurred on May 25, 1637, when the British and their Native allies surrounded a village of about 400 Pequot and set it on fire at daybreak. Only about five Pequot reportedly escaped. This type of indiscriminate killing shocked some of their Narragansett and Mohegan allies who were not used to such wanton slaughter. Some left, some just watched, and others actively participated in the killing.[90] Perhaps they feared the wrath of the English or maybe their hostility to the Pequot overcame their revulsion to the excesses of the colonists, but for whatever reason, the Narragansett, Mohegan, and Niantic remained on the side of the Puritans. It's also likely that they were motivated by a desire to curry favor with the British and profit from their participation, which is indeed what happened. Regardless, the Pequot war was fought and won with the active and usually willing complicity of many Native tribes who assisted in the extermination of the Pequot and sometimes even committed their own atrocities. When a group of Pequot escaped from one massacre into Mohawk territory, for example, they were simply beheaded.[91] To the British, fighting the Indians was "farre less bloudy and devouring than the cruell Warres of Europe."[92] Killed in massacres and skirmishes, executed when captured by the British or their Native allies, or sold into slavery and shipped off to the Caribbean, by the end of the war in September 1638, the Pequot as a people no longer existed. Throughout the conflict, the aim of the Puritans was to eradicate the Pequot as a people. No captives were usually taken and women and children were typically killed, when not being enslaved.

To summarize, then, it is important to recognize that not all massacres were the same in terms of how and why they were perpetrated. Some were part of a systematic pattern of violence, while others tended to be more sporadic. Some were sanctioned, while others were punished. Some were planned, while others were more spontaneous and unanticipated. In many ways, the numerous wars fought between Natives and non-Natives must also be seen as often differing in intent, scope, and outcome. The wars of the colonial era were not the same as the wars of the young nation from 1776 to 1850 or from the 1850s to 1900.[93] Wars are always situated in a particular time and place and the methods and goals of each typically reflect these variances. In turn, the question of genocide in regards to wars and massacres can often hinge upon these more localized questions.

6

EXILES IN THEIR OWN LAND

The Navajos commit their wrongs from a pure love of rapine and plunder. Not a day passes without hearing of some fresh outrage, and the utmost vigilance of the military force in this country is not sufficient to prevent murders and depredations.

—James Calhoun[1]

As a nation of Indians, the Navajoes do not deserve the character given them by the people of New Mexico. From the period of their earliest history, Mexicans have injured and oppressed them to the extent of their power; and because these Indians have redressed their old wrongs, the degenerate Mexicans have represented them as a nation of thieves and assassins.

—Major Electus Backus[2]

A frightened feeling had settled among the Navajo people, a feeling of danger from enemies. Now they were moving into our territory to search for us and kill us all.

—Akinabh Burbank[3]

The Navajo nation comprises the largest tribe in the United States with a growing population of more than 200,000 members, centered around the 25,000-square-mile Navajo reservation in the Four Corners region of Arizona, Utah, Colorado, and New Mexico.[4] When most people think of this area, they envision a spectacular high desert landscape of towering sandstone mesas, deep wrinkled canyons, meandering creek beds lined with shady cottonwoods, and vistas that seem to stretch away forever. It is a harsh, arid, and rocky landscape, but beautiful nonetheless in an austere sort of way. Popular images of the Navajo depict a people renowned for the wool rugs that are still handmade on traditional looms and for the beautiful jewelry that typically features silver and turquoise in intricate and stylized patterns.

This admittedly stereotyped image of the Navajo is nevertheless a common perception since the reservation is a well-known destination for tourists from all over the world who come to see Indian country and get a brief sampling of Native history and culture. In recent years, the Navajo Code Talkers have gained widespread recognition and public acclaim for the contributions they made during the Second World War. Navajo speakers served in the Marine Corps in the Pacific and used their language as a code that the Japanese were unable to decrypt. But things in this region have not always appeared so benign, and one of the most infamous of the events in the long and often turbulent history of this nation concerns what became known as the Navajo "long walk."

Evidence suggests that the Navajo were relative latecomers to the Southwest, arriving in the region sometime before 1400 CE after having slowly made their way down from the Pacific Northwest.[5] The name "Navajo" is a Puebloan word that refers to a region in the Southwest, and when the Spanish arrived in the area, these Puebloans called the Navajo "Apaches de Navajo" to distinguish them from Apaches.[6] The Navajo call themselves "the people," or "Diné" in their language. Always resourceful, the Diné adopted many of the customs, traditions, and lifestyles from the various peoples they encountered. Farming, weaving, pottery, and basket making all appear to be skills that were assimilated from other cultures. The first contact the Navajo had with non-Natives was with Spanish missionaries in the mid-1700s, who met with little success when they attempted to convert the Diné to Catholicism. Importantly, however, the Navajo obtained sheep and goats from the Spanish, and this acquisition helped spark a transition in their culture from hunter-gatherers into pastoralists whose lifestyle largely revolved around their livestock. Much of the subsequent Navajo raiding was centered on stealing livestock to add to their herds.

By the 1700s and 1800s, the Navajo were known primarily for their ability as fighters and marauders and were often in conflict with most of their neighbors, including the Utes, Apache, Comanche, and many of the Puebloan peoples of the region. Importantly, they also often tar-

geted Spanish and Mexicans, especially to the east in New Mexico territory.[7] Engaged in an endless series of hit-and-run attacks against their
enemies, the Navajo would ride out from their homeland to attack
towns and settlements for livestock, supplies, and slaves, and these assaults would typically provoke retaliatory counterraids. This endless cycle of attack and retaliation served to foster and maintain deep-seated
hatreds and animosity for the Navajo among the many victims of their
marauding, and these attitudes would bear bitter fruit for the Diné in
the years to come.

After the United States invaded New Mexico in 1846 and claimed
the territory during the Mexican-American War, the United States offered protection to the settlers, both Mexican and Anglo, but excluded
the Natives from the same such pledge. Specifically, General Stephen
Kearny, the American military leader of the invasion, asserted that the
United States would "protect the persons and property of all quiet and
peaceable inhabitants within its boundaries against their enemies: the
Eutaws, the Navajoes, and others."[8] From the outset, then, the Navajo
were defined as an enemy, and given this oppositional posture, the
stage was set for continued conflict. The raiding continued, and from
the perspective of the Mexicans and Anglo settlers it even increased,
leading General Kearny to complain about "the frequent and almost
daily outrages committed by the Navajos upon the persons and property of the inhabitants of the Rio Abajo, by which several lives have been
lost, and many horses, mules and cattle stolen from them."[9] He even
authorized private citizens to "form war parties, to march into the country of their enemies, the Navajoes, to recover their property, to make
reprisals and obtain redress for the many insults received from them."[10]
Even though Apache, Utes, and other tribes probably conducted many
of the raids, it was the Navajo who received the lion's share of the
blame, and accordingly, the U.S. military commander of the region
mounted an expedition in 1849 through Navajo territory that ultimately
resulted in the signing of a peace treaty. This expedition included not
only American soldiers, but also a detachment of Mexican militia and
Pueblo Indians who were no friends of the Diné, as they were frequent
targets of Navajo raiding.

Unfortunately for the long-term chances of a lasting peace, early in
the expedition the soldiers killed an old man named Narbona who was
one of the most respected and influential of all Navajo leaders. His

death was the result of a dispute over a stolen horse that had escalated needlessly into violence. A fierce fighter in his youth, Narbona had increasingly come to believe in the path of peace, and his killing ended any long-term hope for amity. Not only was he one of the few who had the influence to help persuade large numbers of Diné to abide by the peace agreement, but his completely unjustified killing also fueled resentment and opened the way for young warriors to continue raiding, which they did with renewed vigor. Keep in mind, the Navajo were not uniform in their attitudes toward the Anglos and Mexicans, nor did all accept the constant conflict. Many Navajo disapproved of the constant raiding and feared the consequences of the raiding. One present-day Navajo, Hascon Benally, in speaking about that time, asserted:

> Our late forefathers, those that were wise, begged their fellow *Din é* to stop going around stealing horses, sheep and cattle from the Mexicans; but the stealing went on. One of the men who was begging the *Din é* to quit stealing said, "Don't be sorry when we get enemies like a road covered with ice—starvation, poverty and cold. You will suffer; then you will understand. [11]

Another Navajo, Tlááschchí í Sáni, who was born thirty years after the Diné returned from their exile in the Bosque Redondo, put it bluntly when he stated that

> There was a time when our ancestors hid like the deer in rocks and canyons because they were afraid of being captured, but it was their own fault. There were Navajos then who had nothing. No livestock of any kind. Building a Hogan, planting a crop, hoeing—they never thought of it. Like coyotes or wolves that steal in the night, they were raiding the Utes. . . . Then there were the Mexicans who lived along rivers east of Huerfano Mountain. They had stock in their corrals, too. From as far as Black Mesa Navajos traveled over there like mice in the night and took it. So also with the whites. . . . It was robbery! They told fine stories about "going to war," but they were just saying that. They were stealing. Soon everyone turned against the Navajos, and the word got back to Washington. [12]

Among the Navajo, therefore, it is clear that there was no absolute unanimity of opinion; as with any human community, there was a great deal of division and dissension. Navajo who had sizable herds of livestock typically favored peace over warfare and raiding because they had the most to lose and because their rich herds were likely targets of New Mexican marauders. Poorer Diné, on the other hand, were not averse to increasing their wealth through raiding. The point is that within the larger Navajo nation, there existed a variety of viewpoints and attitudes when it came to conflict versus accommodation. Feeding into this diversity of opinion was the fact that the Diné had a very decentralized and highly democratic political structure. What this meant was that no one particular person or group had any real authority to enforce compliance and any agreement was likely to be violated by those Diné who had a difference of opinion. The only real power any Navajo leader had was through his charisma and personal accomplishments, which was why the death of Narbona, a leader who had that kind of standing, was such a blow to the potential for true peace.

Subsequent to the treaty, the U.S. military built a number of outposts on Diné land, the most well-known of which was named Fort Defiance, and which became a frequent source of contention and conflict over the next decade. Given such a provocative name, it couldn't have been any other way. In fact, in 1860 a large force of around a thousand Navajo warriors attacked and almost overwhelmed the fort before being driven off. Over the decade of the 1850s and into the 1860s, the raiding, skirmishing, and depredations continued on and off, with short intervals of peace that were typically cut short after some dispute or misunderstanding.[13] American authorities spent a great deal of time trying to mediate between the New Mexicans, Navajo, Apache, and Utes, or trying to placate one side or the other, and sometimes they only added fuel to the fire. In 1861, for example, a horse race outside of Fort Fauntleroy ended badly when the Navajo accused the army of sabotaging their horse by slashing the bridle. Fueled by alcohol, the argument escalated into a riot.[14] After a shot rang out, the army unloaded rifles and howitzers on the fleeing Indians, including women and children, and at least twenty Navajo were killed along with many more wounded. Because of events such as this, the Diné felt increasingly besieged by enemies and under continual threat, which only served to heighten the suspicion and levels of hostility and to encourage further raiding.

In 1861, Fort Defiance was abandoned at the outbreak of the Civil War, and many soldiers in New Mexico were sent back east to take part in the war. The territory consequently saw a dramatic increase in the violence as all the parties—Navajo, Mexicans, Anglos, Zuni, Apache, and Utes—used the occasion to raid, loot, get revenge, and wreak whatever havoc they were able to.[15] And so the violence continued. Part of the continuing problem was that New Mexicans continued to encroach on traditional Navajo grazing land, which spurred retaliatory raids as the Diné struggled to resist these incursions and the erosion of their territory. Another reason for the continued hostility displayed by the Navajo was the growing problem of Navajo women and children being kidnapped into slavery. One Navajo leader, Armijo, put it this way:

> Is it American justice that we must give up everything and receive nothing? More than 200 of our children have been carried off and we know not where they are. The Mexicans have lost but few children in comparison with what they have stolen from us. . . . My people are yet crying for the children they have lost.[16]

One contemporary estimate suggested there were six thousand Navajo slaves being held in the New Mexico territory.[17] Trapped in an endless cycle of violence from which they were unable to escape, the Navajo did not realize that times had changed and that the balance of power had shifted decisively against them. Tragically, things were about to get a lot worse.

CARLETON AND THE NAVAJO

In September of 1862, a man named James Carleton took over command of what was known as the Department of New Mexico.[18] Carleton was a career soldier with a distinguished record and many years of service on the frontier, but with an overly rigid and dogmatic personality, well suited perhaps to his Calvinist upbringing. By all accounts he was not a man to admit a mistake, take half measures, or back down. An educated man with eclectic but refined tastes, Carleton was known for being a dynamo who dabbled in various intellectual fields. He also had a well-earned reputation for being a tough disciplinarian and was strongly authoritarian in his leadership style. In his long career, he had also accumulated a great deal of experience working with various Indian tribes. This, then, was the man who was to be the architect of the plan that was to be so devastating to the Navajo. Upon arriving at his new command, he immediately declared martial law and decided to finally bring an end to the raiding and fighting that was so characteristic of the New Mexico territory at that time. As he himself wrote:

> When I came here this time, it not only became my professional business, but my duty to the residents and to the Government, to devise some plan which might, with God's blessing, forever bring these troubles to an end. These Navajo Indians have long since passed that point when talking would be of any avail. They must be whipped and fear us before they will cease killing and robbing the people.[19]

In developing a specific strategy, Carleton built upon some initial ideas proposed by his immediate predecessor in New Mexico, Colonel Edward Canby, who believed that the Navajo must either be eradicated, or be brought under government control in areas so far removed from non-Native settlements that there would be almost no contact between the Diné and New Mexicans.[20] He also relied on some of his earlier experiences to guide him. During his time in California, for example, he had witnessed the birth of what was to become the reservation system.

After gold was discovered in California in 1848, the ensuing Gold Rush proved catastrophic for California's Indians. As gold-obsessed immigrants poured into California to seek their fortunes, the Native Americans were hounded, dispossessed, and murdered to the brink of extinction. In an effort to protect the survivors, the California superintendent for Indian Affairs, Edward Beale, decided to implement a policy of relocation designed to protect the remaining Natives from the depredations of whites. As misguided, patronizing, and culturally devastating as it was, the motivation came from a growing concern among many, Edward Beale included, about the plight of the Indian. It was believed that if they could be separated from white society, then they could be protected and, as an added bonus, taught skills that would help civilize them. Those concerned about the treatment of California's Natives met Beale's ideas with a wide amount of approval. In fact, one newspaper editorial suggested, "Either the whole Indian race in California must be exterminated or they must be brought together, organized into a community, made to support themselves by their own labor; and be elevated above the degraded position they now occupy."[21] Eventually, these ideas were translated into policy, not only in California, but also across the nation as a whole, although that was still years in the future.

Carleton was stationed at Fort Tejon in California, the location of this first experiment with reservations, and so was very much aware of this strategy for dealing with the Natives. After being appointed to the New Mexico territory, Carleton immediately recognized the applicability of the California experiment to his current problem. One other experience also played a role in shaping Carleton's idea for dealing with the Navajo. In 1851, Carleton had surveyed the Pecos River through much of New Mexico and had found a site that quite enchanted him. Located in eastern New Mexico, it was at a horseshoe bend in the river where cottonwood trees grew in a large circle on the inside of the arcing curve of the river. The Spanish name for this place was the Round Forest, or Bosque Redondo. Far away from any settlements, the Bosque Redondo became embedded in Carleton's mind and imagination as a lush and verdant river oasis, fruitful and full of potential and perfect for future settlement.

In 1862, General Carleton began implementing his plan of attack, but his first targets weren't the Navajo. Instead, he focused on a much smaller and more manageable problem: that posed by the Mescalero Apache, a band of about 500 people in southern New Mexico who were engaged in the same style of raiding as the Navajo, albeit on a much smaller scale. Enlisting the aid of his friend Kit Carson, who was serving in the army at the time, Carleton ordered an expedition into Mescalero territory with instructions to kill all the males, but to spare the women and children. Carson had no stomach for this kind of fighting and believed that the Apache should be negotiated with. He had joined the army in order to fight the confederacy as part of the Civil War and did not relish campaigning against the Mescalero. In the actual event, Carson did accept command of the expedition, but chose to ignore some of his instructions and accepted the surrender of at least a hundred fighting males as he fought his way through Mescalero territory. The surviving Apache surrendered unconditionally in November of 1862 and were promptly deported to Fort Sumner at the Bosque Redondo, where they were told that they must henceforth become farmers, an occupation antithetical to Apache tradition and culture.

Next on the hit list were the Navajo, and again Carleton called on Kit
Carson, but at first Carson resisted and even resigned his commission.
Carleton, however, refused to accept his resignation and pressured Car-
son, who finally consented and took charge of a force of about 1,000
soldiers, including regular army, volunteers from New Mexico, and aux-
iliaries and scouts from Puebloan and Ute tribes. On July 7, 1863,
Carson and his troops headed into Navajo-controlled territory under
General Orders No. 15 that read:

> For a long time past the Navajoe Indians have murdered and robbed
> the people of New Mexico. Last winter when eighteen of their chiefs
> came to Santa Fe to have a talk, they were warned—and were told to
> inform their people—that for these murders and robberies the tribe
> must be punished, unless some binding guarantees should be given
> that in future these outrages should cease. No such guarantees have
> yet been given: But on the contrary, additional murders, and addi-
> tional robberies have been perpetrated upon the persons and prop-
> erty of our unoffending citizens. It is therefore ordered, that Colonel
> CHRISTOPHER CARSON, with a proper military force proceed
> without delay . . . and . . . prosecute a vigorous war upon the men of
> this tribe until it is considered at these Head Quarters that they have
> been effectually punished for their long continued atrocities. . . .
> These troops will march from Los Pinos [near Albuquerque] for the
> Navajoe country on Wednesday, July 1, 1863.[22]

This, then, provided the pretext and legal justification for the war
against the Diné. For months, Carson conducted a scorched-earth policy and rampaged through Navajo territory like Sherman on his infamous march to the sea. Whatever misgivings Carson may have harbored
about undertaking this mission, it certainly didn't hinder him in fulfill-
ing his mission to the utmost. Fields and crops were burned, livestock
captured or killed, peach trees and entire orchards chopped down, and
traditional Navajo homes, known as Hogans, razed to the ground. Water holes were guarded or destroyed, and even baskets and pots were
smashed so that no food or supplies—whatever might have escaped
destruction—could be carried anywhere. Anything and everything that
could sustain the Diné was destroyed. Even the traditional stronghold
of Canyon de Chelly succumbed to Carson's destructive rampage. Canyon de Chelly (pronounced "De Shay") is a long and deep sandstone

canyon that winds its way through parts of northeastern Arizona and New Mexico. This is the heart of Dinetah, or the Navajo homeland, and few enemies had ever breached its formidable defenses. Vast, mazelike, and labyrinthine, the canyon had always provided abundant hiding places for refuge and concealment when threatened, but against Carson's destructive thoroughness, even Canyon de Chelly proved vulnerable and was subjected to the same treatment as elsewhere. The canyon's famed peach tree orchards, for example, which had provided a reliable source of food for the Diné for generations, were ruthlessly chopped down and sawn into oblivion.

This campaign was not just about destroying crops, trees, and homes. Carson's troopers killed 301 Navajo, wounded another 87, and captured 703 at a cost of 17 soldiers killed and 25 wounded.[23] We don't know how many others died of starvation and exposure during that terrible winter. During one trip through Canyon de Chelly, for example, one of Carson's units came upon the frozen bodies of a number of Navajo who had apparently starved or froze to death, and it is highly unlikely that these were the only ones to suffer such a fate. One person from a group that surrendered to Carson told him, "Because of what your soldiers have done, we are all starving. Many of our women and children have already died from hunger. We would have come in long ago, but we believed this was a war of extermination."[24] Clearly, many Navajo felt that this was genocide, even if the word hadn't been coined yet.

To compound their suffering, various Native and New Mexican enemies of the Diné took advantage of the situation and conducted raids into Navajo territory in order to loot and take slaves. The practical result of these combined assaults was absolutely devastating. Without food or shelter or the means to acquire them, the Navajo had no choice but to surrender, which they did in increasing numbers during the winter and spring of 1864. In fact, so many gave themselves up that the army did not have enough supplies for the thousands of Navajo who turned themselves in at the rebuilt Fort Canby (formerly Fort Defiance) and Fort Wingate. Beginning at the end of January that year, the Navajos who surrendered were marched to the Bosque Redondo, over 370 to 500 miles away, depending on the route taken. Carson himself escorted the first batch of 500 prisoners to the Rio Grande and then departed for home, while the Navajo were marched the remainder of the distance to the Bosque Redondo. Subsequently, thousands made the arduous march to the lonely plains of eastern New Mexico.

THE LONG WALK

The "Long Walk," as it came to be known, was a horrific tribulation for those who experienced it. Already weakened and destitute from the depredations of their enemies, long and very poorly equipped columns of Navajo, all on foot and many with only the clothes they wore, walked the entire distance to Fort Sumner. Those who left in the winter and spring coped with storms and blizzards during the roughly three-week march. Many died along the way, some from exposure and hypothermia, others from illness, while some were just too young or too old to survive the ordeal. Carleton had directed the soldiers to treat the captives with "Christian kindness" because they were now under the protection of the U.S. army, but long-standing antagonisms and hostility weren't so easily overcome. Soldiers raped women and sometimes shot out of hand those who couldn't keep up. One survivor of the Long Walk testified that "These soldiers did not have any regard for the women folks. They took unto themselves for wives somebody else's wife, and many times the Navajo man whose wife was being taken tried to ward off the soldiers, but immediately he was shot and killed and they took his wife. They did not treat the women like they should have."[25] Another said that "Some were killed on the way for disobedience," and continued by asserting that the bodies "were left to lay right on the spot where they were killed. Left to be devoured by coyotes and other animals."[26]

The soldiers also allowed enemies of the Diné to harass the marchers and to steal women and children in order to sell them into slavery. Part of the breakdown in discipline was likely a result of the large numbers of Navajo who surrendered, which meant that the troops, food, blankets, shelter, and other supplies allocated by the army were often insufficient to meet the needs of the trekkers. One scholar of this period, Frank McNitt, suggests that about eleven thousand Diné were sent on the Long Walk.[27] Overwhelmed by the logistics of handling such a large number of prisoners, the marches usually devolved into anarchy, violence, and chaos, all of which compounded the suffering endured by the Navajo.

Once they were established at the Bosque Redondo, conditions did not improve. Guarded over by soldiers at an adobe stronghold named Fort Sumner, the Indians at Bosque Redondo were expected to raise crops and become self-sufficient. Unfortunately, the Bosque Redondo proved absolutely unsuitable for this plan to turn the Navajo into peaceful farmers, especially given the number of people it was expected to support. The trees of the Bosque, which had made the location initially seem so attractive to Carleton, were soon converted into homes and used for firewood, which meant that everyone had to roam farther and farther afield, sometimes up to twenty or thirty miles to get firewood. Rather than allowing them to live in traditional Hogans, the Diné were asked to build Puebloan-style dwellings. This was a bigger issue than one might initially expect. The Puebloan-style buildings are similar to modern apartment buildings in that many families live in separate rooms within one large building. According to Navajo beliefs and traditions, however, if a person died within a room, that entire building would need to be abandoned.

They therefore strenuously resisted this plan until eventually Carleton was forced to rescind this order. This raised another problem in that there wasn't enough wood to build traditional Hogans, and therefore the Navajo were reduced to living in very primitive mud huts. The farming didn't go well either, since floods, hailstorms, and pests ensured the destruction of most of the crops planted. Dysentery and other intestinal problems were also a common occurrence since the alkaline water of the Pecos proved to be a poor source of drinking water. Smallpox, too, took its deadly toll. In addition, the Navajo and Mescalero Apache were often at each other's throats and needed near-constant policing to prevent riots and attacks. To top it all off, the Bosque became a favorite target of Comanche raiding parties who saw in the now-dispossessed and destitute Navajo an easy target.

All in all, Carleton's vision of the Bosque Redondo as an incubator for reforming the Navajo from their aggressive ways was an utter and abject failure and resulted in a great deal of death and suffering. All told, approximately 2,000 to 3,000 Diné died from various causes during their time at the Bosque Redondo, which, given the size of the total population at the Bosque Redondo, represented a sizable proportion of the population. Through disease, food shortages, raids, and various other tribulations, the Navajo suffered and ultimately endured. Carleton was removed from command in late 1866, as the awful conditions of the Bosque Redondo became widely known.

Finally, in May of 1868, the forty-eight-year-old General William Sherman, he who had sowed such a path of devastation across the South during the Civil War, arrived at the Bosque Redondo to decide what to do with the Navajo. He was part of a commission tasked with deciding the ultimate fate of the people at Bosque Redondo. Earlier in the year, because of a series of clashes with the troops and the worsening situation, a delegation of Navajo leaders was sent to Washington, DC, by the government in order to let them see how powerful the United States was. In no uncertain terms, however, the Navajo told U.S. authorities that unless they were allowed to go home, there would be a serious uprising.[28] With these words in their ears, federal officials decided to send a commission to see conditions for themselves and to decide how to resolve the situation, which was how General Sherman ended up in New Mexico later that spring.

Sherman's first inclination was to send the Diné to Oklahoma territory, a location that had been used as a reservation for Indians since the presidency of Andrew Jackson, but the words of Barboncito, a Navajo elder and spokesman for his people, helped sway Sherman. In part, what Barboncito said was:

> Our grandfathers had no idea of living in any other country except our own, and I do not think it right for us to do so. Before I am sick or older I want to go and see the place where I was born. I hope to God you will not ask me to go to any other country except my own. This hope goes in at my feet and out my mouth as I am speaking to you.[29]

Sherman's reply was equally direct when he said, "I have listened to what you have said of your people and I believe you have told the truth. All people love the country where they were born and raised. We want to do what is right."[30] After getting assurances that the Navajo would forever forswear warfare and raiding, they were granted their fervent wish to return home. On June 1, 1868 a treaty was drawn up and signed, and on June 18 of that same year the Navajo started on their trek back home. Their long and terrible ordeal was over.

How can we understand the "Long Walk" period? It certainly was hugely destructive to the Navajo people, but was it genocide? In addressing this issue, it is helpful to begin with an assessment of General Carleton's intentions in regard to the Navajo and Mescalero Apache. When Carleton ordered Kit Carson after the Apache, he directed that he should:

> Keep after their people and slay them until you receive orders to desist from these headquarters; that this making of treaties for them to break whenever they have an interest in breaking them will not be done any more; that time has passed by; that we have no faith in their promises; that we believe if we kill some of their men in fair, open war, they will be apt to remember that it will be better for them to remain at peace than to be at war. I trust that this severity, in the long run, will be the most humane course that could be pursued toward these Indians.[31]

He furthermore specified that:

> All Indian men of that tribe are to be killed whenever and wherever you find them. The women and children will not be harmed, but you will take them prisoners. If the Indians send in a flag and desire to treat for peace, say that now our hands are untied, and you have been sent to punish them for their treachery and their crimes; that you have no power to make peace; that you are there to kill them wherever you find them.[32]

These orders were harsh in the extreme and, without a doubt, genocidal. By ordering the death of all the men, Carleton was intentionally destroying the ability of the Mescalero Apache to survive, even if some of the women and children were spared. Kit Carson, no shrinking violet when it came to violence, decided not to follow these orders completely and spared the lives of Mescalero men who surrendered, but this doesn't mean that the underlying intention of this directive wasn't genocidal. On the other hand, the evidence suggests that Carleton intended to use the Bosque Redondo as a reservation for the Apache after they surrendered, which certainly seems to suggest that he didn't envision them being attacked into extinction. One possible interpretation of these seemingly contradictory orders is that he may have intended to leave the Apache no other choice but to sign a lasting peace, the alternative being too horrible to contemplate. From his perspective, there had been too many past instances when it appeared that the Mescalero had agreed to peace terms cynically, with no real intention of actually following through. Carleton wrote that this severe course of action was the most reasonable possible alternative: "I trust that this severity, in the long run, will be the most humane course that could be pursued toward these Indians."[33] Additionally, General Carleton never punished Carson for not obeying his orders and, in fact, questioned him about one of his subordinates who had been in a clash with a Mescalero band. Carleton instructed Carson to return the horses and mules of the band if the attack against them had not been "fair and open."[34] His orders and his behavior seem somewhat inconsistent. While he explicitly ordered a potentially genocidal campaign against the Mescalero Apache, his subsequent actions appear to back away from such an extremity.

What is clear, however, is that he appears to have intended to use the Mescalero as a trial run for the assault against and deportation of the larger and more difficult enemy, the Navajo. Carson's assault on the Diné homeland was equally, if not more, brutal than the previous campaign against the Apache. The scorched-earth policy, as devastating as it was, however, was never intended to eliminate the Navajo as a people completely, but rather to eliminate them as a military threat. The goal was to force the Navajo to surrender as quickly and as completely as possible. Sadly, the kinds of absolute and brutal tactics used by Carson against the Navajo are not that unique or uncommon, and have been an all-too-common feature of many wars around the world. The Russians used this tactic against both Napoleon's and Hitler's armies; Hannibal resorted to this strategy against Rome during the Second Punic War; Sherman used this technique on his march through Georgia; and the British also engaged in scorched-earth tactics against the Boers in South Africa during the Boer war.

It's worth noting that the historian Blanca Tovías suggests that these tactics against the Navajo were taken directly from the army's experience in the Civil War. Specifically, she writes that "The concept of total war deployed by Union generals during the Civil War also had an effect on the conduct of the army's campaigns against Indians."[35] These tactics are not always considered legitimate war-fighting measures, but neither are they necessarily considered genocidal. "Total war" refers to a type of warfare that typically involves the mobilization of all resources within a society to support a war effort and a willingness to employ all weapons and strategies, including scorched-earth tactics, to destroy an enemy's military and economic capability.[36] It also often doesn't distinguish between combatants and civilians. During the Civil War, the North employed these tactics in the latter part of the war, as the Union struggled to defeat the Confederacy. One of its most well-known proponents was General William T. Sherman, who once remarked, "We are not only fighting hostile armies, but a hostile people, and must make old and young, rich and poor, feel the hard hand of war."[37] This quote could just as easily have applied to the campaign against the Navajo as to Sherman's march to the sea through Georgia. It is debatable, therefore, whether the violence against the Navajo constituted an example of total war, or, looking at the context of the larger campaign against the Navajo, to make an argument that these tactics were genocidal given the cumulative onslaughts, tactics, and policies pursued so relentlessly against them.

It also should be noted that the Bosque Redondo was also never intended to be an extermination center. It is clear that General Carleton, in designing his grand strategy for the Navajo, never wanted to liquidate the population physically. This spot on the Pecos River that the Diné were forced to call home was not designed to be a concentration camp as some have suggested. Its unsuitability for habitation was something that Carleton was aware of, but stubbornly refused to believe. Shortly after arriving in New Mexico, the general had ordered the creation of a fort at the Bosque Redondo, but an initial survey conducted by a group of army officers indicated that the Bosque was a bad location for any kind of development. Although it appeared to be inviting, the land itself was subject to flooding and the river was alkaline and chalky. Its distance from any other community also meant that supplies would need to be transported a long and difficult way.

Carleton, however, ignored these warnings and proceeded with his plan to pacify the Navajo. He had created an image in his mind of the Bosque as a perfect place to enact his grand strategy of "reforming" the Navajo, and nothing was going to get in the way of that, certainly not inconvenient facts about the unsuitability of his chosen location. When the crops failed, Carleton, realizing how bad the situation was, worked hard to organize emergency food stores and supplies because, as he himself wrote, "These Indians are upon my hands. I cannot see them perish either from nakedness or hunger."[38] To his credit, General Carleton worked tirelessly to ensure that his experiment in the Bosque Redondo was a success, and each setback only seemed to spur him on to greater efforts to provide for the Natives there. Ultimately, it was to no avail, and it is debatable whether these efforts truly served to mitigate or outweigh the tremendous harm that his policies served to inflict on the Navajo. I'm sure his work on their behalf was cold comfort to the Navajo, who suffered because of his grand plan. The Bosque Redondo was simply too inhospitable and the Diné too resistant for Carleton's grand plan to work. With costs mounting—it cost over a million dollars a year in 1860s dollars to run the reservation[39]—and a scandal erupting over the misery and death created by this experiment, Carleton was eventually relieved of command.

Clearly, General James Carleton was guilty of pursuing misguided policies high-handedly and ignoring contradictory information, which resulted in a great deal of suffering and death for the Mescalero Apache and the Diné people. That is not necessarily the same thing as genocide, however. Arrogant and willful he certainly was, but intentionally planning the physical destruction of the Navajo doesn't appear to have been part of the plan. On the other hand, if we focus on outcome rather than intention, a stronger case can be made for genocide. The suffering and death engendered by Carleton's policies were sufficiently widespread that it appears genocidal in retrospect. This is especially true when we look at the combined effects of the campaign, the Long Walk itself, and the time spent at the Bosque Redondo. These events, in quick succession and in combination, produced such high mortality rates as to endanger the continued physical survival of the Navajo, even if that was not the overt or ostensible goal. What was part of the plan, however, was the cultural destruction of the Navajo, and according to many, that can be seen as constituting a form of genocide, specifically ethnocide or cultural genocide.

When Raphael Lemkin created the term "genocide" in 1944, he described the concept in ways that included the destruction of a people's culture. In fact, cultural genocide was central to his articulation of the concept. Unfortunately, the drafters of the U.N. Genocide Convention definition did not see things the same way and specifically excluded cultural genocide from the legal definition they created. That being said, there is evidence, as pointed out by William Schabas, a leading expert on international law and genocide, that the U.N. definition can be interpreted to prohibit acts that are culturally destructive; and this evidence has been somewhat supported by a number of legal judgments.[40] Furthermore, in 1981 the United Nations Educational, Scientific, and Cultural Organization (UNESCO) declared that:

> Ethnocide means that an ethnic group is denied the right to enjoy, develop and transmit its own culture and its own language, whether individually or collectively. . . . We declare that ethnocide, that is, cultural genocide, is a violation of international law equivalent to genocide, which was condemned by the United Nations Convention on the Prevention and Punishment of the Crime of Genocide.[41]

On September 13, 2007, the United Nations Declaration on the Rights of Indigenous Peoples was adopted by the General Assembly. This document specifically protects the cultural survival of indigenous populations.[42] While this declaration does not have the same force or legal authority accorded to international law, it nonetheless represents an acknowledgment of the need to protect indigenous rights, and more specifically acknowledges the threat cultural forms of genocide pose to Native populations. There are many other declarations, covenants, and conventions recognizing the issue of cultural genocide, all of which serve to illustrate the centrality of the concept of cultural genocide to the issue of genocide and indigenous populations. While it might be technically incorrect to suggest that the Bosque Redondo reveals genocidal intent according to the U.N. Genocide Convention, it certainly reveals intent to destroy the culture of the Navajo and can therefore be considered as constituting an example of cultural genocide, or ethnocide as it is also sometimes known, in addition to an outcome-based assessment of genocide.

The intent of the Bosque Redondo was not only to isolate the Navajo and Mescalero from proximity to the settlers, farmers, and shepherds that they were prone to raid, but it was also to transform the culture and lifestyles of the Indians sent to the reservation. As General Carleton himself wrote, "The only peace that can ever be made with them must rest on the basis that they move onto the lands at Bosque Redondo and, like the Pueblos, become an agricultural people and cease to be nomads. Entire subjugation or destruction . . . are the alternatives."[43] In his mind, then, relocation of the Navajo to the Bosque was the preferred and more humane solution for dealing with the Diné. As he saw it, it was an alternative to extinction. It is a terrible irony of human history that so much harm is often caused in the name of helping others. As events turned out, relocation to the Bosque Redondo was anything but humane. But in essence it was created with the explicit purpose of changing the Navajo as a people. Put another way, the Bosque Redondo was intended to kill their culture, but leave the people alive. Simply said, this is the crux of cultural genocide.

FORCED REMOVAL AND RELOCATION

We can also try to make sense of the Long Walk by placing it within the larger context of removal and relocation. While Carleton based his ideas for the Navajo on the earlier attempt to isolate the Indians of California from the whites at El Tejon, this impulse to segregate first appeared even earlier. In 1804, then-President Thomas Jefferson unsuccessfully proposed a constitutional amendment giving Native Americans land west of the Mississippi River in exchange for the land they controlled east of the river. Although it was initially unsuccessful, Congress later provided authorization for such a swap.[44] The young nation was already feeling the tensions of an increasing population that was putting more and more pressure on Native lands in the east.

Even though many treaties had been signed over the years with various tribes guaranteeing their territory and sovereign independence, white settlers and even individual states were encroaching continuously on Indian lands.[45] In Georgia, for example, the state got so aggressive that the Cherokee appealed to the U.S. Supreme Court, which in a landmark ruling (*Cherokee Nation vs. State of Georgia 1831*) ruled that while the Native American tribes had all of the necessary qualities to be considered sovereign nations, the United States could not afford to allow a separate sovereign entity to exist within its borders. Essentially, it defined tribes as domestic and dependent nations, and in the words of the chief justice, "the relationship of the tribes to the United States resembles that of a 'ward to its guardian.'"[46] The solution to the problem was one that had actually begun earlier when, beginning in the 1820s, a number of eastern tribes were removed from their territory into the West, or the Great American Desert as the West was then called. It was believed to be barren and inhospitable for whites and so was thought ideal for the purpose of Native resettlement. With government assistance, it was thought that Native Americans could be taught to change and become more "civilized." In many ways, however, these ostensibly humanitarian or noble sentiments were just window dressing for much baser motives. It was all about the land, and adopting a philosophy of Christian charity toward the Natives made the exploitative and destructive policies all the more palatable. American expansionism lay at the root of American apartheid, not altruism. Comforted by the notion that the Natives had consented to be removed and that they would benefit from the experience and the opportunities that would be provided by the government, Christian organizations and other philanthropic enterprises saw their actions as a humane solution to the "Indian problem."

Indian territory consisted of large amounts of territory in the Great Plains region, mostly centering on what would become the territory and then the state of Oklahoma. In the latter half of the nineteenth century, Natives from all around the country were sent there, including Modoc, Arapahoe, Kiowa, Cheyenne, Comanche, Ponca, Pawnee, Apache, Wichita, Lipan, Kickapoo, Tonkawa, Waco, Tawakoni, Caddo, Hainai, Kichai, Anadarko, Choctaw, Seminole, Creek, Cherokee, Shawnee, Chickasaw, Quapaw, Osage, Kaw, Iowa, Otoe-Missouria, Kaskaskia, Miami, Peoria, Piankashaw, Wea, Sac, Potawatomi, Fox, Delaware, Seneca-Cayuga, Wyandot, and Ottawa.[47] In many ways, the experience of the Navajo was simply one more sad episode among many other similar kinds of occurrences. When thinking of the Long Walk, it's easy to make comparisons with one other deportation in particular, the "Trail of Tears" of the Cherokee.

Over many years the Cherokee, along with a number of other eastern tribes, had adapted to the ways of the Anglos and had developed a thriving agricultural society that was a vibrant blend of old and new.[48] They even worked to protect themselves within the justice system of the United States. Ultimately, however, this was to no avail. President Andrew Jackson signed the Indian Removal Act in 1830, the intent of which was to deport all the eastern tribes to a recently created Indian territory west of the Mississippi River. Resisting legally, the Cherokee took their case all the way to the U.S. Supreme Court and even won a victory of sorts, but President Jackson ignored it and ordered the army to remove the Natives. Pressure had been building for a long time as the needs of the young nation came increasingly into conflict with those of the tribes in the east. The population of whites kept growing and putting more pressure on the besieged Native lands in the east, and the solution was to remove these problem populations into the west.

It was believed that this was a solution that would work for Natives and Anglos alike. The Indians would receive their own land free from conflict with the Anglos, while Anglo-Americans would have more land opened up in the settled areas of the east. The Cherokee, regardless of how they had adapted and assimilated, were simply in the way of expansion and had to be removed. The first to go were the Choctaw, who occupied parts of Mississippi, Alabama, Georgia, and Louisiana. Over the course of about four years, from 1831 to 1834, the Choctaw were rounded up and sent west. As with the Navajo Long Walk, conditions were terrible—so bad, in fact, that about one in every four Choctaws died on the trek to Indian Territory.[49] A lack of funding meant too few supplies and troops, which, when combined with bandits and profiteers, resulted in many deaths from disease, malnutrition, and violence. As if that wasn't bad enough, those that managed to survive the trip often didn't last long, as harsh living conditions on the plains, as well as hostile Native tribes, ensured many more lives lost. The Choctaw were followed by the Creek, the Chickasaw, and the Seminole.

In 1838, it was the turn of the Cherokee. Even though they had taken their case all the way to the Supreme Court and won, the judicial ruling was simply ignored. President Jackson was set on evicting the Cherokee and ordered the army to proceed despite the Supreme Court ruling. From 1838–1839, the Cherokee were moved west 800 miles in conditions so terrible that around 4,000 died in the process of being rounded up and relocated. In its own way, the Trail of Tears and the deportations of the other eastern tribes were as bad as anything that the Navajo and Mescalero Apache experienced. One participant in the Cherokee removal who later fought in the Civil War said, "I fought through the civil war and have seen men shot to pieces and slaughtered by thousands, but the Cherokee removal was the cruelest work I ever seen."[50] Unlike the Navajo, however, it was an exile from which most would not return. Throughout the 1800s and into the early twentieth century, the Indian Territory was systematically reduced in area numerous times as land pressures increased continuously. It wasn't until the

Indian Reorganization Act of 1934 that the continuous loss of land largely ended.[51]

The displacement of the thousands of Native Americans from their lands surely ranks among the least defensible and most reprehensible policies of the U.S. government in its long history of Native/white relations. It reflects a willingness on the part of many politicians, such as President Andrew Jackson, to ignore legal rulings and justice in the face of expediency and pressure from settlers and business interests eager to capitalize on the land and resources held by American Indian tribes and peoples. Comforted by misguided, deceptive, and sometimes cynical notions of protecting Natives by isolating them, proponents of these policies were able to pretend that they were actually assisting the people that they were removing from their homelands. As we have seen, the actual practice of removal was often violent, usually ill organized, and always traumatic and wrenching for those subjected to the experience. As to whether or not these policies constituted genocide, it all depends on how one uses the term, as we have discussed throughout this book.

7

EDUCATION FOR ASSIMILATION

Give the Indian a white man's chance. Educate him in the rudiments
of our language. Teach him to work. Send him to his home, and tell
him he must practice what he has been taught or starve. It will in a
generation or more regenerate the race. It will exterminate the Indian but develop a man.

—Commissioner William A. Jones[1]

We all wore white man's clothes and ate white man's food and went
to white man's churches and spoke white man's talk. And so after a
while we also began to say Indians were bad. We laughed at our own
people and their blankets and cooking pots and sacred societies and
dances.

—Sun Elk[2]

For over a hundred years, the missionary and BIA schools had
sought to reach the core of Indian inner life and destroy that which
made it ethnically and culturally unique.

—Mick Fedullo[3]

By the 1880s the U.S. government had largely defeated Native America militarily. The recognized end of the fighting was still a couple of
years in the future, with the Wounded Knee massacre in 1890, but for
all intents and purposes the Indian wars were over. Native Americans
were no longer able to resist the territorial ambitions of the United
States and had been largely confined to the few territories allocated to
them. The reservation system, while ostensibly designed to protect the

American Indian from extinction, became a tool of suppression and dependence. No longer would the United States sign treaties with tribes. After numerous treaties had been signed and then usually broken, 370 by one count, Congress stopped this procedure in 1871.[4] This symbolized a profound change in status for Indian tribes. Previously, they had been recognized as sovereign and independent nations, albeit often hostile ones, but able to negotiate treaties in the same way that other autonomous political states did.

This tradition actually dated back to the American Revolution when the colonies sought to negotiate alliances with Native tribes. In 1787, the new Congress passed *An Ordinance for the Government of the Territory of the United States, North-West of the River Ohio*, which provided guidelines for the new nation's expansion westward and asserted that

> the utmost good faith shall always be observed towards the Indians, their lands and property shall never be taken from them without their consent; and in their property, rights and liberty, they never shall be invaded or disturbed, unless in just and lawful wars authorized by Congress.[5]

These high-minded words indicated that Native American tribes were supposed to be accorded the same sort of status ascribed to other nations. In practice, these principles were often ignored or overridden by other concerns, but they nevertheless represented a certain legal standing that allowed for treaties and negotiations. But in the wake of the Indian wars, Natives were simply seen as a defeated and conquered people and as dependents and wards of the state, a perception that the reservation system certainly encouraged. With the Natives largely broken and destitute in the wake of numerous wars, relocations, and loss of traditional lifestyles, the reservation system further completed the process of subjugation. Natives were typically forbidden to leave the reservations without permission and were forced to survive on government-provided rations, which could be withheld for various infractions or to enforce compliance and submission to governmental authority.

In many ways, the reservation system was like a vast gulag, a system of incarceration enforced by law and the military and which helped complete the process of conquest. Ironically, the reservation system had originally been introduced, at least partially, for humanitarian reasons. Among those concerned with Native America, it was felt that reservations provided two important things, distance and time: distance in order to survive and time in order to adapt. It was felt that by segregating Natives on reservations, violent conflicts with whites would be reduced and tribes would be able to keep a measure of political autonomy. Underlying these concerns, however, was also the notion that the reservations would allow Indians to become more civilized and assimilate into the larger society.[6] Protected and apart, American Indians living on the reservations would have the time and inclination to adopt supposedly more "civilized" lifestyles, and an important part of this process was to be a system of schools designed to use education as a tool of assimilation.

Keep in mind, however, that this was not a kind and benevolent system. It was a means of forcing Natives to change their ways regardless of their own desires. In the memorable and chilling phrase of the time, "that all the Indian there is in the race should be dead. Kill the Indian in him, and save the man."[7]

The idea of using formal schools and education as a way to forcibly inculcate Western mores, beliefs, and traditions among Native Americans dates back to the first settlements and colonies. The Spanish used schools in their mission stations in an attempt to bring both Christianity and European values to the Natives under their sway, and as early as the 1600s Jesuit missionaries established missions in what would become Maine, New York, Wisconsin, Michigan, Ohio, Illinois, and Louisiana, as well as in Canada. In the British portions of North America, King James ordered the creation of "some churches and schools for ye education of ye children of these Barbarians in Virginia."[8] To this end, the Virginia Company tried to develop a system in which Native youths would be raised and educated in the homes of British colonists and also tried to set up a college for Native Americans, both attempts ultimately failing. In New England, the Puritans put a great deal of effort into converting and educating Natives by creating an entire system of "Indian Praying Towns" where Natives would live, work, dress, and pray in Anglo fashion.[9]

All of these early attempts to use education as a means of transforming Native Americans reveal an ethnocentric mind-set completely devaluing and ignoring local traditions and practices. In other words, these early projects were based on the notion that Indian children did not receive any real education, a view that dismissed the culturally based forms of teaching and learning that were integral to all Native societies. But these colonial and early American efforts at assimilation were sporadic, haphazard, and were largely unsuccessful, usually because of a lack of funds. This all changed in 1879, however, with the creation of the Carlisle Indian Industrial School.

THE BOARDING SCHOOL SYSTEM

The Carlisle Indian Industrial School was the first federally funded boarding school and was created in 1882 on the site of an abandoned military post in Carlisle, Pennsylvania.[10] To understand the creation of the Carlisle School, we need to go back a few years to the summer of 1874, when a number of tribes on the southern plains broke out of the reservation and began an uprising with attacks on settlers, wagon trains, and buffalo hunters. The army, under General Philip Sheridan, commenced operations against those involved, and by the summer of 1875 had largely quelled the violence. The leaders of the uprising were identified and then seventy-two of them were sent in chains to a military prison in St. Augustine, Florida, known as Fort Marion.[11]

The man put in charge of the prisoners was Lieutenant Richard Henry Pratt from the Tenth Cavalry, a unit of African American troopers known as Buffalo Soldiers. A cavalry officer with something of a checkered career—he was even court-martialed at one point—Pratt did have one quality that was to serve him in good stead. He had an interpersonal style that earned the confidence and trust of his prisoners. As a white officer who had successfully commanded African American troopers, he clearly was someone who was able to negotiate the complexities of race and ethnicity, and he evidently transferred these skills to his Native charges. Soon working on their behalf, he even went so far as to pass along a plea for clemency to the War Department when the spokesman for his prisoners, Mah Mante, a Kiowa chieftain, indicated that

> We want to learn the ways of the white men. First we want our wives and children to and then we will go any place and settle down and learn to support ourselves as white men do. . . . We want to learn

how to make corn and work the ground so we can make our living and we want to live in a house just as a white man. [12]

These pleas fell on deaf ears in Washington, but it did spark something in Pratt, who commented that "I believe these protestations to be the result of convictions deep and lasting." [13] Consequently, he began to find the Indians work in the local community and convinced a number of local ladies to come to the fort and volunteer their time to teach the inmates. Essentially, Pratt converted the military prison at Fort Marion into a school and so successful was this largely unsanctioned and unsupported experiment that in 1876 he wrote to his commanding officer:

> There is nothing of note to report regarding these prisoners, unless that fact is of itself important. They are simply under good discipline; quite well behaved, doing the work I can find for them to do cheerfully and industriously. They have abandoned about all the appearance and characteristics of the savage and are as neat and clean in their dress and persons as the men of a disciplined company. My 1st Sgt is about as competent as the average of those we get in the colored troops. I have a two hours school daily with an average of fifty pupils divided into four classes with a good teacher for each. The teachers work from the purest and best motives of Christian charity and as a consequence successfully and there is no cost to the Government. [14]

When the government decided to release these Natives in 1878 and send them back to their homes in the west, twenty-two of the younger inmates wanted to stay with Pratt and so he petitioned for funds and a place to house and continue to educate them. In this he was successful, although it took some time. Their first home was in Hampton Roads, Virginia, where he also succeeded in getting more Native students for his new school. But since Hampton Institute was also a school for African Americans, Pratt felt that this location was unsuitable. He worried that not only would the Natives be kept from interacting with whites and therefore learning from them, but that they would also be tainted by their association with African Americans. Racism sometimes plays out in strange ways. Given that Pratt had formerly commanded Buffalo Soldiers, his stance was in all likelihood less about any personal prejudice, and more about his recognition of the prevailing attitudes of the times in regard to African Americans. He wanted his experiment to succeed and didn't want to stack the deck against his Native charges by having them too closely connected with African Americans.

Finally, in 1879, after a great deal of lobbying, Pratt was able to secure the abandoned military barracks in Carlisle, Pennsylvania, and turned it into the Carlisle Indian School with himself as the superintendent.

With the new school established and funding procured, Pratt's next order of business was to recruit students for this venture, and accordingly, he traveled to the Rosebud and Pine Ridge reservations where the Sioux were located. The initial reactions of the Sioux leaders were negative, to say the least. After Pratt's presentation, one prominent chief named Spotted Tail spoke up, "The white people are all thieves and liars; we do not want our children to learn such things. . . . We are not going to give our children to learn such ways."[15] Pratt's response, for all of its patronizing tone, still managed to be effective. He said, "Spotted Tail, you are a remarkable man. You are such an able man that you are the chief of these thousands of people. But, Spotted Tail, you cannot read or write. You cannot speak the language of this country. You have no education."[16] He then went on to suggest that it would be important for the children to be educated in order to avoid them making the mistakes of their elders and closed by saying, "As your friend, Spotted Tail, I urge you to send your children with me to this Carlisle school and I will do everything I can to advance them in intelligence and industry in order that they may come back and help you."[17]

Amazingly, his speech worked and Spotted Tail changed his mind. In fact, Spotted Tail's children were among the first group sent from the Rosebud agency. Pratt continued his recruiting drive among various other tribes and finally, after having recruited the required 120 students, the Carlisle Indian School officially opened on November 1, 1879. For twenty-five years Pratt guided the Indian school, which reached an annual enrollment of 1,000 students from tribes all across the country. Importantly, it also became the model for boarding schools in places such as Oregon, New Mexico, Arizona, Nebraska, and Oklahoma.[18]

Richard Henry Pratt was successful, in large part, because his ideas were closely in sync with certain ideas that had gained a widespread currency among various groups, especially within various government groups concerned with the issue of Native America. This included the

Bureau of Indian Affairs (BIA).[19] Originally founded in 1824 by the War Department, the BIA was created, in part, to administer treaty funds, make judgments in conflicts between Natives and non-Natives, and oversee and dispense money intended to civilize the Indians.[20] By the late 1800s, the BIA and other concerned groups were worried about the so-called Native problem and believed that Native America was on the verge of extinction. In order to avoid this fate, and also to prevent reoccurrences of open conflict, many believed that the only way forward was through assimilation, and the quickest way to accomplish this was believed to be through education. The idea was that by teaching American Indians to look, act, talk, work, worship, and live as European-style Americans, they would be able to assimilate into the larger society in the same way that other immigrant groups had acculturated into the United States.[21] For many, this cause became a kind of Christian mission or duty, and this sentiment was embodied in the work and words of the Board of Indian Commissioners.

The Board of Indian Commissioners

The Board of Indian Commissioners was established in 1869 by Congress and was created in order to advise the government on supposedly more humane policies toward Native Americans. In their first annual report, the board asserted that

> The legal status of the uncivilized Indians should be that of wards of the Government; the duty of the latter being to protect them, to educate them in industry, the arts of civilization, and the principles of Christianity; elevate them to the rights of citizenship, and to sustain and clothe them until they can support themselves. The payment of money annuities to the Indian should be abandoned, for the reason that such payments encourage idleness and vice, to the injury of those whom it is intended to benefit. Schools should be established and teachers employed by the government to introduce the English language in every tribe. It is believed that many of the difficulties with Indians occur from misunderstandings as to the meaning and intention of either party. The teachers employed should be nominated by some religious body having a mission nearest to the location of the school. The establishment of Christian missions should be encouraged, and their schools fostered. The religion of our blessed

Savior is believed to be the most effective agent for the civilization of
any people. We look forward to success in the effort to civilize the
nomadic tribes with confidence, notwithstanding the many difficulties and obstacles which interpose, but their elevation can only be
the result of patient, persevering, and long-continued effort. To expect the civilization and Christianization of any barbarous people
within the term of a few short years, would be to ignore all the facts
of history, all the experiences of human nature. Within the term of
your administration, their condition may be greatly improved, and
the foundations laid, broadly and firmly, of a policy which the newly
awakened sense of justice and humanity in the American people will
never permit to be abandoned until it has accomplished the intended
result.[22]

These words embody the kinds of sentiments that were ultimately so
destructive to Native America and which reveal an amazing amount of
cultural and religious feelings of superiority. These board members saw
it as their duty to "lift up" the "savage" Natives and bring them to the
light of Christianity and civilization. In their eyes, Native Americans
were little more than children that needed a firm guiding hand to bring
about their secular and religious salvation. This kind of paternalistic
attitude was unfortunately quite common at the time among those concerned with Native American issues and became part of the guiding
philosophy of the Board of Indian Commissioners, which they followed
year after year. Twenty years after its founding, for example, the Board
reported that

The principles and purposes thus set forth at the outset have been
steadily adhered to and pursued throughout the entire history of the
Board. Having advisory functions only, with no executive authority,
we have used our influence in every legitimate way to promote hon-
est dealings with the Indians, to educate and civilize them, and to
give them an equal standing with other men as citizens of a common
country. Our policy and hopes are not yet fully realized, but we still
look forward with confidence to complete success.[23]

What is so paradoxical about the Board of Indian Commissioners and
others concerned about Native American issues is that many of these
concerned and compassionate people truly believed that they were acting in the best interests of Native Americans. Unfortunately, they didn't

seem to understand that this kind of paternalism, which reveals a deep sense of cultural, political, social, and religious ethnocentrism, can be very damaging for the people that are supposed to be assisted. Humanitarianism is all too often predicated upon a platform of superiority. In fairness, Americans were not the only ones to display these kinds of attitudes, which were quite common in European colonies around the world. Many colonial overlords saw themselves as helping educate and Christianize the "childlike" people under their care. The famous British poet Rudyard Kipling referred to this as "The White Man's Burden" in his poem of the same name. It is truly ironic that some of the most destructive actions in history have been perpetrated for ostensibly noble and altruistic reasons.

The Board of Indian Commissioners was no different. They believed that they were saving the Natives from extinction or, in their own words:

> I suppose if anything in the world is certain, it is that the red man's civilization will disappear before the white man's civilization, because, of the two, it is inferior. The Indian problem, in its fundamental aspect, is, then, Must the red man disappear with his civilization? Is it possible that in Christian times the Indians themselves have got to disappear with their inferior civilization? I think we can say certainly that unless we can incorporate the red man into the white man's civilization, he will disappear. Therefore, the one question behind the land question, behind the education question and the law question, is, how can we fit the red man for our civilization?[24]

This is the heart of the matter. These words reveal the mentality behind the boarding schools that became such a prominent part of government policy toward the conquered tribes in the United States. It's also important to note that not everyone concerned with Native America operated under such attitudes. Many advocated assimilation for far baser motives. The historian Carroll Kakel puts it this way,

> While "assimilation" was the oft-stated purpose of US Indian policy, it repeatedly functioned in the Early American settler-colonial context as a convenient rationale for the taking of Indian lands, for the "elimination" of the natives, and for a policy to "kill the Indian" ways of life—and sometimes Indians, regardless of sex or age—in the name of a national homogeneity.[25]

After the Carlisle School gained widespread attention owing to its apparent success, Congress funded a total of twenty-three other schools between 1880 and 1902.[26] These were off-reservation schools that boarded Native American students and that were scattered across the country. In addition to these, a great many reservation schools were also created in which students still lived at home, but were taught during the day at the reservation facility. These schools also served to funnel students into the various boarding schools situated away from the reservation. Pratt himself didn't like these on-reservation schools since he believed that it was crucial to remove Indians completely from their culture in order to help them break away from traditional Native ways, and his educational philosophy reflected this.

By 1900, the government ran 147 reservation day schools with 5,000 students, 81 boarding schools on reservations with 9,600 students, and another 25 off-reservation boarding schools with another 7,430 students.[27] In addition to these, the government also funded another thirty-two private schools that contracted to teach Native children, and there were another twenty-two schools run by various groups, usually religious, which were unaffiliated with the government. These numbers reveal a very extensive system of schools, all with the primary goals of education and assimilation.

The system that began with Pratt and the Carlisle School was a heavy-handed and very strict regimen of teaching and training that shouldn't be surprising, given Pratt's military background. Students at the Carlisle School, for example, were enrolled for a number of years during which they were allowed no visits back to their families. Upon arrival, new students had their hair cut short and were given uniforms. The students were organized into platoons and companies and had to march around campus just like military recruits.[28] Many other schools followed suit with similar kinds of policies. New students often found the transition very difficult and stressful. Taken from all that was familiar, these young Natives had all of the outward trappings of their culture, such as clothing and hairstyles, stripped away and replaced with foreign ones. Their lessons and all instruction were in English, essentially a foreign language for many new students.

The sense of shock, dislocation, and even trauma that many children must have felt at this wrenching experience must have been overwhelming. Keep in mind that not all children went willingly. In fact, at various times the government worked to make it compulsory. In 1891, Congress attempted to make attendance at the various schools mandatory by passing a number of laws authorizing the commissioner of Indian Affairs to create and enforce policies designed to force Native families to send their children to the government schools.[29] Enforcement, however, was very difficult, and Congress went back and forth on the issue of making Native education mandatory. Nevertheless, it wasn't unknown for young children to be kidnapped or forcibly taken from their families and sent to boarding schools. In 1932, for example, a report on the conditions of Native Americans in the United States to a Senate subcommittee was titled, "Kid Catching on the Navajo Reservation" and detailed the following:

> I am making a brief statement of my experience with what I consider the greatest shame of the Indian Service—the rounding up of Indian children to be sent away to government boarding schools. . . . In the fall the government stockmen, farmers, and other employees go out into the back country with trucks and bring in the children to school. Many apparently come willingly and gladly; the wild Navajos, far back in the mountains, hide their children at the sound of a truck. So stockmen, Indian police, and other mounted men are sent ahead to round them up. The children are caught, often roped like cattle, and taken away from their parents, many times never to return. They are transferred from school to school, given white people's names, forbidden to speak their own tongue, and when sent to distant schools are not taken home for three years.[30]

Unfortunately, these kinds of scenes were not that unusual. Earlier, in 1903, a teacher at a day school in the Hopi village of Oraibi, Arizona, gave testimony of Hopi children being rounded up in a series of raids. As she recounted:

> Men, women and children were dragged almost naked from their beds and houses. Under the eyes and the guns of the invaders they were allowed to put on a few articles of clothing, and then—many of them barefooted and without any breakfast, the parents and grandparents were forced to take upon their backs such children as were unable to walk the distance (some of the little ones entirely nude) and go down to the school building, through the ice and snow in front of the guns of the dreaded Navajos.[31]

What this quote also reveals is that, ironically, those who were sent to enforce the government policies on Indian education were themselves Native Americans, albeit from a different tribe. In some ways this is probably a reflection of differences of opinion among Natives about the value of educating children in the ways of the whites, with some supporting and others opposing the schools. It also speaks to tribal differences and rivalries and the ability of governments to co-opt, coerce, and seduce individuals within victimized groups to act against their own collective interest. In many ways this calls to mind the policies in Nazi-occupied Europe, which often depended upon co-opting different populations to assist in the policies of destruction. In the ghettos, for example, the Nazis set up Jewish councils and Jewish police forces that assisted the German authorities in running the ghettos and rounding up Jews for deportation to the death camps.[32] The powerful are often able to exploit the vulnerabilities and self-interest of a few who become willing accomplices in the persecution of their own people. The U.S. government has certainly been no exception to this rule.

Regardless of who was actually doing it, the reality is that many children were forcibly removed from their families and relocated to the boarding schools. In addition to the trauma of being removed from family, friends, and familiar surroundings, students often had to also contend with horrible conditions. One evaluation of the Haskell Indian School in 1907 found that

> The people slept two, three, or more in single beds. Both pulmonary and glandular cases (of tuberculosis) were found occupying beds with supposedly healthy pupils. Common towels, common drinking cups, and no fresh air in the dormitories were the rule rather than the exception. No attention was paid to decayed teeth and tooth brushes were not regularly used or their use insisted upon.[33]

Hoke Denetsosie, a Navajo student at a boarding school in Leupp, Arizona, described conditions at his school this way:

> Conditions at the school were terrible. . . . Food and other supplies were not too plentiful. We were underfed; so we were constantly hungry. Clothing was not good, and, in winter months, there were epidemics of sickness. Sometimes students died, and the school would close the rest of the term.

It was run in a military fashion, and rules were very strict. A typical day went like this: Early in the morning at 6 o'clock we rose at the sound of bugles. We washed and dressed; then we lined up in military formation and drilled in the yard. For breakfast, companies formed, and we marched to the dining room, where we all stood at attention with long tables before us. We recited grace aloud, and, after being seated, we proceeded with our meal. . . .

Some teachers and other workers weren't very friendly. When students made mistakes they often were slapped or whipped by the disciplinarian who usually carried a piece of rope in his hip pocket.[34]

The issue of food seems to have been a common complaint among many former students who remembered that it was strange to their tastes and that there was never enough. While conditions varied between different schools, malnourishment appears to have been fairly common. One former student, Helen Sekaquaptewa, remembered that "I was always hungry and wanted to cry because I didn't get enough food. They didn't give second helpings, and I thought I would just starve. You can't go to sleep when you are hungry."[35] These kinds of sentiments do not appear to have been unique, as many others testified to.

A key element of the Carlisle model was something known as the "outing system" in which students were placed with white families for a period of time in order to learn by association. As Pratt, the architect of this arrangement, asserted to the Board of Indian Commissioners in 1889:

I say, and have said the same in effect many times before, that if we take a dozen young Indians and place one in Dr. Buckley's family and another in the chairman's family, and so on, taking those so young they have not learned to talk, and will train them up as the children of those families, I defy you to find any Indian in them when they are grown. We are not born with ideas. God did not make us that way. The ideas come afterwards; they come as we grow up; they come through environment. I believe that if Dr. Buckley would take one of those Indians he has seen in the West a little papoose from his mother's back, always "looking backward" into his family, face it the other way, and keep it under his care and training until grown, it would then be Anglo-Saxon in spirit and American in all its qualities.

Color amounts to nothing. The fact that they are born Indians does not amount to anything.[36]

In his testimony to the commission, Pratt was partially responding to those critical of his ideas who felt that the answer was not to integrate in order to assimilate, but rather to segregate and educate apart from whites, hence the schools on the reservations. This was an idea that Pratt whole-heartedly refused to sanction, or as he put it, "It is not practicable to educate them on the reservation if we desire them to be anything else than Indians."[37] To educate Native Americans on the reservation, according to Pratt, was to condemn them to failure since they would not have the skills or preparation for competing within the larger society.[38] They wouldn't be able to overcome the cultural isolation engendered by tribal life on the reservation. What is important to note is that these competing visions of Native education did not differ on one important point. Specifically, adherents of both philosophies agreed that Native Americans needed to be assimilated and as part of that process their traditional culture had to be eradicated and replaced with the European-based culture of the dominant white society.

While it is true that the experience of the boarding schools was not always perceived as negative—some students valued their educational experience and remembered it as a positive experience and found the skills useful in their lives—it is also true that the overall effect of the push to assimilate Native Americans through education and schools was a very negative one. It was also largely unsuccessful. In this the U.S. government was not alone. The residential schools in Canada were so bad, for example, that in 2008 it prompted then–Prime Minister Stephen Harper to offer an apology on behalf of the Canadian government for the treatment young First Nations children experienced in those schools. In part he stated that "While some former students have spoken positively about their experiences at residential schools, these stories are far overshadowed by tragic accounts of the emotional, physical and sexual abuse and neglect of helpless children, and their separation from powerless families and communities."[39]

Rather than creating new generations of young Natives who were able to integrate fully into the larger society of the United States, what the schools were successful in creating were groups of young American Indians who were never acculturated fully into either world. White society never accepted Native Americans as equal citizens and fellow human beings, largely because of the widespread racism and the accompanying negative stereotypes of them. At the same time, many of these students also didn't fit into their home communities and culture anymore. They had lost their language, traditions, and customs and struggled to readapt and reintegrate into their tribes. Additionally, all the vocational training was useless if Natives were unable to find work and acceptance in the white world, and jobs were few and far between on the reservations. Throughout much of the twentieth century, as various debates raged about the utility and morality of the reservation and boarding schools, support gradually declined, although Indian education of this kind never went away completely.

Looking back at this particular aspect of the history between Natives and non-Natives, it's fairly clear that the explicit and overt intention of the U.S. government, acting through various agencies, such as the Bureau of Indian Affairs, was to eradicate Native American culture. Education, as we have just seen, was a particularly important tool in pursuing this strategy. It should be noted that education was not the only instrument of forced assimilation. The infamous Dawes Act, for example, is another. Known formally as the 1887 General Allotment Act, it was also intended to destroy Native American culture, albeit in a more roundabout way. [40] The act itself divided up tribal land, historically held communally, into private property given to individual tribal members. Individuals were given 80 acres, while families were granted 160. The excess land was then sold off with the profits supposedly going to pay for education.

The idea was that by dividing up the land into private property holdings, Western values emphasizing individualism and private ownership would take hold among the Natives and would thus serve to help "civilize" them. Unfortunately, the only thing it achieved ultimately was to separate many Natives physically, since their holdings weren't always next to each other, and to reduce further the size and amount of tribal lands since the sold-off lands typically did not end up in Native hands. Ironically, the Navajo reservation was largely preserved from allotment because whites did not see the arid landscape as being very desirable. Today, the Navajo reservation is consequently the largest reservation in the United States. But the Navajo experience is the exception. In 1887, tribal lands consisted of about 138 million acres. This had fallen to

around 78 million acres in 1900. Ultimately, the Dawes Act was reversed in 1934 with the Indian Reorganization Act, but by then much of
the damage had been done. Essentially, the Dawes Act served largely to
benefit only white settlers regardless of the ostensible motivation. Even
with the Dawes Act, however, education remained the most potent
weapon of assimilation in terms of importance and impact, and it is in
that arena that we can more closely examine the issue of boarding
schools, forced assimilation, and genocide.

FORCED ASSIMILATION AND CULTURAL GENOCIDE

Culture was central to Raphael Lemkin's notions of genocide. In his
seminal work, *Axis Rule in Occupied Europe*, Lemkin focused a great
deal of attention on attacks against culture as expressed through language and historical and religious artifacts.[41] In fact, he identified six
types of cultural genocide, consisting of destruction of leadership,
forced conversion, prohibition of cultural activities, destruction of religious and cultural symbols, destruction of cultural centers, and looting.[42]
Lemkin quite rightly understood that a people's culture—their language, traditions, shared history, customs, etc.—is central to any
group's identity and continued survival. Destroy the bonds that unite a
people as a people and you effectively destroy that population. During
the debates and committee work leading up to the United Nations
Genocide Convention, the notion of cultural genocide appears to have
been fairly popular with a great deal of support, but for a variety of
political and definitional issues, it was eventually dropped and never
appeared in the final convention draft.[43] One reason for its exclusion
was that many delegates felt that the issues of the destruction of a
culture were more properly addressed as a human rights issue, and
consequently, albeit many years later, the United Nations approved
language affirming the rights of minority groups to practice and maintain their cultures and cultural traditions. Specifically, Article 27 of the
International Covenant on Civil and Political Rights asserts that

> In those states in which ethnic, religious or linguistic minorities exist
> persons belonging to such minorities shall not be denied the right, in
> community with the other members of their groups, to enjoy their

own culture, to profess and practice their own religion, or to use their own language. [44]

Various other international legal instruments also define and protect the rights of minority groups during various conflicts, and these support the notion that, legally speaking, the destruction of a culture is recognized as a form of human rights violation, but not genocide. Nevertheless, cultural genocide continues to be widely considered a form of genocide by many scholars who see it as a valuable concept for understanding the ways in which groups are victimized and who remain true to the original vision of Raphael Lemkin. If we ignore the legal recognition of cultural genocide and simply focus on the issue of intent, the issue of the boarding schools appears to quite clearly meet the criteria for intentionality of destruction. Clearly, the schools were intended to destroy Native culture. But there is a terrible irony here. Remember, if you will, that the ostensible purpose of the reservations and the system of boarding schools was to save Native Americans from extinction. The paradox of this situation is that in trying to save Native Americans physically, well-meaning public officials and humanitarians decided to destroy Native Americans culturally. We also need to acknowledge that not everyone had such ostensibly noble motivations. Many used these lofty goals as a convenient pretext to act out their prejudices and capitalize on the vulnerability of Native populations to exploitation. So we have a situation in which good intentions and bad intentions were fused together in a way that defies easy explanation. The case of the boarding-school system is one that certainly calls to mind the old saying that the road to hell is paved with good intentions.

8

WHAT'S IN A NAME?

If the moral and emotional satisfaction of identifying and excoriating the evil-doers strikes a symbolic blow for surviving victim communities, writing as a hanging judge brings with it the danger of oversimplifying the historical record by casting each genocidal conjuncture as a tidily organized drama of passive victims, wicked perpetrators, and craven bystanders.

—A. Dirk Moses[1]

To characterize the processes through which Native American lives and cultures were degraded and destroyed as "genocidal" may express proper moral indignation, but it does not necessarily help us understand the complex, multi-faceted and often contradictory patterns of inter-racial and inter-cultural interaction on colonial frontiers and within colonies in the Americas.

—Alfred A. Cave[2]

To look at Native America in the contemporary world is to understand the legacy of conquest. Many, if not most, Native American tribes suffer from a wide variety of significant social problems. The rates of violent crime on reservations tend to be about two and a half times higher than in the nation as a whole.[3] In fact, according to the Bureau of Justice Statistics, the violent crime rate in every age group below thirty-five is higher for Native Americans than for any other racial or ethnic group in the United States.[4] This works out to be about one violent crime for every ten Native Americans aged twelve or older.[5] According to some statistics, one out of every three Native women has been the victim of an attempted or completed rape, a rate that is more than two times the national rate, and in rural Alaska the rate of rape among Native populations may be twelve times higher than that of the United States as a whole.[6] These are extreme statistics that speak to a great deal of pain and suffering.

Other social problems also abound. Arrest rates for alcohol violations such as DUI and drunkenness are significantly higher on reservations than for non-Native populations. Alcoholism is such a problem that a report from the Center for Disease Control and Prevention reveals that almost 12 percent of all Native deaths are alcohol related compared with 3.3 percent for the country as a whole.[7] Suicide rates for American Indians also tend to be 50 percent higher than the national average.[8] In addition to these statistics, Native American reservations tend to have very high rates of unemployment, homicide, drug abuse, child abuse, and domestic violence. On the Pine Ridge reservation in South Dakota, for example, these problems are so bad that the average male life expectancy is forty-eight years.[9] One older woman from Pine Ridge, Verlyn Long Wolf, summarized the situation this way, "I'll say about three-quarters of the people I've grown up with are dead. Very few still alive. Alcohol. Drugs. Violence."[10]

While there is no single answer as to why Native communities suffer from such a constellation of ills and difficulties, some have suggested that it is, at least in part, a product of the historical experiences endured by Native peoples in the Americas. While the question of genocide may be debated, what is not in dispute is that Native tribes and their cultures often suffered terribly, especially in the long run, from contact with the Europeans. Samuel Totten and Robert Hitchcock put it this way:

> Even a cursory study of the history of contacts between indigenous peoples and other groups, government officials, transnational corporations, and non-indigenous organizations and institutions reveals that indigenous peoples are usually the losers and bear the costs of contact and incorporation into state systems.[11]

For all the complexity and varied experiences of the American Indians, the end result was all too often violence, destruction, and pain. The costs of contact, in other words, were paid and continue to be paid for in the blood and suffering of human beings. In many ways, their victimization has never ended. The problems that continue to plague Native communities are clear evidence of this and may be explained, at least in part, with reference to the phenomenon of posttraumatic stress disorder (PTSD), which refers to a variety of physical and psychological dysfunctions that sometimes arise after a person has experienced some sort of traumatic event.[12] Typically, this anxiety disorder arises after someone:

> Has been exposed to a traumatic event in which both of the following were present:
>
> 1. the person experienced, witnessed, or was confronted with an event or events that involved actual or threatened death or serious injury, or a threat to the physical integrity of self or others; and
> 2. the person's response involved intense fear, helplessness, or horror.[13]

Essentially, living through or seeing something deeply harmful can dramatically affect somebody's emotional and physical well-being. Events that cause someone to experience intense fear, horror, and a strong sense of helplessness can generate PTSD.[14] Symptoms can include flashbacks, nightmares, sleeplessness, anger, difficulty concentrating, hypervigilance, and an exaggerated startle reflex. Other related manifestations of this disorder can include acute anxiety, depression, suicide, alcohol and drug use, and paranoia. These symptoms can persist for a very long time and dramatically impact a person's quality of life. While we usually think of PTSD in terms of how it impacts individuals, it's important to understand that it can also harm communities. In recent years scholars have increasingly explored the multigenerational effects of PTSD.[15] Often referred to as historical trauma, this concept can be defined as the "cumulative emotional and psychological wounding across generations, including the lifespan, which emanates from massive group trauma."[16] In other words, this theory asserts that damage can persist over generations and this is what is largely responsible for the high rates of dysfunction and violence experienced by many Native American populations. The author Chris Hedges puts it more simply when he writes, "The violence imposed on Indian culture has become internalized. Despair and pain of this magnitude lead to lives dedicated to self-immolation. The agony is expressed in self-defeating and self-destructive urges that shred what is left of dignity and hope."[17]

Clearly, Native America is still struggling with the legacy of colonialism and military and cultural conquest. Because of these massive and ongoing problems, it's easy to understand why the question of genocide has become so important in relation to Native American history, and it is to this issue that we now turn.

In recent years, applying the label of genocide to the experiences of Native America in the wake of contact with Europeans has become increasingly common. This has often been accompanied by a great deal of resistance to the idea of perceiving the history of Native America as consisting of anything other than genocide. Why? Genocide is, after all, just a word. But what is it about that specific word that calls forth such strong reactions? Part of the answer lies in the ongoing efforts of many Native American groups to overcome the historical trauma briefly discussed above and to revitalize their cultures, assert their identity, and reclaim tribal autonomy in modern American society.[18] But another part of the answer lies in the power we assign to words. They have meaning and can powerfully influence and shape our perceptions and emotions around many issues and topics. The old saying that sticks and stones can break bones, but words can never hurt us is simply incorrect. We are often profoundly moved by words, sometimes positively and sometimes negatively. Words can bring forth tears of joy or of suffering depending on the meaning that those sounds convey. Words can also elicit actions, whether it is a command, a speech, a taunt, a threat, or a cry for help. We are, after all, symbolic beings whose experience of the world is mediated through the prism of words. Should we be surprised, therefore, that some words, such as "genocide," can be so tremendously important and meaningful to many people? So words have power, but what is it about this particular word?

In a relatively few short years, genocide has been transformed from a largely obscure word used only by a handful of scholars who study mass atrocity to a mainstream term understood and used by many people, not just academics. There appear to be a number of reasons for this remarkable change. Since its inception in 1944, "genocide" has come to represent the most heinous possible crime in the minds of many, or as one writer suggests, "Genocide is the supreme crime."[19] What could be more horrific than cold-bloodedly trying to wipe out an entire population?

Much of this perception is due to the Holocaust, arguably one of the most studied and written-about events in history. Ever since the Nuremberg trials first brought international attention to the crimes of the Nazis, the Holocaust has become emblematic of genocide, and the imagery of the concentration camps, death's head insignia, and gas chambers have become ubiquitous and synonymous with unbridled evil. Say "Auschwitz," or "Dachau," and most people will understand immediately what you are referring to. So genocide, especially as exemplified by the Holocaust, has become shorthand for the worst possible kind of violence and criminality. It has become, to borrow David Moshman's phrase, "the ultimate human rights catastrophe, and thus the measure of all catastrophes."[20]

More recent examples of genocide in places such as Bosnia, Rwanda, and Darfur have also served to bring the concept of genocide into the mainstream of popular consciousness. While the violence in these places was usually geographically distant for many Americans, it also tended to be emotionally close given the widespread coverage of these genocides in various television, radio, print news, and Internet forums. The end result is that "genocide" has become an iconic word that represents the cruelest behavior that humans can inflict upon one another. In short, it has come to represent pure distilled evil and unimaginable horror, loss, and tragedy. When Raphael Lemkin first coined this word in 1944 in his book *Axis Rule in Occupied Europe*, he did so because he felt that traditional words and terms used to describe large-scale mass atrocities simply did not capture the full extent and nature of the Nazi-perpetrated outrages.[21] In his eyes, the terms "mass murder" and "war crimes," for example, could not encompass the broad range of tactics, the systematic nature, or the deadly intent of the Holocaust, and so a new word was needed. The vocabulary of atrocity was and still is quite limited. Genocide, therefore, was conceived in order to fill a perceived need in the language surrounding certain kinds of crimes and because of this, it has become the preferred word whenever individuals and/or groups want to suggest that something is the absolute worst and condemn it in the strongest possible way.

These reasons suggest why it seems to be so important for some individuals and groups to apply the word "genocide" to the victimization suffered by their group at some point in the past. Because genocide has assumed this special status as being the apex of evil, the term has been used increasingly to acknowledge extreme victimization. It is largely about the belief that only the word "genocide" suffices to describe the suffering of a population group, especially if that group is one's own. After all, what other words are there that represent the same level of heinousness or that carry the same amount of moral condemnation? It is only natural to want to highlight the suffering your people may have experienced, especially if the consequences are still evident and ongoing. But there is a danger here, which is the often closely related belief that if a group's victimization does not meet the definitional criteria for genocide, then somehow that group's history is discounted and the suffering minimized. If the word genocide represents the worst fate that could befall a group, then by implication if it is not considered genocide, the suffering and victimization experienced by those people is somehow perceived to be diminished. At its worst, the desire to apply the designation of genocide may appear to have overtones of elevating one people's suffering over that of other similarly victimized groups. It's as if there's some sort of perverse status or exalted victimhood in having suffered more than others. These easily understood sentiments reveal why the definition and application of the term genocide is such a fraught and politicized issue. This is as true for the academic community as it is for activists and others.

Genocide has always been an intensely debated topic, even among Holocaust and genocide scholars, and this has only increased in recent years. As genocide studies has developed and grown as a field of study, and as more and more scholars have expanded their domains of interest into genocide studies, the conceptual and definitional debates have often grown more vociferous and heated. I have been in conferences with genocide scholars in which some have explicitly suggested that a rigid focus on intentionality is a form of denial. This kind of charge is particularly disturbing because of the history of Holocaust denial. Over the years a number of organizations and individuals have aggressively worked to discredit Holocaust survivors and deny that the Holocaust ever took place.[22] These groups and individuals have clearly been motivated by an anti-Semitic agenda that seeks to rehabilitate the Nazi regime and denigrate Jews. Similarly, the Turkish government's continued denial of the Armenian genocide has also been part of a deliberate campaign of disinformation for political purposes. To suggest, therefore, that academics who rely on a legalistic definition of genocide, one based on the United Nations Genocide Convention definition, are acting as genocide deniers is not only factually incorrect, but also a gross mischaracterization. This type of rhetorical excess can only serve to discourage legitimate debate and discussion about how we understand and define the term of genocide. This isn't to suggest that the positions of some genocide scholars are always completely tenable or that some aren't overly restrictive, but to impute a denialist motive to all of those attempts to wrestle with the complexities of genocide is, in my opinion, inappropriate. It does, however, raise an important question in regard to those who study genocide.

What obligation do genocide scholars have when it comes to genocide? Some have suggested that focusing on overly legalistic and arguably restrictive definitions of genocide essentially gives aid and comfort to past and future perpetrators and helps to create a culture of impunity.[23] In other words, by creating a high threshold that atrocities need to meet in order to qualify as genocide, future genocides may become more likely. Yet on the other hand, a certain amount of definitional rigor and detachment is necessary if we are to truly come to grips with this complicated phenomenon in order to better understand it, to influence policy, and to potentially prosecute perpetrators. Balancing these two opposing objectives can be quite tricky, as the debates and controversies attest. Of this, the scholar Uğur Üngör correctly notes, "All social research operates amidst the tension between involvement and detachment."[24] Üngör explicitly warns against the two extremes of what he terms sacralization and trivialization, the tendency either to portray genocide as a mystical event that is both inexplicable and unknowable on the one hand, or, on the other hand, to suggest that any and every outrage or atrocity is genocide. Both ends of this continuum are to be avoided. Somewhere in the middle between these two poles lies a reasonable approach to analysis and discussion of genocide. In some ways, the crux of this struggle concerns the issue of ownership.

Who owns genocide? Who has the right to impose their interpretation on this concept? These questions are not easily answered. The sociologist and genocide scholar Scott Straus points out that genocide means different things to different people when he writes:

> To one person, "genocide" means evil and demands a preventive or punitive action by a government; to another, "genocide" carries a circumscribed juridical meaning, while to still others it designates a specific type of mass violence. These wide-ranging and powerful dimensions—and the relatively small number of terms that connote unspeakable atrocity—ironically have made "genocide" an attractive concept. But these multiple dimensions also have made for a conceptual muddle.[25]

Straus is absolutely correct in assessing that genocide can assume multiple meanings depending on who is defining it. So who owns genocide? Whose interpretation of this heinous crime do we give greater weight or more legitimacy to? Is it the activist calling attention to the plight and suffering of a people; the scholar intent on categorizing, delineating, and describing; the politician eliciting moral outrage and condemnation in the name of human rights or geopolitical advantage; or perhaps the lawyer attempting to build a case against a human rights violator? Ultimately, who's to say which definition is right and which others are wrong? Does one group or person have a stronger moral claim to this contested concept we call genocide? In many ways, one term such as genocide can never completely encompass such a complicated phenomenon. As the well-known Holocaust historian Yehuda Bauer points out, reality is always far more complicated than our attempts to define it.[26] The world is endlessly more varied and intricate than we often allow for, and attempts to theoretically encapsulate and define phenomena within one set of criteria often fall short. In many ways, genocide is no one thing, and attempts to wrestle with it must acknowledge this fundamental truth.

As this book has illustrated, the question of genocide in the Americas is a much more complicated issue than has often been suggested. Part of this is due to the long time period and the multiplicity of tribes, policies, and experiences. On the part of the Europeans, there were many different governments, at least initially, that developed a multitude of policies and relationships with the Native peoples they encountered. These policies and relationships evolved and changed over time as the people and the circumstances shifted, and while many of these policies and relationships ended up being destructive to Native lives and culture, not every experience can readily be defined as constituting genocide. Not every atrocity or outrage is genocide. On the part of the

Natives of the Americas, there was a great diversity of tribes and tribal leaders who resisted, negotiated, accommodated, and otherwise struggled to adapt and cope with the changing circumstances with varying degrees of success.

Another part of the complexity of this topic is a result of the lack of conceptual clarity regarding genocide. Genocide, as we have seen, is inherently a problematic topic. This reality has meant that there is no one single definition of genocide that all who use the term can agree upon. This has resulted in a proliferation of interpretations and applications. This definitional confusion means that there is no single definitive answer to the question of Native America and genocide. Depending on which version one subscribes to and which specific incident or situation under examination, it's possible to arrive at very different conclusions regarding the central question of this book.

In assessing the question of genocide, the reality is that the term used to describe a people's suffering and/or victimization is ultimately irrelevant to their lived experience as human beings. While these definitional debates are important to help us conceptualize and understand the past and present, the reality of the experience for those involved isn't altered by what we decide. The meaning and import of an event is always different for those who actually experience it as a lived event compared to those who experience it intellectually from a distance. While the words we use have meaning and power, they do not encompass everything. The fact that academics, scholars, and activists argue definitional issues related to genocide doesn't take anything away from those who lived through the events briefly reviewed and described in this book. In closing, then, I can think of no better way to conclude than to refer to the words of the historian and genocide scholar Paul Bartrop, who summarizes this issue beautifully when he writes:

> In the long term, of course, none of this mattered to those who were the victims; but it makes a great deal of difference to those who remain, to those who seek some acknowledgement of past wrongs, to those with a commitment to seeing that the story is told accurately, and to those who would try to know how the term genocide should properly be employed—and when, according to those with the legal competence to do something about it, it should not.[27]

NOTES

INTRODUCTION

1. Oscar Wilde quote, accessed September 23, 2010, http://thinkexist.com/quotation/the_truth_is_rarely_pure_and_never_simple/153927.html.

2. Patricia Nelson Limerick, forward to *Shadows at Dawn: An Apache Massacre and the Violence of History*, by Karl Jacoby (New York: Penguin Books, 2008).

3. See, for example, Alex Alvarez, *Genocidal Crimes* (London: Routledge, 2010); Alex Alvarez, *Governments, Citizens, and Genocide: A Comparative and Interdisciplinary Approach* (Bloomington: Indiana University Press, 2001).

4. James Axtell, *Natives and Newcomers: The Cultural Origins of North America* (New York: Oxford University Press, 2001), 296.

5. Roger Moorhouse, *Berlin at War* (New York: Basic Books, 2010), 3–4.

6. James Axtell, *Beyond 1492: Encounters in Colonial North America* (New York: Oxford University Press, 1992), 19.

7. Carl Waldman, *Encyclopedia of Native American Tribes*, 3rd ed. (New York: Checkmark Books, 2006).

8. James Axtell, *Beyond 1492: Encounters in Colonial North America* (New York: Oxford University Press, 1992).

1. BEGINNINGS

1. Adam Jones, *Genocide: A Comprehensive Introduction* (London: Routledge, 2006), 70.

2. Quoted in Russell Thornton, *American Indian Holocaust and Survival: A Population History Since 1492* (Norman: Oklahoma University Press, 1987), x.

3. The archeologist Brian Fagan presents a very accessible narrative of this climatic period in Brian Fagan, *The Great Warming: Climate Change and the Rise and Fall of Civilizations* (New York: Bloomsbury Press, 2008).

4. See Robert Ferguson, *The Vikings: A History* (New York: Viking Press, 2009).

5. Ferguson, *The Vikings*.

6. Jared Diamond, *Collapse: How Societies Choose to Fail or Succeed* (New York: Penguin Books, 2005); Fagan, *The Great Warming*.

7. Ferguson, *The Vikings*.

8. Samuel Eliot Morison, *The European Discovery of America: The Northern Voyages* (New York: Oxford University Press, 1971).

9. Ferguson, *The Vikings*.

10. Morison, *The European Discovery of America*, 55.

11. Ferguson, *The Vikings*.

12. Quoted in Diamond, *Collapse*, 268.

13. Quoted in Ferguson, *The Vikings*, 288.

14. Diamond, *Collapse*.

15. Tony Horwitz, *A Voyage Long and Strange* (New York: Picador, 2008).

16. See, for example, Thornton, *American Indian Holocaust and Survival*, or David Henige, *Numbers from Nowhere* (Norman: Oklahoma University Press, 1998).

17. Nancy Shoemaker, *American Indian Population Recovery in the Twentieth Century* (Albuquerque: University of New Mexico Press, 1999).

18. James Wilson, *The Earth Shall Weep: A History of Native America* (New York: Grove Press, 1998), 19.

19. For a more detailed discussion of the political nature of the population debate see Thornton, *American Indian Holocaust and Survival*, or Henige, *Numbers from Nowhere*.

20. Frederick E. Hoxie, "The Indians versus the Textbooks: Is There Any Way Out?" *Perspectives* 23 (April 1985): 1–36, 3.

21. Thornton, *American Indian Holocaust and Survival*; Shoemaker, *American Indian Population Recovery*.

22. "U.S. Census. American Indians: Census Facts," Infoplease.com, accessed October 20, 2010, http:www.infoplease.com/spot/aihmcensus1.html.

23. Depending on which paleontologist or archaeologist one subscribes to, the dates range from as early as 70,000 to as late as 10,000 years ago. The general consensus suggests, however, that around 14,000 years is most likely.

24. See for example Jason A. Eshleman, Ripan S. Malhi, and David Glenn Smith, "Mitochondrial DNA Studies of Native Americans: Conceptions and Misconceptions of the Population Prehistory of the Americas," *Evolutionary Anthropology* 12, no. 1 (2003):7–18; Terrence Kaufman and Victor Golla, "Language Groupings in the New World: Their Reliability and Usability in Cross-disciplinary Studies." in *America Past, America Present: Genes and Languages in the Americas and Beyond*, ed. Colin Renfrew (Cambridge: McDonald Institute for Archeological Research, 2000), 57–67.

25. It's quite possible that the Bering land bridge was not the only route to the Americas. Some have suggested, for example, that Polynesian sailors were early arrivals in South America, while others have speculated about very early European arrivals during the same historic era. See, for example, Jake Page, *In the Hands of the Great Spirit: The 20,000-Year History of American Indians* (New York: Free Press, 2003).

26. Francis Jennings, *The Founders of America: From the Earliest Migrations to the Present* (New York: W. W. Norton and Company, 1994).

27. Brian Fagan, *The Long Summer: How Climate Changed Civilization* (New York: Basic Books, 2004).

28. Page, *In the Hands of the Great Spirit*.

29. Shepard Krech, *The Ecological Indian: Myth and History* (New York: W. W. Norton and Company, 1999).

30. Ted Morgan, *Wilderness at Dawn: The Settling of the North American Continent* (New York: Touchstone Books, 1993).

31. Fagan, *The Long Summer*.

32. See, for example, Clifford Geertz, *The Interpretation of Cultures* (New York: Basic Books, 1973); Raymond Williams, *The Sociology of Culture* (Chicago: University of Chicago Press, 1995).

33. David Maas, "Native Peoples of Alaska," in *Native America: Portrait of the Peoples*, ed. Duane Champagne (Detroit: Visible Ink, 1994).

34. Robin Ridington, "Northern Hunters," in *America in 1492: The World of the Indian Peoples before the Arrival of Columbus*, ed. Alvin M. Josephy (New York: Vintage Books, 1991).

35. Richard D. Daugherty, "People of the Salmon," in *America in 1492: The World of the Indian Peoples before the Arrival of Columbus*, ed. Alvin M. Josephy (New York: Vintage Books, 1991).

36. Krech, *The Ecological Indian*.

37. Charles C. Mann, *1491: New Revelations of the Americas before Columbus* (New York: Alfred A. Knopf, 2005).

38. Timothy R. Pauketat, *Cahokia: Ancient America's Great City on the Mississippi* (New York: Penguin Books, 2009); Peter Nabokov, with Dean Snow, in *America in 1492: The World of the Indian Peoples before the Arrival*

of Columbus, ed. Alvin M. Josephy (New York: Vintage Books, 1991); see also, Mann, *1491*.

39. Mann, *1491*, 19.

40. Mann, *1491*.

41. Edward Hyams, and George Ordish, *The Last of the Incas: The Rise and Fall of an American Empire* (New York: Dorset Press, 1963).

42. Hoxie, "The Indians versus the Textbooks: Is There Any Way Out?" 24.

43. John C. Mohawk, *Utopian Legacies: A History of Conquest and Oppression in the Western World* (Santa Fe: Clear Light Publishers, 2000), 1.

44. Quoted in Mark Cocker, *Rivers of Blood, Rivers of Gold: Europe's Conquest of Indigenous Peoples* (New York: Grove Press, 1998), 10.

45. Christopher Columbus, *The Four Voyages of Christopher Columbus: Being His Own Log Book, Letters, and Dispatches with Connecting Narrative Drawn from the Life of the Admiral by his Son Hernando Colon and Other Contemporary Historians*, ed. and trans. J. M. Cohen (New York: Penguin Books, 1969).

46. Victor Kiernan, *The Lords of Human Kind: European Attitudes to Other Cultures in the Imperial Age* (London: Serif, 1995).

47. For a good discussion of this issue, see Steven A. LeBlanc, with Katherine E. Register, *Constant Battles: Why We Fight* (New York: St. Martin's Griffin, 2003).

48. See, for example, G. B. Nash, *Red, White, and Black: The Peoples of Early America* (Englewood Cliffs, NJ: Prentice-Hall, 1982).

49. See, for example, Richard J. Chacon and Rubén G. Mendoza, eds., *North American Indigenous Warfare and Ritual Violence* (Tucson: University of Arizona Press, 2007).

50. Ernest S. Burch, Jr., "Traditional Native Warfare in Western Alaska" in *North American Indigenous Warfare and Ritual Violence*, eds. Richard J. Chacon and Rubén G. Mendoza (Tucson: University of Arizona Press, 2007), 11–29.

51. Jeffrey P. Blick, "The Iroquois Practice of Genocidal Warfare (1534–1787)," *Journal of Genocide Research* 3, no. 3 (2001): 405–429.

52. Page, *In the Hands of the Great Spirit*.

53. For a very readable history of the Comanche, see S. C. Gwynne, *Empire of the Summer Moon: Quanah Parker and the Rise and Fall of the Comanches, the Most Powerful Indian Tribe in American History* (New York: Scribner, 2010).

54. Steven LeBlanc, *Prehistoric Warfare in the American Southwest* (Salt Lake City: University of Utah Press, 1999).

55. Richard A. Gabriel and Karen S. Metz, "A Short History of War: The Evolution of Warfare and Weapons, Professional Readings in Military Strate-

gy," no. 5 (Carlisle Barracks, Pennsylvania: Strategic Studies Institute, U.S. Army War College, 1992), accessed December 12, 2012,http://www.au.af.mil/au/awc/awcgate/gabrmetz/gabr0001.htm.

56. Hyams and Ordish, *The Last of the Incas*.

57. Heather Pringle, "Vikings and Native Americans," *National Geographic*, November 2012.

58. Heather Pringle, "Evidence of Viking Outpost Found in Canada," *National Geographic Daily News*, accessed December 12, 2012, http://news.nationalgeographic.com/news/2012/10/121019-viking-outpost-second-new-canada-science-sutherland/#ng_comments.

2. GENOCIDE

1. Brenden Rensink, "Genocide of Native Americans: Historical Facts and Historiographic Debates," in *Genocide of Indigenous Peoples, Genocide: A Critical Bibliographic Review*, vol. 8, eds. Samuel Totten and R. K. Hitchcock (New Brunswick: Transaction Publishers, 2011), 16.

2. Laurence M. Hauptman, *Tribes and Tribulations: Misconceptions about American Indians and Their Histories* (Albuquerque: University of New Mexico Press, 1995), 5.

3. William A. Schabas, *Genocide in International Law: The Crimes of Crimes* (Cambridge: Cambridge University Press, 2000), 9.

4. See, for example, Helen Fein, *Genocide: A Sociological Perspective* (London: Sage Publications, 1993); Mark Levene, *The Meaning of Genocide, Vol. 1: Genocide in the Age of the Nation State* (London: I.B. Taurus, 2005).

5. Samantha Power, *A Problem from Hell* (New York: Basic Books, 2002).

6. Lawrence J. LeBlanc, *The United States and the Genocide Convention* (Durham, NC: Duke University Press, 1991).

7. The complete text is available at the United Nations website, http://www.un.org/millenium/law/iv-1.htm.

8. Yusuf Aksar, "The Specific Intent (Dolus Specialis) Requirement of the Crime of Genocide: Confluence or Conflict between the Practice of Ad Hoc Tribunals and the ICJ," *International Relations* 6, no. 23(2009):113–126.

9. See Ben Kiernan, *Blood and Soil: A World History of Genocide and Extermination from Sparta to Darfur* (New Haven: Yale University Press, 2007).

10. LeBlanc, *The United States and the Genocide Convention*.

11. Schabas, *Genocide in International Law*; The International Criminal Tribunal for Rwanda. "Proseuctor v. Jean-Paul Akayesu" Case no. ICTR-96-4-T. 2 Dec. 1998.

12. See, for example, A. L. Kroeber and Clyde Kluckhorn, *Culture: A Critical Review of Concepts and Definitions* (New York: Vintage Books, 1952); Clifford Geertz, *The Interpretation of Cultures* (New York: Basic Books, 1973).

13. UNESCO Latin American Conference, Declaration of San José, 11 December 1981, UNESCO Doc. FS 82/WF.32, reproduced in Martin Shaw, *What is Genocide?* (Malden, MA: Polity Press, 2007).

14. Robert Melson, *Revolution and Genocide: On the Origins of the Armenian Genocide and the Holocaust* (Chicago: University of Chicago Press, 1992), 26.

15. Alex Alvarez, *Governments, Citizens, and Genocide: A Comparative and Interdisciplinary Approach* (Bloomington: Indiana University Press, 2001).

16. Frank Chalk and Kurt Jonassohn, *The History and Sociology of Genocide: Analyses and Case Studies* (New Haven: Yale University Press, 1990), 23.

17. Martin Shaw, *War and Genocide* (Malden, MA: Polity Press, 2003); Shaw, *What is Genocide?*

18. Fein, *Genocide*, 24.

19. See, for example, Mary Anne Warren, *Gendercide: The Implications of Sex Selection* (Totowa, NJ: Rowman and Allenheld, 1985). See also, Adam Jones, "Gendercide and Genocide," *Journal of Genocide Research* 2, no. 2 (2000): 185–211.

20. For a thorough review of these variations on genocide see Shaw, *What is Genocide?*

21. William A. Schabas. 2006. "The "Odious Scourge": Evolving Interpretations of the Crime of Genocide." *Genocide Studies and Prevention* 1, no. 2 (September): 93–106.

22. See, for example, Alex Alvarez, *Governments, Citizens, and Genocide*.

23. David E. Stannard, *American Holocaust: The Conquest of the New World* (New York: Oxford University Press, 1992), x.

24. Ward Churchill, *A Little Matter of Genocide: Holocaust and Denial in the Americas 1492 to the Present* (San Francisco: City Lights Books, 1997), 97.

25. Rebecca Joyce Frey, *Genocide and International Justice* (New York: Facts on File, 2009), 10.

26. In the Summary Records of the meetings of the Sixth Committee of the General Assembly, 21 September–10 December 1948, Official Records of the General Assembly, 109.

27. Alex Alvarez and Ronet Bachman, *Murder American Style* (Belmont, CA: Thomson/Wadsworth, 2003).

28. Alvarez and Bachman, *Murder American Style*.

29. See, for example, Kai Ambros, "What Does 'Intent to Destroy' in Genocide Mean?" *International Review of the Red Cross* 91, no. 876 (December 2009): 833–858.

30. Kiernan, *Blood and Soil*, 17.

31. Alexander Statiev, "Soviet Ethnic Deportations: Intent versus Outcome," *Journal of Genocide Research* 11, no. 2–3 (June–September 2009): 243–264.

32. Statiev, "Soviet ethnic deportations: intent versus outcome," 259.

33. Israel Charny, "Toward a Generic Definition of Genocide," in *Genocide: Conceptual and Historical Dimensions*, ed. George J. Andreopoulos (Philadelphia: University of Pennsylvania Press, 1994), 64–94.

34. Kai Ambos, "Criminologically Explained Reality of Genocide, Structure of the Offence and the 'Intent to Destroy' Requirement," in *Collective Violence and International Criminal Justice*, ed. Alette Smeulers (Antwerp: Intersentia, 2010), 153–173.

35. Ambos, "Criminologically Explained Reality of Genocide," 171.

36. See, for example, The International Criminal Tribunal for Rwanda. "The Prosecutor versus Jean-Paul Akayesu." Case no. ICTR-96-4-T, accessed November 18, 2011, http://www.unictr.org/tabid/128/Default.aspx?id=18& mnid=4; also see, The International Criminal Tribunal for Rwanda. "The Prosecutor v. Sylvestre Gacumbitsi." Case no. ICTR-2001-64-T, accessed November 18, 2011, http://www.unictr.org/tabid/128/Default.aspx?id=21&mnid=4. For a brief summary, see Kiernan, *Blood and Soil*.

37. See, for example, David Scheffer, "The World Court's Fractured Ruling on Genocide," *Genocide Studies and Prevention* 2, no. 2 (August 2007): 123–136.

38. The International Tribunal for the Prosecution of Persons Responsible for Serious Violations of International Humanitarian Law Committed in the Territory of the Former Yugoslavia since 1991. "The Prosecutor v. Goran Jelisic" Case no. IT-95-10-T. 14 Dec. 1999, accessed November 21, 2011, http://www.icty.org/case/jelisic/4.

39. The appeals judgment is available online, accessed November 21, 2011, http://www.icty.org/case/jelisic/4.

40. Both the trial judgment and appeals judgments are available online, accessed November 23, 2011, http://www.icty.org/case/stakic/4.

41. The indictment is available online, accessed February 7, 2010, http://www.icc-cpi.int/iccdocs/doc/doc279813.PDF.

42. Ward Churchill, "Genocide by Any Other Name: North American Indian Residential Schools in Context," in *Genocide, War Crimes, and the West: History and Complicity*, ed. Adam Jones (London: Zed Books, 2004), 78–115.

43. Churchill, *A Little Matter of Genocide*, 156.

44. Stannard, *American Holocaust*, xii.

45. Stannard, *American Holocaust*, xii.

46. Quoted in Russell Thornton, *American Indian Holocaust and Survival: A Population History since 1492* (Norman: University of Oklahoma Press, 1987), 101.

47. Donald Jackson, ed., *Letters of the Lewis and Clark Expedition with Related Documents*, 2nd ed. (Urbana: University of Illinois Press, 1978).

48. See, for example, The International Criminal Tribunal for Rwanda. "The Prosecutor versus Jean-Paul Akayesu." Case no. ICTR-96-4-T, accessed November 18, 2011, http://www.unictr.org/tabid/128/Default.aspx?id=18&mnid=4. Also see, The International Criminal Tribunal for Rwanda. "The Prosecutor versus Sylvestre Gacumbitsi." Case no. ICTR-2001-64-T accessed November 18, 2011, http://www.unictr.org/tabid/128/Default.aspx?id=21&mnid=4. For a brief summary, see Kiernan, *Blood and Soil*.

49. Alan Taylor, *American Colonies: The Settling of North America* (New York: Penguin Books, 2001).

50. Irving Louis Horowitz, *Taking Lives: Genocide and State Power*, 4th ed. (New Brunswick: Transaction Publishers, 1997), 39.

51. Karl Jacoby, *Shadows at Dawn: An Apache Massacre and the Violence of History* (New York: Penguin Books, 2009), 18.

52. Samuel P. Huntington, *The Clash of Civilizations and the Remaking of World Order* (New York: Simon and Schuster, 1998).

3. DESTRUCTIVE BELIEFS

1. Quoted in Lotte Hughes, *The No-Nonsense Guide to Indigenous Peoples* (London: Verso, 2003), 29.

2. Bartolomé de Las Casas, *The Devastation of the Indies: A Brief Account*, trans. Herma Briffault (Baltimore: Johns Hopkins Press, 1992), 31.

3. Cormack was speaking of the Beothuk people. Quoted in Tony Horwitz, *A Voyage Long and Strange* (New York: Picador, 2008), 35.

4. Christopher Columbus, *The Four Voyages*, trans. J. M. Cohen (New York: Penguin Books, 1969).

5. Contrary to popular opinion, Columbus did not sail across the Atlantic to prove the world was round or for a particular love of exploration; rather, he sailed for riches. He was seeking the famed wealth of the Orient. More specifically, he was looking for a shortcut to the spices of Asia that were so valuable in the marketplaces of Europe. Pepper, nutmeg, ginger, and cinnamon, to name just a few, were the most valuable commodities of the age, and a single shipload could make a person wealthy for life, hence the driving desire to find shorter trade routes to the sources of spice.

6. Columbus, *The Four Voyages*, 55.

7. Columbus, *The Four Voyages*, 56.

8. Columbus, *The Four Voyages*, 118.

9. Laurence Bergreen, *Columbus: The Four Voyages* (New York: Viking Books, 2011).

10. Columbus, *The Four Voyages*; Bergreen, *Columbus*.

11. Bergreen, *Columbus*.

12. Bergreen, *Columbus*.

13. See, for example, Alex Alvarez, *Governments, Citizens, and Genocide: A Comparative and Interdisciplinary Approach* (Bloomington: Indiana University Press, 2001); Alex Alvarez, *Genocidal Crimes* (New York: Routledge, 2010): Ervin Staub, *The Roots of Evil: The Origins of Genocide and Other Group Violence* (New York: Cambridge University Press, 1989).

14. Leonard S. Newman and Ralph Erber, eds., *Understanding Genocide: The Social Psychology of the Holocaust* (Oxford: Oxford University Press, 2002): Christopher Powell, *Barbaric Civilization: A Critical Sociology of Genocide* (Montreal: McGill-Queen's University Press, 2011): Ervin Staub, *The Psychology of Good and Evil: Why Children, Adults, and Groups Help and Harm Others* (Cambridge: Cambridge University Press, 2003); James Waller, *Becoming Evil: How Ordinary People Commit Genocide and Mass Killing* (New York: Oxford University Press, 2002).

15. J. Ross Eshleman, Barbara G. Cashion, and Laurence A. Basirico, *Introduction to Sociology*, 2nd ed. (Reno, NV: Best Value Textbooks, 2005).

16. Richard J. Gelles and Ann Levine, *Sociology: An Introduction*, 6th ed. (Boston: McGraw Hill, 1999).

17. E. O. Wilson, *On Human Nature* (New York: Bantam Books, 1982).

18. Robin I. M. Dunbar, "Sociobiological Explanations and the Evolution of Ethnocentrism," in *The Sociobiology of Ethnocentrism*, eds. Vernon Reynolds et al. (Athens: University of Georgia Press, 1987).

19. Carl Waldman, *Encyclopedia of Native American Tribes*, 3rd ed. (New York: Checkmark Books, 2006).

20. Waldman, *Encyclopedia of Native American Tribes*.

21. Olive P. Dickason, *The Myth of the Savage and the Beginnings of French Colonialism in the Americas* (Edmonton: The University of Alberta Press, 1997).

22. Derek W. Lomax, *The Reconquest of Spain* (London: Longman, 1978); Joseph F. O'Callaghan, *Reconquest and Crusade in Medieval Spain* (Philadelphia: University of Pennsylvania Press, 2003).

23. See, for example, Gabriel Jackson, *The Making of Medieval Spain* (New York: Harcourt Brace Jovanovich, Inc., 1972); Angus MacKay, *Spain in the Middle Ages: From Frontier to Empire, 1000–1500* (New York: St. Martin's

Press, 1977); John Fraser Ramsey, *Spain: The Rise of the First World Power* (University of Alabama Press, 1973).

24. Peter Rietbergen, *Europe: A Cultural History* (London: Routledge, 1998).

25. O'Callaghan, *Reconquest and Crusade in Medieval Spain.*

26. Joseph R. Strayer and Dana C. Munro, *The Middle Ages, 395–1500*, 5th ed. (New York: Appleton-Century-Crofts, 1970).

27. O'Callaghan, *Reconquest and Crusade in Medieval Spain.*

28. David J. Weber, *The Spanish Frontier in North America* (New Haven: Yale University Press, 1992).

29. Lauren Faulkner Rossi, 2012, Comment made on earlier draft of this chapter.

30. Thomas R. Berger, *A Long and Terrible Shadow: White Values, Native Rights in the Americas since 1492* (Seattle: University of Washington Press, 1999), 2.

31. Weber, *The Spanish Frontier in North America.*

32. Bartolomé de Las Casas, *The Devastation of the Indies: A Brief Account*, trans. Herma Briffault (Baltimore: Johns Hopkins Press, 1974), 29.

33. Bartolomé de Las Casas, *The Devastation of the Indies: A Brief Account*, trans. Herma Briffault (Baltimore: Johns Hopkins Press, 1974), 33–34.

34. See, for example, Ben Kiernan, *Blood and Soil: A World History of Genocide and Extermination from Sparta to Darfur* (New Haven: Yale University Press, 2007).

35. Translated text of the requerimiento available online athttp://www.ciudadseva.com/textos/otros/requeri.htm.

36. Charles Selengut, *Sacred Fury: Understanding Religious Violence* (Walnut Creek, CA: Altamira Press, 2003).

37. Dickason, *The Myth of the Savage.*

38. Jürgen Osterhammel, *Colonialism*, 2nd ed., trans. Shelley Frisch (Princeton: Markus Wiener Publishers, 2005).

39. Patrick Wolfe, "Settler Colonialism and the Elimination of the Native," *Journal of Genocide Research* 8, no. 4 (December 2006): 387–409.

40. See, for example, Tony Barta, "After the Holocaust: Consciousness of Genocide in Australia," *Australian Journal of Politics and History* 31, no. 1 (1984); Tony Barta, "Relations of Genocide: Land and Lives in the Colonization of Australia," in *Genocide and the Modern Age: Etiology and Case Studies of Mass Death*, eds. Isidor Wallimann and M. N. Dobkowski (New York: Greenwood Press, 1987).

41. Ben Kiernan, *Blood and Soil: A World History of Genocide and Extermination from Sparta to Darfur* (New Haven: Yale University Press, 2007); Ann Curthoys, "Genocide in Tasmania," in *Empire, Colony, Genocide: Occu-*

pation and Subaltern Resistance in World History, ed. A. Dirk Moses (New York: Berghahn Books, 2008); A. Dirk Moses, "An Antipodean Genocide: The Origins of the Genocidal Moment in the Colonisation of Australia," *Journal of Genocide Research* 2, no. 1 (2000): 89–106; A. Dirk Moses, ed., *Genocide and Settler Society* (New York: Berghahn Books, 2003).

42. See, for example, Carroll P. Kakel, *The American West and the Nazi East: A Comparative and Interpretive Perspective* (New York: Palgrave McMillan, 2013).

43. Kakel, *The American West and the Nazi East*.

44. A. Dirk Moses, "Empire, Colony, Genocide: Keywords and the Philosophy of History," in *Empire, Colony, Genocide: Conquest, Occupation, and Subaltern Resistance in World History*, ed. A. Dirk Moses (New York: Berghahn Books, 2008), 7.

45. Peter Iadicola and Anson Shupe, *Violence, Inequality, and Human Freedom* (Lanham, MD: Rowman & Littlefield, 2003).

46. Osterhammel, *Colonialism*.

47. Dickason, *The Myth of the Savage*, 277.

48. Quoted in Daron Acemoglu and James A. Robinson, *Why Nations Fail: The Origins of Power, Prosperity, and Poverty* (New York: Crown Business, 2012), 22.

49. Daron Acemoglu and James A. Robinson, *Why Nations Fail*, 26.

50. David E. Stuart, *Anasazi America* (Albuquerque: University of New Mexico Press, 2000).

51. David Roberts, *The Pueblo Revolt: The Secret Rebellion that Drove the Spaniards Out of the Southwest* (New York: Simon and Schuster, 2004); Waldman, *Encyclopedia of Native American Tribes*.

52. Waldman, *Encyclopedia of Native American Tribes*.

53. Edward H. Spicer, *Cycles of Conquest: The Impact of Spain, Mexico, and the United States on the Indians of the Southwest, 1533–1960* (Tucson: University of Arizona Press, 1992).

54. Weber, *The Spanish Frontier in North America*.

55. Gregory D. Smithers, "Rethinking Genocide in North America," in *The Oxford Handbook of Genocide Studies*, eds. Donald Bloxham and A. Dirk Moses (Oxford: Oxford University Press, 2010), 322–341.

56. Roberts, *The Pueblo Revolt*; Joe S. Sando, *Pueblo Nations: Eight Centuries of Pueblo Indian History* (Santa Fe: Clear Light Publishers, 1992).

57. Bartolomé de Las Casas, *The Devastation of the Indies: A Brief Account*, trans. Herma Briffault (Baltimore: Johns Hopkins Press, 1992).

58. Paul Schneider, *Brutal Journey: Cabeza De Vaca and the Epic First Crossing of North America* (New York: Holt Paperback, 2007).

59. Alvar Nunez Cabeza de Vaca, *Castaways: The Narrative of Alvar Núñez Cabeza De Vaca*, ed. Enrique Pupo-Walker, trans. Frances M. Lopez-Morillas (Berkeley: University of California Press, 1993).

60. Andres Resendez, *A Land So Strange: The Epic Journey of Cabeza de Vaca* (New York: Perseus Books, 2007).

61. Resendez, *A Land So Strange*; Schneider, *Brutal Journey*.

4. DISEASE

1. R. G. Robertson, *Rotting Face: Smallpox and the American Indian* (Caldwell, ID: Caxton Press, 2001), ix.

2. Andrew Nikiforuk, *The Fourth Horseman: A Short History of Epidemics, Plagues, Famines, and Other Scourges* (New York: M. Evans & Company, Inc., 1991), 64.

3. David P. Clark, *Germs, Genes, and Civilization: How Epidemics Shaped Who We Are Today* (Upper Saddle River, NJ: FT Press, 2010).

4. Clark, *Germs, Genes, and Civilization*.

5. See, for example, J. M. Blaut, *The Colonizer's Model of the World: Geographical Diffusionism and Eurocentric History* (New York: The Guilford Press, 1993).

6. Ian K. Steele, *Warpaths: Invasions of North America* (New York: Oxford University Press, 1994).

7. The writer was Cabeza de Vaca, who would gain fame after being shipwrecked and spending many years wandering through much of the southern half of North America. Quoted in Steele, *Warpaths*, 13.

8. Hugh Thomas, *Conquest: Montezuma, Cortés, and the Fall of Old Mexico* (New York: Touchstone Books, 1993).

9. Mark Cocker, *Rivers of Blood, Rivers of Gold: Europe's Conquest of Indigenous Peoples* (New York: Grove Press, 1998).

10. Bernal Diaz Del Castillo, *The Conquest of New Spain* (n.p.: Snowball Publishing, 2009).

11. Thomas, *Conquest*.

12. Ronald Wright, *Stolen Continents: The "New World" through Indian Eyes* (Boston: Houghton Mifflin, 1992).

13. Some recent scholarship challenges this assertion and points out that all we know about this story comes from postconquest Spanish sources.

14. Quoted in James Cross Giblin, *When Plague Strikes: The Black Death, Smallpox, AIDS* (New York: HarperCollins Publishers, 1995), 69.

15. Wright, *Stolen Continents*.

16. Donald R. Hopkins, *The Greatest Killer: Smallpox in History* (Chicago: University of Chicago Press, 1983).

17. Massimo Livi Bacci, *Conquest: The Destruction of the American Indios* (Malden, MA: Polity Press, 2008).

18. Quoted in Alfred W. Crosby, "Conquistador y Pestilencia: The First New World Pandemic and the Fall of the Great Indian Empires," *Hispanic American Historical Review* 47 (1967): 321–337, 329.

19. This quote was translated from the original Nahuatl language by a Spanish historian in the 1500s named Fray Bernardino de Sahagún. Quoted in Sheldon Watts, *Epidemics and History: Disease, Power and Imperialism* (New Haven, CT: Yale University Press, 1997), 89.

20. Crosby, "Conquistador y Pestilencia," 329.

21. Watts, *Epidemics and History*.

22. Watts, *Epidemics and History*.

23. Giblin, *When Plague Strikes*.

24. Terence N. D'Altroy, *The Incas* (Oxford: Wiley-Blackwell, 2003).

25. Quoted in Dorothy H. Crawford, *Deadly Companions: How Microbes Shaped Our History* (Oxford: Oxford University Press, 2007), 116.

26. See, for example, Henry F. Dobyns, "An Outline of Andean Epidemic History to 1720," *Bulletin of the History of Medicine* 37 (1963): 493–515.

27. Quoted in Giblin, *When Plague Strikes*, 73–74.

28. Watts, *Epidemics and History*.

29. Clark, *Germs, Genes, and Civilization*.

30. Charles C. Mann, *1491: New Revelations of the Americas before Columbus* (New York: Alfred A. Knopf, 2005).

31. Russell Thornton, *American Indian Holocaust and Survival: A Population History since 1492* (Norman: Oklahoma University Press, 1987).

32. Robertson, *Rotting Face*.

33. Robertson, *Rotting Face*, 43.

34. Charles C. Mann, "1491," *Atlantic Monthly*, March 2002, accessed September 7, 2010, http://cogweb.ucla.edu/Chumash/Population.html.

35. Neil Salisbury, *Manitou and Providence: Indians, Europeans, and the Making of New England, 1500–1643* (New York: Oxford University Press, 1982).

36. Robertson, *Rotting Face*.

37. Quoted in Mann, *1491*, 110.

38. Mann, *1491*.

39. Henry Dobyns, *Their Numbers Become Thinned* (Knoxville: University of Tennessee Press, 1983).

40. Mark Kurlansky, *Cod: A Biography of the Fish That Changed the World* (New York: Penguin Books, 1997).

41. Robertson, *Rotting Face*.

42. Quoted in Alan Taylor, *American Colonies: The Settling of North America* (New York: Penguin Books, 2001), 39.

43. Mann, "1491," http://cogweb.ucla.edu/Chumash/Population.html.

44. Quoted in Charles C. Mann, "Native Intelligence: The Indians Who First Feasted with the English Colonists Were Far More Sophisticated Than You Were Taught in School. But That Wasn't Enough to Save Them," *Smithsonian Magazine*, December 2005, accessed September 13, 2010, http://www.smithsonianmag.com/history-archaeology/squanto.html.

45. Mann, "Native Intelligence."

46. Francis Jennings, *The Invasion of America: Indians, Colonialism and the Cant of Conquest* (Chapel Hill: University of North Carolina Press, 1975), 30.

47. Taylor, *American Colonies*.

48. See Ann F. Ramenofsky and Patricia Galloway, "Disease and the Soto Entrada," in *The Hernando de Soto Expedition: History, Historiography, and Discovery in the Southeast*, ed. Patricia Galloway (University of Nebraska Press, 2006), 259–280.

49. Susan Scott and Christopher Duncan, *Return of the Black Death: The World's Greatest Serial Killer* (Chichester: Wiley, 2004), 49.

50. Mark Wheelis, "Biological Warfare at the 1346 Siege of Caffa," *Emerging Infectious Diseases* 8 (September 2002), accessed on September 14, 2010, http://www.cdc.gov/ncidod/eid/vol8no9/01-0536.htm.

51. Quoted in Mann, "Native Intelligence," 10.

52. Mann, "1491," http://cogweb.ucla.edu/Chumash/Population.html.

53. Seymour I. Schwartz, *The French and Indian War. 1754–1763. The Imperial Struggle for North America* (Edison, NJ: Booksales, 1999).

54. Robert Leckie, *"A Few Acres of Snow:" The Saga of the French and Indian Wars* (New York: John Wiley & Sons, Inc., 1999).

55. Daniel K. Richter, *Facing East from Indian Country: A Native History of Early America* (Cambridge, MA: Harvard University Press, 2001); Steele, *Warpaths*.

56. David Dixon, *Never Come to Peace Again: Pontiac's Uprising and the Fate of the British Empire in North America* (Norman: University of Oklahoma Press, 2005), 109.

57. Steele, *Warpaths*.

58. Steele, *Warpaths*.

59. Walter R. Borneman, *The French and Indian War: Deciding the Fate of North America* (New York: Harper Perennial, 2006).

60. Quoted in Ben Kiernan, *Blood and Soil: A World History of Genocide and Extermination from Sparta to Darfur* (New Haven: Yale University Press, 2007), 244.

61. Ted Morgan, *Wilderness at Dawn: The Settling of the North American Continent* (New York: Touchstone Books, 1993), 345.

62. Colin G. Calloway, *The Scratch of a Pen: 1763 and the Transformation of North America* (New York: Oxford University Press, 2006); Morgan, *Wilderness at Dawn.*

63. John W. Harpster, ed., *Pen Pictures of Early Western Pennsylvania* (Pittsburgh: University of Pittsburgh Press, 1938), 99, 103–4, accessed on September 17, 2010, http://www.nativeweb.org/pages/legal/amherst/trent.html; See also, Morgan, *Wilderness at Dawn*, 345.

64. The entire text of the journal is available at http://hsp.org/sites/default/files/legacy_files/migrated/pagesfromwilliamtrentsjournal.pdf, accessed on September 17, 2010. Also see, Spencer C. Tucker, *The Encyclopedia of North American Indian Wars, 1607–1890* [3 volumes]: *A Political, Social, and Military History* (n.p.: ABC Clio, 2011), 1024.

65. Calloway, *The Scratch of a Pen*, 1360 in Kindle version.

66. Fred Anderson, *Crucible of War: The Seven Years' War and the Fate of Empire in British North America, 1754–1766* (New York: Vintage Books, 2000).

67. See, for example, Ward Churchill, *Indians Are Us? Culture and Genocide in Native North America* (Monroe, ME: Common Courage Press, 1994); Ward Churchill, *A Little Matter of Genocide: Holocaust and Denial in the Americas, 1492 to the Present* (San Francisco: City Lights Books, 1997).

68. For a fuller account, see Thomas Brown, "Did the U.S. Army Distribute Smallpox Blankets to Indians? Fabrication and Falsification in Ward Churchill's Genocide Rhetoric," *Plagiary: Cross-Disciplinary Studies in Plagiarism, Fabrication, and Falsification* (2006): 100–129; Landon Y. Jones, "Tribal Fever," *Smithsonian Magazine*, May 2005; Robertson, *Rotting Face.*

5. WARS AND MASSACRES

1. Quoted in Dee Brown, *Bury My Heart at Wounded Knee: An Indian History of the American West* (New York: Bantam Books, 1970), 86; see also, Stan Hoig, *The Sand Creek Massacre* (Norman: University of Oklahoma Press, 1961), 142–143.

2. Quoted in Brown, *Bury My Heart at Wounded Knee*, 166.

3. Stan Hoig, *The Sand Creek Massacre.*

4. Robert M. Utley, *The Indian Frontier of the American West, 1846–1890* (Albuquerque: University of New Mexico Press, 1984).

5. Utley, *The Indian Frontier of the American West*.

6. See Brown, *Bury My Heart at Wounded Knee*, 89.

7. Utley, *The Indian Frontier of the American West*.

8. Quoted in Brown, *Bury My Heart at Wounded Knee*, 85.

9. *Report of the Joint Committee on the Conduct of the War at the Second Session Thirty-Eighth Congress.* United States. Congress. Washington: Government Print Office, 1865. University of Michigan Digital Library Production Service , accessed on September 22, 2010, http://quod.lib.umich.edu/cgi/t/text/text-idx?c=moa;idno=ABY3709.0003.001;rgn=full%20text;view=toc;cc=moa.

10. Thom Hatch, *Black Kettle: The Cheyenne Chief Who Sought Peace But Found War* (New York: John Wiley & Sons, 2004).

11. Gary L. Roberts and David Fridtjof Halaas, "Written in Blood: The Soule-Cramer Sand Creek Massacre Letters," *Colorado Heritage* (Winter 2001): 22–32.

12. Ari Kelman, *A Misplaced Massacre: Struggling Over the Memory of Sand Creek* (Cambridge, MA: Harvard University Press, 2013).

13. Hampton Sides, *Blood and Thunder: An Epic of the American West* (New York: Doubleday Books, 2006), 379.

14. *Report of the Joint Committee*, http://quod.lib.umich.edu/cgi/t/text/text-idx?c=moa;idno=ABY3709.0003.001;rgn=full%20text;view=toc;cc=moa.

15. *Report of the Joint Committee*.

16. *Report of the Joint Committee*.

17. *Report of the Joint Committee*.

18. Kelman, *A Misplaced Massacre*; David Svaldi, *Sand Creek and the Rhetoric of Extermination: A Case Study in Indian-White Relations* (Lanham: University Press of America, 1989).

19. The War of the Rebellion: A Compilation of the Official Records of the Union and Confederate Armies, volume 34, http://ehistory.osu.edu/osu/sources/recordView.cfm?Content=064/0354.

20. Quoted in Hoig, *The Sand Creek Massacre*, 147.

21. Quoted in Hoig, *The Sand Creek Massacre*, 176.

22. Quoted in Svaldi, *Sand Creek and the Rhetoric of Extermination*, 117.

23. Quoted in Svaldi, *Sand Creek and the Rhetoric of Extermination*, 120.

24. Quoted in Svaldi, *Sand Creek and the Rhetoric of Extermination*, 120.

25. Quoted in Svaldi, *Sand Creek and the Rhetoric of Extermination*, 118.

26. Rob Harper, "Looking the Other Way: The Gnadenhütten Massacre and the Contextual Interpretation of Violence," in *Theatres of Violence: Massa-*

cres, Mass Killing and Atrocity throughout History, eds. Philip G. Dwyer and Lyndall Ryan (New York: Berghahn Books, 2012).

27. Quoted in Harper, "Looking the Other Way," 85.

28. Harper, "Looking the Other Way," 85.

29. Thomas Goodrich, *Scalp Dance: Indian Warfare on the High Plains, 1865–1879* (Mechanicsburg, PA: Stackpole Books, 1997).

30. Stan Hoig, *The Battle of the Washita: The Sheridan-Custer Indian Campaign of 1867–69* (Lincoln: University of Nebraska Press, 1976).

31. In Brown, *Bury My Heart at Wounded Knee*, 164.

32. Evidently, he was among the first to be killed and was shot off his horse as he attempted to escape the massacre. Hatch, *Black Kettle*.

33. Hoig, *The Battle of the Washita*.

34. Custer's orders from General Philip Sheridan were, "To proceed south in the direction of the Antelope Hills, thence toward the Washita River, the supposed winter seat of the hostile tribes; to destroy their villages and ponies; to kill or hang all warriors and bring back all women and children." Quoted in Dee Brown, *The American West* (New York: Charles Scribner's Sons, 1994), 102.

35. Hatch, *Black Kettle*.

36. Quoted in Richard E. Jensen, R. Eli Paul, and John E. Carter, *Eyewitness at Wounded Knee* (Lincoln: University of Nebraska Press, 1991), 6.

37. Quoted in Robert M. Utley and Wilcomb E. Washburn, *Indian Wars* (Boston: Mariner Books, 2002), 294.

38. Utley and Washburn, *Indian Wars*, 294.

39. Paul M. Robertson, "Wounded Knee Massacre," in *Encyclopedia of North American Indians*, ed. Frederick E. Hoxie (Boston: Houghton Mifflin, 1996), 694–697.

40. Robertson, "Wounded Knee Massacre," 694–697.

41. Brown, *Bury My Heart at Wounded Knee* (New York: Bantam Books, 1970).

42. Bill Yenne, *Indian Wars: The Campaign for the American West* (Yardley, PA: Westholme, 2006).

43. Jensen, Paul, and Carter, *Eyewitness at Wounded Knee*.

44. Brown, *Bury My Heart at Wounded Knee*; Michael Blake, *Indian Yell: The Heart of an American Insurgency* (Flagstaff, AZ: Northland Publishing, 2006); Carl Waldman, *Encyclopedia of Native American Tribes*, 3rd ed. (New York: Checkmark Books, 2006).

45. Brown, *Bury My Heart at Wounded Knee*.

46. John G. Neihardt, *Black Elk Speaks: Being the Life Story of a Holy Man of the Oglala Sioux, The Premier Edition* (Albany: State University of New York Press, 2008).

47. See, for example, Russell Thornton, *American Indian Holocaust and Survival: A Population History Since 1492* (Norman: University of Oklahoma Press, 1987). Thornton writes, "The distinction between war and genocide often is not well defined: atrocities of American Indian genocide have been called war by non-Indians. For example, the so-called battle at Wounded Knee Creek in South Dakota, where several hundred old men, women, and children were massacred, was not a battle; it was genocide, as was the Sand Creek Massacre of some 150 Cheyenne" (49).

48. Brenda Uekert, *Rivers of Blood: A Comparative Study of Government Massacres* (Westport, CT: Praeger, 1995).

49. Paul R. Bartrop, "Punitive Expeditions and Massacres: Gippsland, Colorado, and the Question of Genocide," (unpublished article).

50. Israel W. Charny, "Toward a Generic Definition of Genocide," in *Genocide: Conceptual and Historical Dimensions*, ed. George J. Andreopoulos (Philadelphia: University of Pennsylvania Press, 1994); Helen Fein, *Genocide: A Sociological Perspective* (Newbury Park, CA: Sage Publications, 1990); Robert Melson, *Revolution and Genocide: On the Origins of the Armenian Genocide and the Holocaust* (Chicago: University of Chicago Press, 1992).

51. William A. Schabas, *Genocide in International Law: The Crime of Crimes* (Cambridge: Cambridge University Press, 2000).

52. Duane Champagne, *Native America: Portrait of the Peoples* (Detroit: Visible Ink Press, 1994).

53. Sherburne F. Cook, *The Population of the California Indians, 1769–1970* (Berkeley: University of California Press, 1976).

54. William S. Simmons, "Indian Peoples of California." in *Contested Eden: California before the Gold Rush*, eds. Ramón A. Gutiérez and Richard J. Orsi (Berkeley: University of California Press, 1998), 48–77.

55. M. Kat Anderson and Michael G. Barbour, "A World of Balance and Plenty: Land, Plants, Animals, and Humans in a Pre-European California," in *Contested Eden: California before the Gold Rush*, eds. Ramón A. Gutiérez and Richard J. Orsi (Berkeley: University of California Press, 1998), 12–47; Champagne, *Native America*.

56. James A. Sandos, "Between Crucifix and Lance: Indian-White Relations in California, 1769–1848," in *Contested Eden: California before the Gold Rush*, eds. Ramón A. Gutiérez and Richard J. Orsi (Berkeley: University of California Press, 1998), 196–229.

57. Clifford E. Trafzer and Joel R. Hyer, eds., *Exterminate Them!: Written Accounts of the Murder, Rape, and Enslavement of Native Americans during the California Gold Rush* (East Lansing: Michigan State University Press, 1999).

58. Albert L. Hurtado, *Indian Survival on the California Frontier* (New Haven: Yale University Press, 1988).

59. Jerry Stanley, *Digger: The Tragic Fate of the California Indians from the Missions to the Gold Rush* (New York: Crown Books, 1997).

60. Quoted in Trafzer and Hyer, eds., *Exterminate Them!* 18; Robert F. Heizer, ed., *The Destruction of California Indians: A Collection of Documents from the Period 1847 to 1865 in Which Are Described Some of the Things That Happened to Some of the Indians of California* (Lincoln: University of Nebraska Press, 1974).

61. Quoted in Stanley, *Digger*, 67; Heizer, ed., *The Destruction of California Indians*.

62. Stanley, *Digger*.

63. Stanley, *Digger*, 68–69.

64. Stanley, *Digger*.

65. Trafzer and Hyer, eds., *Exterminate Them!*

66. "Message to the California State Legislature," January 7, 1851, *California State Senate Journal*, 1851, 15.

67. McDougal was warning of what he believed would happen if the treaties with the Indians failed and was speaking to the Indian commissioners, January 25, 1851, *California State Senate Journal*, 1851, 677.

68. William B. Secrest, *When the Great Spirit Died: The Destruction of the California Indians, 1850–1860* (Sanger, CA: Word Dancer Press, 2003), xiv.

69. Heizer, ed., *The Destruction of California Indians*, 268–269.

70. In Stanley, *Digger*, 67.

71. Heizer, ed., *The Destruction of California Indians*.

72. Helen Fein, *Genocide: A Sociological Perspective* (London: Sage Publications, 1993).

73. This quote is from an Indian agent named Redick McKee. Quoted in Stanley, *Digger*, 68.

74. The first quote was from the *San Francisco Chronicle* while the second was from a local Humboldt county newspaper. In Stanley, *Digger*, 66.

75. Secrest, *When the Great Spirit Died*, xiv.

76. Heizer, ed., *The Destruction of California Indians*, 36.

77. Albert L. Hurtado, *Indian Survival on the California Frontier* (New Haven: Yale University Press, 1988).

78. Hurtado, *Indian Survival*; Stanley, *Digger*.

79. Stanley, *Digger*.

80. Cook, *The Population of the California Indians*.

81. Laurence M. Hauptman, *Tribes and Tribulations: Misconceptions about American Indians and Their Histories* (Albuquerque: University of New Mexico Press, 1995).

82. Carl Waldman, *Encyclopedia of Native American Tribes*, 3rd ed. (New York: Checkmark Books, 2006).

83. Alfred A. Cave, *The Pequot War* (Amherst: University of Massachusetts Press, 1996).

84. Steele, *Warpaths*.

85. Hauptman, *Tribes and Tribulations*.

86. Russell Bourne, *Gods of War, Gods of Peace: How the Meeting of Native and Colonial Religions Shaped Early America* (New York: Harcourt Press, 2002).

87. Alan Taylor, *American Colonies: The Settling of North America* (New York: Penguin Books, 2001).

88. Steele, *Warpaths*.

89. Carl Waldman, *Atlas of the North American Indian*, 3rd ed. (New York: Checkmark Books, 2009).

90. Steele, *Warpaths*.

91. Waldman, *Atlas of the North American Indian*.

92. Jill Lepore, *The Name of War: King Philip's War and the Origins of American Identity* (New York: Vintage Books, 1998).

93. See, for example, Francis Jennings, "Wars: Colonial Era," in *Encyclopedia of North American Indians*, ed. Frederick E. Hoxie (Boston: Houghton Mifflin Company, 1996), 668–670; Donald L. Fixico, "Wars: 1776–1850," in *Encyclopedia of North American Indians*, ed. Frederick E. Hoxie (Boston: Houghton Mifflin Company, 1996), 670–672; Tom Holm, "Wars: 1850–1900," in *Encyclopedia of North American Indians*, ed. Frederick E. Hoxie (Boston: Houghton Mifflin Company, 1996), 672–674.

6. EXILES IN THEIR OWN LAND

1. Calhoun was an Indian agent for the New Mexico territory. Quoted in Hampton Sides, *Blood and Thunder: The Epic Story of Kit Carson and the Conquest of the American West* (New York: Anchor Books, 2006).

2. Backus was the commander of Fort Defiance for a period after it was created. Quoted in Peter Iverson, *Diné: A History of the Navajos* (Albuquerque: University of New Mexico Press, 2002), 42.

3. Quoted in Sides, *Blood and Thunder*, 431.

4. Taken from the Navajo Nation website, accessed on November 8, 2010, http://navajonationcouncil.org/NNprofile.htm.

5. They were preceded by their linguistic cousins, the Apache, who had made the same journey a bit earlier. Both groups speak an Athapaskan language that is quite distinct from the language of other Southwestern peoples.

See Stephen Trimble, *The People: Indians of the American Southwest* (Santa Fe: SAR Press, 1993).

6. Carl Waldman, *Encyclopedia of Native American Tribes*, 3rd ed. (New York: Checkmark Books, 2006).

7. Iverson, *Diné*.

8. Quoted in Iverson, *Diné*, 34.

9. Quoted in Iverson, *Diné*, 38.

10. Quoted in Iverson, *Diné*, 38.

11. Cited in Tom Dunlay, *Kit Carson and the Indians* (Lincoln: University of Nebraska Press, 2000), 266.

12. Quoted in Dunlay, *Kit Carson and the Indians*, 264.

13. Lynn R. Bailey, *The Long Walk: A History of the Navajo Wars, 1846–68* (Tucson: Westernlore Press, 1988).

14. Sides, *Blood and Thunder*.

15. Garrick Bailey and Roberta Glenn Bailey, *A History of the Navajos: The Reservation Years* (Santa Fe, NM: School of American Research Press, 1986).

16. Quoted in Iverson, *Diné*, 42.

17. Trimble, *The People*.

18. Dunlay, *Kit Carson and the Indians*.

19. Quoted in Sides, *Blood and Thunder*, 403.

20. Gerald E. Thompson, ed., "'To The People of New Mexico' Gen. Carleton defends the Bosque Redondo," *Arizona and the West* 14, no. 4 (Winter 1972): 347–366.

21. Quoted in Sides, *Blood and Thunder*, 402.

22. In Robert A. Roessel, Jr., "Navajo History, 1850–1923," in *Handbook of North American Indians: Volume 10 Southwest*, ed. Alfonso Ortiz (Washington, DC: Smithsonian Institution, 1983), 506–23, accessed on November 21, 2010, http://www.unco.edu/library/gov/middle_ground/books/HONAI-%20Navajo%20HIstory,%201850-1923.pdf.

23. In Roessel, "Navajo History, 1850–1923."

24. Quoted in Sides, *Blood and Thunder*, 440.

25. Crawford R. Buell, "The Navajo 'Long Walk.' Recollections by Navajos," in *The Changing Ways of Southwestern Indians: A Historic Perspective*, ed. Albert H. Schroeder (Glorieta, NM: The Rio Grande Press, Inc., 1973), 177.

26. Buell, "The Navajo 'Long Walk,'" 177.

27. Frank McNitt, "The Long March, 1863–1867," in *The Changing Ways of Southwestern Indians: A Historic Perspective*, ed. Albert H. Schroeder (Glorieta, NM: Rio Grande Press, 1973).

28. Iverson, *Diné*.

29. Quoted in Sides, *Blood and Thunder*, 496.

30. Quoted in Sides, *Blood and Thunder*, 496.

31. Cited in Dunlay, *Kit Carson and the Indians*, 305.

32. Quoted in Sides, *Blood and Thunder*, 412.

33. Quoted in Dunlay, *Kit Carson and the Indians*, 241.

34. Quoted in Dunlay, *Kit Carson and the Indians*, 245.

35. Blanca Tovías, "A Blueprint for Massacre: The United States Army and the 1870 Blackfeet Massacre," in *Theatres of Violence: Massacres, Mass Killing and Atrocity throughout History*, eds. Philip G. Dwyer and Lyndall Ryan (New York: Berghahn Books, 2012).

36. Peter Rowe, "Total War," in *Crimes of War: What the Public Should Know*, eds. Roy Gutman and David Rieff (New York: W. W. Norton and Company, 1999), 355.

37. Quoted in James M. McPherson, *Drawn with the Sword: Reflections on the American Civil War* (Oxford: Oxford University Press, 1996), 66.

38. Quoted in Sides, *Blood and Thunder*, 471.

39. Gerald E. Thompson, ed., "'To the People of New Mexico' Gen. Carleton defends the Bosque Redondo," *Arizona and the West* 14, no. 4 (Winter 1972): 347–366.

40. See, for example, William A. Schabas, "The Law and Genocide," in *The Oxford Handbook of Genocide Studies*, eds. Donald Bloxham and A. Dirk Moses (Oxford: Oxford University Press, 2010), 123–141: William A. Schabas, *Genocide in International Law* (Cambridge: Cambridge University Press, 2000).

41. UNESCO Latin American Conference, Declaration of San José, 11 December 1981, UNESCO Doc. FS 82/WF.32, reproduced in Martin Shaw, *What is Genocide?* (Malden, MA: Polity Press, 2007).

42. Available online at http://www.un.org/esa/socdev/unpfii/en/declaration.html.

43. Quoted in Sides, *Blood and Thunder*, 405.

44. Jack Utter, *American Indians: Answers to Today's Questions*, 2nd ed. (Norman: University of Oklahoma Press, 2001).

45. Klaus Frantz, *Indian Reservations in the United States: Territory, Sovereignty, and Socioeconomic Change* (Chicago: The University of Chicago Press, 1993).

46. C. Wilkinson, *American Indians, Time, and the Law: Native Societies in a Modern Constitutional Democracy* (New Haven: Yale University Press, 1988).

47. Utter, *American Indians*.

48. Carl Waldman, *Atlas of the North American Indian*, 3rd ed. (New York: Checkmark Books, 2009).

49. Waldman, *Atlas of the North American Indian*.

50. James M. Mooney, *Historical Sketch of the Cherokee* (Chicago: Aldine Transaction, 1975), 124.

51. Carl Waldman, *Encyclopedia of Native American Tribes*, 3rd ed. (New York: Checkmark Books, 2006).

7. EDUCATION FOR ASSIMILATION

1. Quoted in Michael C. Coleman, *American Indian Children at School, 1850–1930* (Jackson: University of Mississippi Press, 1993), 46.

2. Quoted in Jack Utter, *American Indians: Answers to Today's Questions*, 2nd ed. (Norman: University of Oklahoma Press, 2001), 315.

3. Mick Fedullo, *Light of the Feather* (New York: Morrow, 1992), 54.

4. Klaus Frantz, *Indian Reservations in the United States: Territory, Sovereignty, and Socieoeconomic Change* (Chicago: University of Chicago Press, 1993).

5. Available online, accessed December 21, 2011, http://www.ourdocuments.gov/doc.php?flash=true&doc=8&page=transcript.

6. Frederick E. Hoxie, *A Final Promise: The Campaign to Assimilate the Indians, 1880–1920* (Lincoln: University of Nebraska Press, 1984).

7. Official Report of the Nineteenth Annual Conference of Charities and Correction (1892), 46–59. Reprinted in Richard H. Pratt, "The Advantages of Mingling Indians with Whites," in *Americanizing the American Indians: Writings by the "Friends of the Indian" 1880–1900* (Cambridge, MA: Harvard University Press, 1973), 260.

8. Quoted in Report on Indian Education, Task Force Five: Final Report to the Indian Policy Review Commission (Washington, DC: U.S. Government Printing Office, 1976), 26.

9. Report on Indian Education, Task Force Five; see also, Jon Reyhner and Jeanne Eder, *American Indian Education: A History* (Norman: University of Oklahoma Press, 2004).

10. Carl Waldman, *Atlas of the North American Indian*, 3rd ed. (New York: Checkmark Books, 2009).

11. Louis Morton, "How the Indians Came to Carlisle," *Pennsylvania History* 29, no. 1 (January 1962): 53–73.

12. Quoted in Morton, "How the Indians Came to Carlisle," 59.

13. Quoted in Morton, "How the Indians Came to Carlisle," 60.

14. Quoted in Morton, "How the Indians Came to Carlisle," 62.

15. Quoted in Morton, "How the Indians Came to Carlisle," 69.

16. Quoted in Morton, "How the Indians Came to Carlisle," 69.

17. Quoted in Morton, "How the Indians Came to Carlisle," 69.

18. Waldman, *Atlas of the North American Indian*.

19. Utter, *American Indians*.

20. Utter, *American Indians*.

21. David H. Dejong, *Promises of the Past: A History of Indian Education* (Golden, CO: North American Press, 1993).

22. Quoted in Board of Indian Commissioners, Annual Report (Washington, DC: Government Printing Office, 1888), 3.

23. Board of Indian Commissioners, Annual Report (Washington, DC: Government Printing Office, 1888), 3.

24. Board of Indian Commissioners, Annual Report (Washington, DC: Government Printing Office, 1888), 58.

25. Carroll P. Kakel, *The American West and the Nazi East: A Comparative and Interpretive Perspective* (New York: Palgrave McMillan, 2013), 168.

26. Reyhner and Eder, *American Indian Education*.

27. Scott Riney, *The Rapid City Indian School, 1898–1933* (Norman: University of Oklahoma Press, 1999).

28. Riney, *The Rapid City Indian School*.

29. Michael C. Coleman, *American Indian Children at School, 1850–1930* (Jackson: University Press of Mississippi, 1993).

30. Senate Subcommittee of the Committee on Indian Affairs. 1932. Conditions of the Indians. Seventy-first Congress, second session, part 18. 81–84.

31. Quoted in Reyhner and Eder, *American Indian Education*, 173.

32. Gustavo Corni, *Hitler's Ghettos: Voices from a Beleaguered Society, 1939–1944* (London: Arnold Press, 2003).

33. Cited in Dejong, *Promises of the Past*, 108.

34. Quoted in Reyhner and Eder, *American Indian Education*, 169.

35. Quoted in David Wallace Adams, *Education for Extinction: American Indians and the Boarding School Experience* (Lawrence: University Press of Kansas, 1995), 115.

36. Board of Indian Commissioners, Annual Report (Washington, DC: Government Printing Office, 1889), 82.

37. Hoxie, *A Final Promise*.

38. Adams, *Education for Extinction*.

39. Text of speech online at http://www.cbc.ca/news/canada/story/2008/06/11/pm-statement.html, accessed on December 20, 2012.

40. Reyhner and Eder, *American Indian Education*.

41. For a thorough discussion, see Schabas, *Genocide in International Law*.

42. Raphael Lemkin, *Axis Rule in Occupied Europe: Laws of Occupation, Analysis of Government, and Proposals for Redress* (Washington, DC: Carnegie Foundation for International Peace, 1944).

43. Schabas, *Genocide in International Law*.

44. Quoted in Schabas, *Genocide in International Law*.

8. WHAT'S IN A NAME?

1. A. Dirk Moses, "Empire, Colony, Genocide: Keywords and the Philosophy of History," in *Empire, Colony, Genocide: Conquest, Occupation, and Subaltern Resistance in World History*, ed. A. Dirk Moses (New York: Berghahn Books, 2008), 3–54, 6.
2. Alfred A. Cave, "Genocide in the Americas" in *The Historiography of Genocide*, ed. Dan Stone (New York: Palgrave Macmillan, 2008), 275–276.
3. Timothy Williams, "Higher Crime, Fewer Charges on Indian Land," *The New York Times* (2012), accessed on February 11, 2012, http://www.nytimes.com/2012/02/21/us/on-indian-reservations-higher-crime-and-fewer-prosecutions.html?pagewanted=all&_r=0.
4. Steven W. Perry, *American Indians and Crime: A BJS Statistical Profile, 1992–2002* (Washington, DC: U.S. Department of Justice, December 2004) NCJ 203097.
5. Perry, *American Indians and Crime*.
6. Timothy Williams, "For Native American Women, Scourge of Rape, Rare Justice," *The New York Times*, May 22, 2012, accessed on January 1, 2013, http://www.nytimes.com/2012/05/23/us/native-americans-struggle-with-high-rate-of-rape.html.
7. "Alcohol-Attributable Deaths and Years of Potential Life Lost Among American Indians and Alaska Natives—United States, 2001–2005," *Morbidity and Mortality Weekly Report*, August 29, 2008, 57(34)938-941, accessed on January 7, 2013, http://www.cdc.gov/mmwr/preview/mmwrhtml/mm5734a3.htm.
8. U.S. Department of Health and Human Services, *Mental Health: Culture, Race and Ethnicity, A Supplement to Mental Health: A Report of the Surgeon General* (Rockville, MD: DHHS, 2001).
9. Chris Hedges and Joe Sacco, *Days of Destruction, Days of Revolt* (New York: Nation Books, 2012).
10. Hedges and Sacco, *Days of Destruction, Days of Revolt*, 8.
11. Samuel Totten and Robert K. Hitchcock, "Introduction: The Genocide of Indigenous Peoples," in *Genocide of Indigenous Peoples, Genocide: A Critical Bibliographic Review*, vol. 8, eds. Samuel Totten and Robert K. Hitchcock (New Brunswick, NJ: Transaction Publishers, 2011), 7.
12. American Psychiatric Association, *Diagnostic and Statistical Manual of Mental Disorders: DSM-IV* (Washington, DC: American Psychiatric Association, 1994).

13. American Psychiatric Association, *Diagnostic and Statistical Manual*, 427.

14. R. Barry Ruback and Martie P. Thompson, *Social and Psychological Consequences of Violent Victimization* (Thousand Oaks, CA: Sage Publications, 2001).

15. See, for example, Eduardo Duran, *Healing the Soul Wound: Counseling with American Indians and Other Native Peoples* (New York: Teachers College, Columbia University, 2006); L. B. Whitbeck, G. W. Adams, and D. R. Hoyt, "Conceptualizing and Measuring Historical Trauma among American Indian People," *American Journal of Community Psychology* 33, no. 3–4 (2004): 119–130; R. Struthers and J. Lowe, "Nursing in the Native American Culture and Historical Trauma," *Issues in Mental Health Nursing* 24, no. 3 (2003): 257–272; M. Y. H. Brave Heart, "The Return to the Sacred Path: Healing the Historical Trauma Response among the Lakota," *Smith College Studies in Social Work* 68, no. 3 (1998): 287–305; Robert Morgan and Lyn Freeman, "The Healing of Our People: Substance Abuse and Historical Trauma," *Substance Abuse and Misuse* 44 (2009): 84–98; Shelly A. Wiechelt, Jan Gryczynski, Jeannette Johnson, and Diana Caldwell, "Historical Trauma among Urban American Indians: Impact on Substance Abuse and Family Cohesion," *Journal of Loss and Trauma* 17, no. 4 (July/August 2012): 319–336.

16. Maria Yellow Horse Brave Heart, Josephine Chase, Jennifer Elkins, and Deborah B. Altschul, "Historical Trauma among Indigenous Peoples of the Americas: Concepts, Research, and Clinical Considerations," *Journal of Psychoactive Drugs* 43, no. 4 (2011): 282–290.

17. Hedges and Sacco, *Days of Destruction, Days of Revolt*, 4.

18. See, for example, Marianne O. Nielsen and Linda Robyn, "Stolen Lands, Stolen Lives: Native Americans and Criminal Justice," in *The Criminology and Criminal Justice Collective of Northern Arizona University. Investigating Difference: Human and Cultural Relations in Criminal Justice*, 2nd ed. (Upper Saddle River, NJ: Prentice Hall, 2009).

19. Kenneth Campbell, *Genocide and the Global Village* (New York: Palgrave, 2001), 25.

20. David Moshman, "Conceptual Constraints on Thinking about Genocide," *Journal of Genocide Research* 3, no. 3(2001): 431–450, 431.

21. See, for example, Alex Alvarez, *Governments, Citizens, and Genocide: A Comparative and Interdisciplinary Approach* (Bloomington: Indiana University Press, 2001).

22. Michael Shermer and Alex Grobman, *Denying History: Who Says the Holocaust Never Happened and Why Do They Say It?* (Berkeley: University of California Press, 2000).

23. See for example Roger Smith, Erik Markusen, and Robert Jay Lifton, "Professional Ethics and the Denial of the Armenian Genocide," *Holocaust and Genocide Studies* 91, no. 1(1995): 1–22; and Hannibal Travis, "On the Original Understanding of the Crime of Genocide," *Genocide Studies and Prevention* 7, no. 1 (April 2012): 30–55.

24. Uğur Üngör, "Studying Mass Violence: Pitfalls, Problems, and Promises," *Genocide Studies and Prevention* 7, no. 1 (April 2012): 68–80.

25. Scott Straus, "Contested Meanings and Conflicting Imperatives: A Conceptual Analysis of Genocide," *Journal of Genocide Research* 3, no. 3 (2001): 349–375, 359.

26. Yehuda Bauer, *Rethinking the Holocaust* (New Haven: Yale University Press, 2001).

27. Paul R. Bartrop, "Punitive Expeditions and Massacres: Gippsland, Colorado, and the Question of Genocide," (unpublished article).

INDEX

ABOUT THE AUTHOR

Alex Alvarez is a professor in the Department of Criminology and Criminal Justice at Northern Arizona University. From 2001 until 2003, he was the founding director of the Martin-Springer Institute for Teaching the Holocaust, Tolerance, and Humanitarian Values. His main focus of study is in the area of collective and interpersonal violence, including homicide and genocide. His first book, *Governments, Citizens, and Genocide*, was a nominee for the Academy of Criminal Justice Sciences book of the year award, as well as a Raphael Lemkin book award nominee from the International Association of Genocide Scholars in 2003. His other books include *Murder American Style, Violence: The Enduring Problem*, and *Genocidal Crimes*. He has also served as an editor for the journal *Violence and Victims*, was a founding coeditor of the journal *Genocide Studies and Prevention*, was a coeditor of the H-Genocide List Serve, and is an editorial board member for the journals *War Crimes, Genocide, and Crimes Against Humanity: An International Journal* and *Idea: A Journal of Social Issues*. He has been invited to present his research in various countries such as Austria, Bosnia, Canada, Germany, the Netherlands, and Sweden.